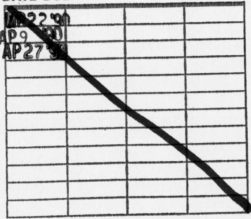

Outdoor Recreation in America

In its own setting nature has always been a creator of drama.

Outdoor Recreation in America

Trends, Problems, and Opportunities

Third Edition

Clayne R. Jensen

Brigham Young University
Provo, Utah

Burgess Publishing Company
Minneapolis, Minnesota

The natural things of this earth are not ours to abuse and do with as we please. They have been given to us in trust, and we must account for them to the generations which will come after us and audit our procedures.

Preface

The forests, prairies, streams, lakes, skies, and shorelines were once abundant with game, fish, fowl, and pleasant scenes. Mountain streams ran clear as they found their way to the rivers which funneled to the scenic Atlantic and Pacific. Nature's gifts to Americans were rich, abundant, and unequaled. But due to lack of appreciation, planning, and foresight, these gifts were abused, mismanaged, and lost, never to be restored, no longer a symbol of life in America.

Surely the chronicles of history will not include such a statement. Americans will certainly be wise enough to retain their precious gifts of nature, even though retaining them has become extremely difficult, and will be even more so in the future.

In recent decades the population of the U.S. has changed from rural to predominantly urban. Americans have moved from close touch with the out-of-doors. Open space no longer lies in the family backyard or around the corner of the next block. Yet our need for outdoor experiences and our appreciation for nature still persist. As a result, the big outdoor recreation rush is on. People from all walks of life travel long distances to hunt, fish, camp, picnic, boat, ski, take pictures, hike, study nature, and just relax in a peaceful setting.

The outdoors has always been a great laboratory for learning, a museum for study, and a playground for wholesome fun and enjoyment. It affords people a special kind of fulfillment not available in any other setting. Thus, there must be fish in the lakes, deer in the forests, scenery to paint and to photograph, groves in which to camp and picnic, trails to hike, and wilderness to explore. Rob Americans of these opportunities and you take away one of the great urges to live.

Every generation of Americans has a rendevous with the land. If our generation is to meet this rendezvous, we must show special respect for the fundamental values of nature and of natural beauty, and we must pay special attention to the way these relate to the good of the individual and to the society as a whole.

Many agencies and organizations have undertaken programs of preservation, conservation, and education to guarantee continued enjoyment and satisfaction derived from contact with nature — to guarantee high-quality outdoor recreation. Numerous government agencies at federal, state, and local levels are involved in outdoor recreation either as a primary or secondary function. Professional and service organizations have interests in this field, and it is now becoming important as private enterprise.

There have been articles written on specific topics of outdoor recreation, and some textbooks deal with certain phases of the field. But at the present time there is no book which covers outdoor recreation as a field of study or a field of special interest. To be more specific, there is no book which (a) interprets the present and future significance of outdoor recreation, (b) describes the responsibilities of the numerous agencies and organizations involved, (c) covers the recent legislation and programs which will significantly influence outdoor recreation in the future, (d) points out the need for interagency cooperation at different levels, and (e) identifies current and potential future problems.

This book is designed to cover the aforementioned areas. Essentially, it contains factual information about agencies, programs, problems, and trends. It also contains projections based on current facts.

The book should be especially meaningful to (a) teachers and students in recreation, natural resource management, and outdoor education, (b) employees of resource management agencies, both governmental and private, (c) park and recreation administrators, and (d) laymen concerned with the use of natural resources for the enjoyment of the people.

C.R.J.

America today is in a state of transition and so is the park and recreation movement. The philosophy and attitudes of many people interested and concerned with the leisure era, now upon us, have also changed.

It is timely, then, to examine and study the changing times and trends and problems that confront us in the park and recreation field.

OUTDOOR RECREATION IN AMERICA deals effectively not only with trends and problems but available outdoor recreation opportunities, now and in the future.

The National Recreation and Park Association believes that the caliber and scope of Clayne Jensen's writings deserve the attention of all citizens interested in coping with the struggle that faces America in this new decade — a decade of concern for Environmental Quality and the Quality of Life.

Sal J. Prezioso
Past President
National Recreation and
Park Association

Contents

1 Important Meanings and Interpretations   1

2 The Need for Outdoor Opportunities   13

3 Significant Social and Economic Forces   25

4 Historical Development of Outdoor Recreation   47

5 Federal Government Involvement   57

6 Recent Legislation and Special Government Programs   97

7 The Roles of State Agencies   115

8 Local Government Participation   139

9 Outdoor Recreation on Private Lands   161

10 Outdoor Recreation Resources — Supply and Demand   175

11 Economic Impact of Outdoor Recreation   195

12 The Struggle for a Pleasant Environment   205

13 Education for Outdoor Recreation   225

14 Professional, Service, and Educational Organizations   239

15 A Look into the Future   251

Selected References   259

Photo Credits   263

Index   265

Chapter 1 Important Meanings and Interpretations

In the Declaration of Independence it is proclaimed that "the pursuit of happiness" is a basic human right. Since that important proclamation (and also previous to it) many papers have been written and multitudes of orations given on what we should achieve for ourselves in this life, and for what we should hope and strive. One frequent answer seems to be the achievement of satisfaction, joy, and well-being, a condition known as happiness. The pursuit of true happiness is today, as it has always been, the main business of the human race.

Without taking the time to thoroughly analyze all the circumstances of the happy person, it is important to say that this book is based on the thesis that significant work and recreation, particularly of the outdoor type, contribute significantly to the lives of people. Furthermore, the book is based on the idea that an intellectual treatment must be given to the study of outdoor recreation and the factors which influence it. Such an approach involves at least serious consideration of (a) our time and the use we make of it, (b) socioeconomic forces that influence work, leisure, and recreation, (c) organizations, agencies, and programs concerned with people's outdoor recreation, (d) supply and demand with respect to outdoor recreation resources, (e) economic impact of outdoor recreation pursuits, and (f) what we might expect in the future as opposed to the present and the past.

Before the subject at hand can be discussed intelligently some basic interpretations and concepts must be established. For instance, what is the meaning of leisure time, recreation, and outdoor recreation? What determines whether an activity is or **1**

> Recreation in the outdoors is a pleasurable reuniting of human beings with a part of their natural environment.

is not recreational in nature? What have our outstanding leaders said of the significance of leisure and recreation? Following are some answers to these important questions.

Meaning of Leisure Time

Leisure time is "choosing time," free of the tensions associated with the necessities of living and available for use according to one's wishes. Time can logically be divided into three classes: (a) time for existence — biological requirements, such as sleeping, eating, sanitation, and the like; (b) time for subsistence — economic requirements, such as working on one's job; and (c) leisure time — the time remaining after a minimum level of existence and subsistence have been accomplished. For the typical American adult, this classification of time may be represented on a 24-hour scale as follows:

Existence (biological requirements)	Subsistence (work)	Leisure time
10 hours	9 hours (including travel time)	5 hours

Some authorities say *free time* and *leisure time* are not the same. They distinguish between them by defining leisure time as "that portion of available free time devoted to the pursuit of leisure values." This definition indicates that one's leisure time is only a portion of one's free time, depending on whether it is devoted to leisure values. This fine line of differentiation probably cuts too thin to add real meaning for most people. The differentiation is not in harmony with dictionary definitions or with definitions commonly accepted by most authorities in recreation and related fields. Therefore, in this text, free time and leisure time are considered to be synonymous.

Meaning of Leisure

Several superior thinkers and writers have declared that leisure and leisure time are the same. Others declare that leisure is not simply a block of time but a *state of being*. Following are interpretations given by some prominent leaders who believe that leisure and leisure time are the same.

> Leisure, then, is essentially a *block of time*. The fact that the word "leisure" conjures up many things in our minds should not blind us to the fact that when we are concerned with leisure we are primarily concerned with a period of time in which the feeling of compulsion is minimized. This is in contrast to those hours when we are compelled to work or prepare for work.[1]

[1]Charles K. Brightbill, *Man and Leisure, A Philosophy of Recreation,* Prentice-Hall, Englewood Cliffs, N.J., 1961, p. 21.

Leisure — unobligated time, free time or spare time; time when one is free to do what one chooses.[2]

Leisure: "For purposes of social analysis the concept is usually narrowed and widened to mean simply freedom from activities centering around the making of a livelihood."[3]

Leisure is commonly thought of as surplus time remaining after the formal duties and necessities of life have been attended to. It is the free time, enabling a person to do as he or she chooses.[4]

Leisure is a condition in which an individual is free from all obligations and thus is enabled to engage in activities without any compulsion whatsoever. Thus, the outstanding characteristics of leisure are freedom and the absence of necessity.[5]

Some leaders interpret leisure not as a block of time, but a state of being or a condition in which the person exists. They believe that some people are not capable of leisure, even when an abundance of free time is available.

Miller claims that leisure is quite different from leisure time, and says that leisure is "the complex of self-fulfilling and self-enriching values achieved by the individual as he uses leisure time in self-chosen activities that recreate him."[6]

In his comprehensive discussion of leisure, Sebastian de Grazia reviews the serene concept of leisure held by some ancient philosophers. He does not equate leisure with unproductiveness. He believes that free time is thought of as the opposite of work and therefore unproductive. But he believes that leisure and free time are entirely different, stating, "...today's time is considered free when not at grips with work. Work is the antonym of free time. But not leisure. Leisure and free time live in two different worlds."[7]

Nash claims, "It is possible to be freed from the pressures of daily life and still not have leisure." This occurs when one has no interest in leisure and no ability to make worthy use of free time, is subject to conditions that are not propitious, or lacks the facilities that enable expression of one's interests, use of one's abilities, and taking advantage of the conditions.[8]

It is apparent that in order to have leisure one must have a block of time available. But whether people have leisure during their free time depends on whether they engage in self-enriching and self-fulfilling pursuits — pursuits that add balance and meaning to their lives. Leisure is a state of being — a condition of the individual.

Significance of Time and Leisure

The amount of free time people have and how they use it have great significance. It has been said that the final test of a civilization is its ability to use free time wisely

---

[2]Harold D. Meyer and Charles K. Brightbill, *Community Recreation, A Guide to Its Organization,* 4th edition, Prentice-Hall, Englewood Cliffs, N.J., 1969, p. 29.

[3]Howard G. Danford, *Creative Leadership in Recreation,* 2nd edition, Allyn & Bacon, Boston, 1970, p. 9.

[4]Martin H. Neumeyer and Esther S. Neumeyer, *Leisure and Recreation,* A.S. Barnes & Co., New York, 1936, 1949, 1958, p. 14.

[5]Danford, *op. cit.,* p. 9.

[6]Norman P. Miller and Duane M. Robinson, *The Leisure Age, Its Challenge to Recreation,* 2nd edition, Wadsworth Publishing Co., Belmont, Calif., 1966, p. 6.

[7]Sebastian de Grazia, *Of Time, Work, and Leisure,* Doubleday & Co., Garden City, N.J., 1964, p. 233.

[8]Jay B. Nash, *Philosophy of Recreation and Leisure,* Wm. C. Brown Co. Publishers, Dubuque, Iowa, 1964, p. 161.

and profitably. Furthermore, it has been observed that individuals, communities, and nations are made and unmade by the way they use free time; and the use of time helps to determine the final quality of individuals and societies.

Aristotle described leisure as "the first principle of all action." Leisure has also been described as the main content of a free life and the nurse of civilization. Like virtue and unlike labor, leisure is its own chief reward. The amount and quality of any society's leisure activities set the tone, define its version of the good life, and measure the level of its civilization.

Bertrand Russell said, "To be able to fill leisure time intelligently is the last product of civilization." And a century earlier Disraeli stated: "Increased means and increased leisure are the two civilizers of man." Long before that, Socrates said, "Leisure is the best of all possessions." Time to do as one pleases — to create, to play, to do things enriching and satisfying — has long been a dream of the common man. The dream to be freed from the heavy waves that have beaten upon his craft has become at least partly true, with the promise of still more to come. But with such freedom of time must come understanding of its potential for quality or lack of quality, for good or for bad.

Arnold Toynbee, one of our most renowned historian-philosophers, stated that the three great dangers facing the contemporary American society are world warfare, overpopulation, and too much leisure time. David Sarnoff said that leisure time rather than labor will be the great problem in the years ahead. Other prominent leaders have given strong warnings about leisure time and the significance of its influence. Some pertinent quotations about this follow.

We should be able not only to work well but to use leisure (time) well; for, as I repeat once more, the first principle of all action is leisure. Both are required, but leisure is better than work and is its end. — Aristotle.

If we survive the leisure (time) which the atomic age will bring it may make peace more horrible than war. We face the dreadful prospect of hour after hour, even day after day, with nothing to do. After we have read all the comic books, traveled all the miles, seen all the movies, what shall we do then? — Robert Hutchins, former president of the University of Chicago.

A new colossus has been formed by the millions of leisure hours which have developed out of the forty-hour work week. This colossus has more leisure time at his disposal than all of the aristocracies of history. What will he do with it? Will he make of himself a full or an exact man, or will he be content to be merely a ready man — a measure of muscle and a shout from the mob? The choice lies before him. Who will help him make it? — A. Whitney Griswold, former president of Yale University.

We are simply going to have to adopt the credo that the wise use of leisure (time) is more wholesome, creative and elevating than is work. But as W. H. Ferry of the Center for the Study of Democratic Institutions has pointed out, "This means we will have to change our basic cultural standards — and that isn't easy." — James Charlesworth, president of the American Academy of Political and Social Science.

Leisure (time) can be a real friend if you know how to use it; a formidable enemy if you abuse it. — Thomas G. Desmond, former New York State Senator.

For the first time in human history leisure, rather than work, is becoming the factor which integrates the life of the average man; it becomes the dominating factor in his expectations in relation to the content of time. Such about-face constitutes a primary revolution: to take our leisure as seriously as we once did our work places a new perspective on life.— Paul Douglas.

Leisure with dignity is the supremely desirable object of all sane and good men. — Cicero.

Sebastian de Grazia[9] has warned us that if the trend toward automation continues, one of our great challenges is to construct a worthwhile society largely on the concept of leisure rather than totally on the concept of work. He indicates that America stands on the threshold of an era when the opportunity for a good life through increased leisure time is unequaled. Dr. Alexander Reid Martin of the American Psychiatric Association calls this time "the latest and greatest freedom of all."

The basic problem associated with increased leisure time is that it is not inherently good or bad, but has tremendous potential for either. It is simply a key which unlocks a new door but brings no guarantee of improved individuals or a better society. Increased leisure time simply presents a new opportunity to succeed to greater heights or to fail in the attempt. It requires the making of choices, and in order to assure wise choices we must provide adequate education and good leadership.

One author depicted the significance of leisure time choices as follows:

During leisure man may choose to eat and drink. The quality and quantity of the food and drink, and the wisdom of his choices in relation to his needs, may determine his capacity to live fully, to be only half alive, or to contribute to his own destruction.

During leisure man may also seek spiritual sustenance. He may do this through organized religion, or he may establish certain values by which he chooses to live. Outlets for spiritual activity must be a part of a man's leisure hours....

Another pursuit of leisure is the maintenance of a sense of physical well-being....Still another component is the recreative process through which man seeks to refresh himself, to relax, or, as the word itself means, to be created anew.[10]

Leisure time that is available to an individual will influence his or her life. And if it is present on a large scale in a society it will strongly influence the molding of that society. We cannot eliminate the influence of leisure time, but we can determine the quality of its influence by making wise decisions.

Meaning of Recreation

Recreation is a term which people use freely as if everyone understood its meaning. Yet, even people who have specialized in recreation and related fields differ in their interpretations of the term.

According to dictionary definitions, recreation is derived from the Latin word *recreare,* which means to create anew, to become refreshed. The dictionary further defines the term as the act of recreating, refreshment of strength or spirit, invigoration, or rebirth.

Outstanding leaders have used different phrases to define the term. George But-

[9]de Grazia, *op. cit.*
[10]Nash, *op. cit.*, p. 157.

> Outdoor activity is essentially a "renewing" experience — a refreshing change from the workaday world and the domestic routine.

ler[11] states, "Recreation may be considered as any form of leisure-time experience or activity in which an individual engages from choice because of enjoyment and satisfaction which it brings directly to him." Harold Meyer[12] defines it as "activity voluntarily engaged in during leisure time and primarily motivated by the satisfaction and pleasure derived from it." Frank Brockman[13] claims that recreation is "the pleasurable and constructive use of leisure time." According to Reynold Carlson[14] recreation is "any enjoyable leisure experience in which the participant voluntarily engages and from which he receives immediate satisfaction." Howard Danford[15] says it is "any socially desirable leisure activity in which an individual participates voluntarily and from which he derives immediate and continuing satisfaction." Sebastian de Grazia[16] considers recreation to be "activity that rests men from work, often by giving them a change (diversion), and restores (re-creates) them for work." Howard Braucher[17] said, "It is the things in which we engage because of inner desire and not because of any outer compulsion." Others have said that recreation is not a matter of motions — but rather emotions. It is a personal response, a psychological reaction, an attitude, an approach.

Of course, other outstanding leaders have used different words to tell what they think recreation means — what it includes and excludes. Upon analysis of the definitions it seems that many of them, even though stated differently, say essentially the same. The following elements are common to the several definitions.

1. Recreation directly involves the individual.
2. It is entered into voluntarily.
3. It occurs during leisure time.
4. The motivating force is enjoyment and satisfaction, as opposed to material gain.
5. Recreation is wholesome to the individual and his or her society.

The term recreation implies that the participants are re-created in some aspect — physically, psychologically, spiritually, or mentally; that they become refreshed and enriched; that they are revitalized and more ready to cope with their trials. In order to qualify as recreation, an activity must do something desirable to the participants. It must enrich them and add joy and satisfaction to an otherwise routine day. Recreation should be clearly distinguished from amusement, time-filling, or low-quality participation. Its meaning includes a characteristic of quality.

If we accept the idea that recreation actually re-creates the participant, then many

[11]George D. Butler, *Introduction to Community Recreation*, 4th edition, McGraw-Hill Book Co., New York, 1967, p. 10.

[12]Harold D. Meyer and Charles K. Brightbill, *op. cit.*

[13]C. Frank Brockman, *Recreational Use of Wild Lands,* 2nd edition, McGraw-Hill Book Co., New York, 1973, p. 1.

[14]Reynold E. Carlson, Theodore R. Deppe, and Janet R. MacLean, *Recreation in American Life,* 2nd edition, Wadsworth Publishing Co., Belmont, Calif., 1972, p. 7.

[15]Danford, *op. cit.*, p. 21.

[16]de Grazia, *op. cit.*, p. 233.

[17]Howard Braucher, *A Treasury of Living,* National Recreation Association, New York, 1950, p. 23.

of the so-called recreation pursuits are not recreational at all, but are only amusers, time-fillers, and time-wasters, which are actually detrimental rather than constructive, which fatigue rather than rejuvenate, "decreate" rather than recreate, and actually deprive participants of the enrichment opportunities vital to them.

In his book titled *Philosophy of Recreation and Leisure*, J. B. Nash[18] added meaning to the "quality concept" of recreation by placing different kinds of pursuits into a hierarchy on the basis of their potential value to the individual and to society. Following is a modified version of Nash's original interpretation of the hierarchy.

Recreation takes several forms, and it is so varied that any of a great number of activities may be recreational to someone at some time. Those activities that are recreational to one person may not be so to another. Furthermore, that which recreates a person at one time may have a different effect at another time, because one's appeal for a given activity changes from time to time, depending on one's particular needs. For instance, a person who is physically fatigued has little need for vigorous physical recreation, and one who is mentally or emotionally fatigued is not attracted to activities that require heavy concentration. Recreation usually takes the form of diversion and helps bring one's life into balance.

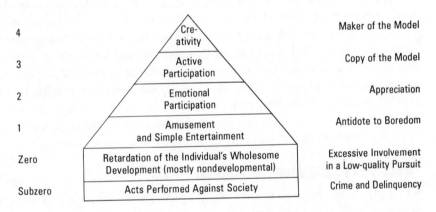

4	Cre-ativity	Maker of the Model
3	Active Participation	Copy of the Model
2	Emotional Participation	Appreciation
1	Amusement and Simple Entertainment	Antidote to Boredom
Zero	Retardation of the Individual's Wholesome Development (mostly nondevelopmental)	Excessive Involvement in a Low-quality Pursuit
Subzero	Acts Performed Against Society	Crime and Delinquency

Because people have different needs and interests they enjoy different pursuits, even in the same setting and while utilizing the same resources. For this reason a recreation agency cannot plan a narrow program to meet the needs of many people. For instance, some lovers of the outdoors enjoy hunting and fishing, while others prefer to photograph and study forms of wildlife. To some the park is a place to play, while to others it is a place to enjoy beauty, meditate, and study the balances of nature. Some want to preserve resources in order to enjoy them in their present state, while others see little value to them unless they are used in some activity or to produce material goods.

Classification of Recreational Pursuits

Due to the large number and great variety of pursuits included under the term recreation, a logical classification seems necessary. Recreation is commonly

[18]Nash, *op. cit.*, p. 69.

classified as (a) resource oriented and (b) activity oriented. *Resource-oriented* recreation includes those forms that depend strongly on the utilization of natural resources, such as the study of botany and wildlife, camping, hiking, fishing, boating, and hunting. *Activity-oriented* recreation includes the performance or the witnessing of a performance such as athletics, dramatics, art, music, crafts, and so on. Obviously, there is no sharp line of distinction between these two categories. For example, both water and snow skiing utilize natural resources to a large extent and at the same time they require a skilled performance. The same is true with fishing, hunting, and camping to a lesser degree. But classification into these two large divisions does help to enhance communication and planning. However, such classification should not be restrictive to the extent that it divides recreation into two completely separate areas.

Outdoor recreation is a commonly used term meaning essentially the same as resource-oriented recreation. It is defined as those *recreational activities which occur in an outdoor (natural) environment and which relate directly to that environment.*

Because this book deals with the large area of recreation known as outdoor (or resource-oriented) recreation it is important to reemphasize that this field is growing rapidly, and the growth has caused some critical problems to develop. The developments have required a reanalysis of the supply of resources and the amount and kinds of uses to which they should be put in the future. Many agencies and organizations have had to reevaluate their present and future roles relative to outdoor recreation, and drastic changes have occurred in the philosophies of many conservationists and preservationists. Recently outdoor recreation has become recognized as a field deserving greater emphasis and more thorough attention. Especially it demands an increasing amount of consideration among resource management personnel, park and recreation administrators, and educators.

Objectives of Outdoor Recreation

Objectives are the goals toward which a program or endeavor is pointed, serving as guides, adding purpose and direction. In identifying the importance of having well-established objectives, Socrates once stated, "If a man does not know to what port he is sailing, no wind is favorable." In our present society, no social or economic trend is favorable to a program for which no clear purpose has been established.

Many years ago John Collier, a great friend and critic of recreation, charged the recreation leaders in this country with "conducting pigmy programs seeking pigmy results amid giant opportunities." There is still some validity in Collier's criticism.

For a century Americans labored to settle and subdue a continent. For half a century they called upon unbounded invention and untiring industry to create an order of plenty for all. A challenge of the future is whether we have the wisdom to use that wealth to enrich and elevate our lives and to advance the quality of our civilization.

Certainly a weakness of the recreation profession is that its leaders do not have great purposes which unite them for achievement, because objectives have not been clearly established.

It seems that up to this time the objectives of most agencies involved in outdoor recreation have been to yield to the pressures of public demand with strong reservation and little long-range planning. Until recently very few agencies have taken aggressive and positive approaches to planning in advance of public demand. For the most part, it seems that no one has wanted to take command in developing outdoor recreation to its maximum potential for the good of the people. Many resource management agencies are involved, and each agency has objectives of its own relative to its total program, of which recreation is only one part. But in spite of this difficulty, if outdoor recreation as a field of study and as an area of great public interest and public spending is to approach its potential, then some guiding purposes must be stated.

The objectives of outdoor recreation in America should include at least the following:

1. Develop appreciation for nature. Today the majority of people in our urbanized society have limited opportunities for contact with the great outdoors. They have little chance to develop knowledge of and appreciation for nature's processes. Without such knowledge and appreciation it is difficult for people to become interested in the conservation and preservation of natural resources. For increasing numbers of people, contact with a natural environment occurs during outdoor recreation experiences on an occasional trip to the country or a visit to a nearby scenic or historic area. In view of this, it is important that outdoor recreation be aimed toward increasing people's knowledge of an appreciation for nature, and making them aware of the importance of sound conservation and preservation practices.

2. Enhance individual satisfaction and enjoyment. People participate in outdoor recreation primarily for joy and satisfaction. This contributes to happiness, the ultimate desire of all. Since people resort to the outdoors for satisfaction and joy, and since this achievement is desirable, then outdoor recreation agencies should try to enhance these qualities. Each agency involved in outdoor recreation ought to develop an aggressive program of identifying and developing those resources which have unusual potential for creating in people a feeling of satisfaction and well-being. Included should be areas which are significant from the standpoint of aesthetics, history, geology, archeology, biology (including wildlife resources), and a certain amount of just "open space."

3. Provide opportunity for diversion and relaxation. For the most part people go to the outdoors to divert themselves from their usual rapid pace, routine patterns, and the restrictions under which they ordinarily live. Therefore, agencies should help them to achieve this much-sought-after diversion. This will become increasingly difficult as the number of users continues to increase at a rapid rate. In the outdoors, people must find opportunity to relax, to live at their own desired pace, to find time to identify their place in the scheme of things, and to renew and refresh themselves in preparation for a return to their usual patterns of living.

4. Develop physiological fitness. The increasing lack of physiological fitness has been recognized as one of the crucial problems facing the American society, and much emphasis is currently placed on remedying this situation. Many forms of outdoor recreation are vigorous and tax participants far beyond their usual levels of performance. For instance, hiking, swimming, hunting, fishing, skiing, and camping often provide unusual physical challenges. In many instances, participants in such activities condition themselves to meet the occasion. Special attention should be given to promoting fitness through outdoor recreation. People should be encouraged to do a wholesome amount of hiking to points of interest and to participate in other vigorous outdoor activities. The idea should be developed that in order to fully enjoy the outdoors one must become vigorous and somewhat "rugged."

5. Develop desirable behavioral patterns. There was a time when an individual going to the outdoors was alone, but for the most part those days are gone. Today's typical outdoor participant finds many people wherever he or she goes, driving most of the way to the destination on a superhighway where thousands of cars pass in a day, fishing on a lake where boat traffic is so heavy that strict controls are required, hunting where more hunters are seen than game, and camping each night within a colony of other campers. The fact that today's outdoor recreationist must share his or her resources with many other people requires the development of desirable patterns of social outdoor conduct. Attitudes of courtesy, consideration, and sincere interest in each other must be fostered. Each recreationist should recognize that others have come for essentially their own same purposes. Agencies involved in outdoor recreation must take the lead in stimulating desirable social conduct.

The Total Recreation Experience

At first thought a recreation experience appears to be confined to the block of time during which participation actually occurs. But, upon further analysis, it becomes apparent that the total experience extends far beyond the time of actual participation. The value and usefulness of the experience may be part of a person's life long before, and remain long after, the participation itself. A total recreation experience includes the following four phases: anticipation, planning, participation, and recollection.

The *anticipation phase* is that time during which the person foresees the greatness of the coming event — the time of anxiously awaiting the day when the experience will become a reality. It is during this time that enthusiasm develops. This phase includes the anticipation of catching a big trout, climbing a high mountain, bagging another deer, elk, or moose; the thought of next summer's canoe trip, learning to ski, or ride horseback. Some "would-be" recreation events never progress beyond the anticipation phase, but even then they make some contributions to one's life.

The *planning phase* involves the actual preparation for the coming event — the gathering of equipment and supplies, preparation of food and clothes, and other such necessary matters.

The *participation phase* is the period of the actual activity and the duration of the event. It extends from the time of departure until the time of return. Sometimes this phase is relatively short and may seem almost insignificant in terms of time. Yet it is the core around which the other three phases are built. This is the actual experience

> The fact that we live in a world that moves crisis by crisis does not make a growing interest in outdoor activities frivolous, or ample provision for them unworthy of the nation's concern.

of fishing, hunting, canoeing, swimming, camping, skiing, hiking, or whatever the activity may be.

The *recollection phase* may take the form of thought, expression in oral or written form, or displaying pictures, slides, movies, etc. This phase is the thinking, telling, and showing about the direct experiences that have occurred.

Sometimes anticipation, planning, and recollection are more exciting than the participation itself, but it takes all four phases to make the recreational experience complete. None of the four phases should be played down in terms of its contributions.

Chapter 2 The Need for Outdoor Opportunities

The outdoors is a great laboratory for learning, a museum for study, a playground for wholesome fun and enjoyment. It affords a special kind of fulfillment not available in other settings. It has meaning and significance in the lives of people, and it has importance to our society and our nation. The outdoors has special meaning to young people.

It Became Part of Him

A boy went into the woods amidst the beauty of deep-toned spruce mixed with pines, and the lime and yellow aspens. He enjoyed the mellow texture of the rolling hills, and felt the vastness of the great open spaces, and what he saw and felt became part of the boy. In the distance he gazed at rugged peaks as they reached beyond the treeline for the clouds. He studied their contours and felt their strength, and they too became a part of him. The grass-covered valley, lying between the foothills and extending toward the peaks, was interrupted with a lake, and a stream carved a path to carry the strength of the land all the way to the sea. As he studied the valley and the lake and the stream and saw them in harmony and purpose, they also became part of him.

The boy lay back on the spongy grass and caught a glimpse of scattered clouds riding the wind to their place of rendezvous as they gathered to shadow the sun. And in the far distance a thunderhead hung heavy above the skyline and connected to it with a stream of raindrops. And all of this became part of the boy.

He watched closely a colony of ants as they went about their chores, and he saw two squirrels play hide-and-seek, and he studied a leaf and counted the pine needles in a cluster. He wondered why moss grew on the north side of trees. The shriek of the

This absolute freedom gives every hour an intense lucidity.

A day filled with only the sand and the sea and me.

red-tailed hawk, the caw of a crow, and the chirp of a bluejay as it hurried to its nesting young all became part of the boy. The evening call of the moose was echoed by the trumpet of an elk, and the yapping of a coyote, and the shriek of the night hawk. He watched swallows dart about in search of food on the wing, and later he heard the hooting of an owl as it welcomed the night and darkness overcame the day. All of these things became part of the boy, to remain permanently with him, and at the end of the day he was more complete than at its beginning.

At another time and another place the boy stood on the seashore and watched the breakers softly push sand crabs onto the beach and a sanderling moved quickly after them as they scurried into the sand. A great pelican dove awkwardly from aloft and plucked an anchovy from the sea. Picking a shell from the sand, the boy carefully studied its structure, contour, and hue, and he tried to interpret all of life that had related to it. He splashed in the brine, tasting the salt, and he felt its stickiness on his skin. He gathered kelp from the water's edge and studied the shellfishes clinging to an old raft, and watched an elderly seaman take a fish from the surf.

He looked out across the sea at a half a sail, then saw only the tip of the sail. Finally the sail disappeared over the horizon. He watched the tide move away from the shore, revealing the bottom of the sea for anyone to witness and study. Later he saw the sun cast a brilliant glow through the haze before it passed from sight. All of this became part of the boy and filled his day with meaning and satisfaction. It brought him closer to becoming a complete person.

People have always treasured experiences in the outdoors, and in one way or another tracts of land and water have been reserved throughout history for their pleasure. Such areas were not uncommon in the great civilizations of Thebes, Greece, and Rome, and during the Renaissance a revival of contact with the beauties of nature was expressed largely in the development of formal gardens. In hunting and fishing there is even a closer affinity between primitive and modern concepts of outdoor recreation. It is true that early humans hunted and fished primarily as a means of sustaining life and not for purposes of pleasure, but various primitive peoples recognized their dependence upon a continuing supply of wildlife. Many of our present ideas on conservation and preservation evolved from practices that date from antiquity.

Modern recreation on wild lands has a close relationship to medieval practices in Great Britain. In feudal England, some forests were more important for game than for timber, and certain lands were customarily reserved for the recreation of the nobility. Such recreational privileges of the ruling classes, greatly extended by William the Conqueror and other Norman kings, were not modified until after the adoption of the Magna Carta in 1215. Today most of these medieval English preserves are but historic relics, but two areas exist as modern memorials of that period. Both the Forest of Dean, west of Gloucester, and New Forest, near Southampton, can trace their existence directly from the Norman period.

The first great lovers of the outdoors in America were the Indians. These people were born into the out-of-doors, and it was their heritage in the truest sense. In their daily living nature was a part of every phase of their lives. They were truly agrarian, living directly from the resources of the land and putting what they could back into it. Their diets were geared to the vegetation of their particular locale. Their clothing and crude utilities were made of the resources at hand. And even their places of domicile shifted northward and southward with the seasons. The high mountains, plateaus, plains, rivers, trees, shrubs, and the wild animals of the land and water all had deep and special meaning to these people.

The great days of the American Indians are gone, and with them went an era of rugged outdoor living. Since then, we have moved through other great eras. The conquering of the wilderness, the isolated farm, the plantation, the self-contained New England town, the detached neighborhood are all phases of the American past. And now all of the nation is gradually becoming a city.

In one great stride the United States has changed from a rural to an urban nation, and as a result we have encountered new problems that require new solutions. We have few, if any, similar experiences on which to base our solutions. It has become apparent that despite the advantages inherent in urban living, there is something lacking in city life: the fundamental values of nature, the wholeness concept of life, the satisfaction of seeing things born and seeing things grow, admiring the scenery, and observing nature's processes. Today these elements are not common in the lives of most Americans, and indeed, to many Americans they are not even accessible.

To the slum child of Harlem and Chicago's South Side, the conservation epic, the wilderness, the great outdoors are unfamiliar phrases of little meaning. In the central portions of Boston and New York City there are countless children and adults who have never walked on wet sand or tasted the salt of the nearby sea. There are children in the midwest cities of Detroit, St. Louis, and Kansas City who have never seen corn growing in fertile fields. For a great many people of northern California cities the redwoods could just as well be on the moon. In some cities, children look out of their bedroom windows upon foul rivers, masses of railroad cars, or abandoned industrial sites. To them, the beauty of the great outdoors is only a storybook tale of another time and another place.

In the memorable phrase of former Secretary of the Interior Stewart Udall, "Every generation of Americans has a rendezvous with the land." If our generation is to meet this rendezvous, we must show special respect for the fundamental values of nature and of natural beauty, and we must pay special attention to the way these relate to the good of the people and the society. We must learn that people cannot live by science and technology alone. The natural world is the human world. Having evolved in it for many centuries, we are not far removed by a thin clothing of civilization. It is packed into our genes. There is in nature a wisdom that seems to shape all earth's experiments with life.

The fact that we live in a world that moves crisis by crisis does not make a growing interest in outdoor activities frivolous, or ample provision for them unworthy of the nation's concern. In fact, the more power-driven, complex, and delicate our society becomes, the more meaningful a touch with nature can become.

There needs to be public understanding that outdoor recreation is not only a renewing experience but also serious business, both because of its economic impact and its beneficial effect on the physical, cultural, social, and moral well-being of the people. It is a partial solution to the social problems created by urbanization and increased leisure time. It is a solution in part to the problem that human beings are not wholly suited physiologically or psychologically to meet the technological demands upon them. The recreation business is the great hope for economic improvement of certain depressed rural portions of this country. Further, the manufacturing and marketing of recreation equipment and the provision of recreation facilities have a major impact on our economy. Think of what is involved in the manufacturing, marketing, and use of sporting arms, fishing tackle, camping equipment, pleasure boats, winter sports equipment, camp trailers, recreation roads, resort hotels, motels, lodges, dude ranches, and the recreation press.

Cultural Values

Throughout history people have gradually added beauty to utility. The first pots or vessels were made for utility alone; then a touch of decoration was added. As civilization advanced, pots became known more for beauty than utility. The same pattern has followed in architecture, clothing, design of cities, and many other things created, used, and treasured by people.

There was a time in history when our natural resources were valued almost exclusively for their utility, for the goods which they provided for people's use as they attempted to conquer the wilderness and survive. Little by little, priority of beauty over utility has occurred in the use of certain resources, as it has in other phases of life. The beauty in this case is described in our use of nature for enjoyment, the enrichment and fulfillment of life. Essentially, this is what outdoor recreation is all about: the use of the great outdoors for fulfillment of life.

In America the time has finally come when the recreational use of many natural resources equals or supersedes in importance the more traditional uses. Outdoor recreation has become recognized as essential in the lives of the people, recognized as a great national asset. Specific cultural values are derived from such activities as scenic and historic study, photography, painting, and investigation into the meditation about the outdoor heritage of our nation. As stated in the Outdoor Recreation Resources Review Commission (ORRRC) report,

> The outdoors lies deep in American tradition. It has had immeasurable impact on the Nation's character and on those who made its history. When an American looks for the meaning of his past, he seeks it not in ancient ruins, but more likely in mountains and forests, by a river, or at the edge of the sea. The tale is one of discovery, of encounter, of hard-won settlement.

Psychological Values

One of the great comforting influences comes from being in contact with nature, aware of a presence beyond and around us which manifests itself in all living things — the marvel of the smallest snowflake, the grandeur of the Milky Way, the return of every spring, each bird in its own nest, each bee with its own discipline. These are all evidences of the order and creation of which we are a part. These daily miracles can be visible on every side, and they can help to mold secure and happy personalities. The wholeness concept of life, the awareness of interactions and interrelationships, and the balance of nature are all important in our lives. Robert Frost said it well:

> Here are your waters and your watering place. Drink and be whole again beyond confusion.

Some of our wisest leaders have emphasized that the goals of life should be the full unfolding of a person's potentials; what matters is that a person is much, not that he or she has or uses much. They have emphasized that having much and using much are, at best, only means toward being much. Retaining a feeling of significance is becoming ever more difficult in our society of giant enterprises, directed by bureaucracy in which the individual becomes a smaller cog in a bigger machine. In many cases, people find themselves economic puppets who dance to the tune of automated machines and bureaucratic management. They become anxious, not only because their economic security depends directly upon others, but because they fail to derive satisfaction in their everyday lives. In too many cases they live and die without having confronted the fundamental realities of human existence. Their fragmented and piecemeal lives do not teach them the wholeness, unity, and purpose that they need in order to be satisfied and secure. Wholesome outdoor

"Give me health and a day. He is only rich who owns the day." Ralph Waldo Emerson.

experiences can help mold into people the wholeness concept and the balance that are essential to a satisfying life.

The outdoors embodies something that cannot be found anywhere else. It is not merely the scenery, or the mountain breeze, or the open spaces that delight us. The outdoors embodies history, primitive experiences, and elements capable of lifting the spirit. Intangible and imponderable qualities abound. The outdoors has greatly influenced America's history and her character, but its great impact is its contribution to the health and sanity of man. John Muir stated:

> Everybody needs beauty as well as bread, places to play in and pray in, where Nature may heal and cheer and give strength to body and soul alike.

Sociological Values

In most people there exists an innate drive for adventure, excitement, and challenge. If this drive is not satisfied by high-quality activities, then it will be satisfied by less desirable ones. But it will be satisfied. When a young boy was brought before a renowned judge on a charge of theft, the judge made the classic statement, "This boy should have been stealing second base." His statement implied that the boy ought to have challenging and exciting experiences through socially acceptable activities. The same statement could have been made about an adventure to the top of a mountain, or about the pursuit of a large fish, or a vigorous hike through the woods, or the study of nature, or one of many other wholesome outdoor experiences.

Another social aspect of outdoor activities is that people of like interests draw close together, causing them to develop friendships. Often, a person's circle of friends is developed around a special recreational interest. People with common interests tend to attract each other and enjoy each other's companionship. Many wonderful friendships are based on mutual appreciation of outdoor activities.

Still another aspect is learning desirable behavior and conduct. Learning to keep camp and picnic areas clean, to avoid marring the landscape, and to be considerate of the rights and enjoyment of others are important social attributes, and they are rapidly becoming more important in outdoor recreation because of the tremendous increase in participants. In the future good manners in the out-of-doors will have great influence on how much people enjoy their outdoor experience.

Physiological Values

A nation is no stronger than its people. The physical vigor of people is as much a part of a nation's strength as good education. In our present pattern of sedentary living, it is difficult to keep the body in good condition. Because of this, numerous worthy programs and many leaders are devoted to improving the physical fitness of the American people. Outdoor recreation has a contribution to make. Hiking, mountain climbing, hunting, fishing, canoeing, bicycling, skiing, and swimming tax the body beyond its usual performance level, and thereby stimulate the organism to improve its condition. Those who participate regularly in outdoor activities generally improve their fitness. Enjoyment in vigorous outdoor activities is directly dependent upon a high level of fitness. If all of us were rugged outdoors

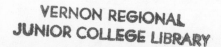

people, our physical fitness would be greatly improved. The following statement was taken from the ORRRC report.

> The most basic thing that can be done to improve physical fitness is to encourage the simple pleasures of walking and cycling. It is something of a tribute to Americans that they do as much cycling and walking as they do, for very little has been done to encourage these activities, and a good bit to discourage them.[1]

Educational Values

Outdoor recreation has educational values that are essential to the health of society. The outdoors provides a part of education that strengthens people's minds as well as their bodies, that broadens their understanding of the laws of nature, that sharpens their appreciation of its manifold beauties, that fortifies their most precious possession — the spirit which gives life its meaning.

The outdoors offers a laboratory in living where all people who love the outdoors can make discoveries that vest life with value. Discovering things for oneself is one of the most satisfying occupations. Each of us is on a separate voyage of exploration, and there is no limit to the exciting things we may find, if we place ourselves in an environment where we may discover and observe firsthand the wonders of nature.

Some of the specific educational values that may be obtained through outdoor experiences are an awareness and observation of
1. life's processes and their great variety,
2. geological formations and the content of soil and rock,
3. the importance and the practice of conservation,
4. beautiful scenery and the joy of experiencing it,
5. one's own self through being somewhat alone with nature,
6. good outdoor manners,
7. the benefit of mastery of outdoor skills.

Spiritual Values

In outdoor experiences, as in no other way save a good home or a good church, spiritual values may be realized. In such experiences a person may feel freedom and serenity and develop humility, inner warmth, and a sense of security, all of which are necessary for true satisfaction. To quote Ralph Waldo Emerson:

Whoso walketh in solitude,
and inhabiteth the wood,
Choosing light, wave, rock, and bird,
Before the money-loving herd,
Into that forester shall pass,
From these companions, power and grace.

Of all the outdoor settings that appeal to people perhaps rivers are the most unique, the most meaningful, and the most eternal.

[1]Outdoor Recreation Resources Review Commission, *Study Report Summary*, 1962, p. 26.

Rivers

There is water to feed and cleanse and water to quicken the earth. Water is in all shapes and sizes from babbling brooks to the great sea. But a river is the friendliest because the river is a traveler. It bears life and stimulates life, and protects life; a joy to all who share its presence.

Long before a river acquires enough authority, it earns a name and a place on the map. Maybe it is a child of the Rocky Mountains, shimmering through green-sided valleys. It may be a daughter of the Cascades made of milk water, hurrying down the church aisle to marry the sea. Or it might be a sentry of the great plains meandering slowly toward the ocean as it keeps its watch over all of life that depends upon it. It passes fifty towns or more and witnesses every kind of land and living thing. It seems to say, "Let all who will come seeking; no treasures shall be hidden."

Before a river settles in its summer bed, early spring campers come to its side to shed the bonds of winter. The fresh smell of snowfed waters holds a promise for new beginnings. Man, child, and river reunite for another long season of sunlight and blooming.

Along a western river freshly watered horses carry adventurers alongside a swift stream as they weave their way upward to the high country, and they see the river gradually dwindle as it branches into many tributaries.

The trout angler seeks a river's loneliness and a touch-and-go acquaintance with a speckled life. He comes to claim the river, and in perfect privacy he stands in the current hypnotized by the river's voice, listening to the monologue of his thoughts; and he calls this fishing. Dressed against the chilliness and mist of a mountain valley, another angler takes his rivers swift, deep, and cold where strong salmon test his tackle. For him, the river holds no easy prize.

Rushing down a deep gorge of the high country is a special kind of river that jumps, thrusts, strikes, and whirls. Its violence and speed cause men to want to conquer it. After the first river riders came down alive, one of them said, "It's ours now; we have mastered the river."

In a less violent setting, a lazy river, clear as window glass, meanders along the valley showing off its sapphires and emeralds to the sky, sliding over limestone, stealing catnip in Missouri on its way to Arkansas. Slow travelers follow this river as they drift in their boats and explore and dream.

Look across the middle of the land and there are wild hills and prairies divided by another river. It is clean and dependable, and long ago it provided the buffalo with drink. After the buffalo, longhorned cattle grazed on the same banks, and now the longhorns are also gone. Beneath the hoof marks and deep in the hills, lie fossils of life long ago. Prehistoric mammals trace close to the surface. Scientists listen and learn what the earth has been preaching. The river is a museum guarding records of voyagers who came with bows and arrows, rifles, and traps, and traders who came to sell pelts of mink and beaver.

Today another kind of voyager comes by canoe to the same place, trading a few hours of youth for a reunion with the past. For this generation of traders there is only a trace of the olden days on the river, but other things have changed only in small ways. This is a river, serenely independent and timeless. "Come back when you can," it says, "I'll be waiting."

In the East, a man in no particular hurry can take his stand in a square stern boat and ease along the trail straight out of American history. The scene hasn't changed much since the first man floated down. Fences along the quiet river signify the partnership of man and river. Like so many rivers which run over rocks, this one sparkles in the sun like specks of gold in a prospector's pan. Here the dreamer could ask no more than time and the river's music.

Somewhere in late September a river comes to a lonely, quiet time. Summer slips

"A River is more than an
Amenity — it is a Treasure."
Oliver Wendell Holmes.

...every river is a world of its
own, unique in pattern and
personality...

"There's no music like a little river's...It takes the mind out of doors...and...sir, it quiets a man down like saying his prayers." Robert Louis Stevenson.

One cannot say that aimless hours of youth were wasted on the river. One can only make sure that the river is a fit companion. So it has been and so it should always be.

away into the mist like the wake of a canoe on a foggy day. Schoolboys return to their more practical errands, and the waterfowl rehearse their journey to the South. Now the late hikers discover the river's summer handiwork, the driftwood. This is the time when a river flows through the countryside as a thin thread of nature, appealing for a thicker screen of trees and a wider apron of beauty to guard its privacy and enhance its charm.

The smartest of the curious are brought to the river to make one final probe of shell and pebble before the days turn dark too soon. Shopping for an autumn wardrobe, the river borrows colors and textures from sky and shore, altering them with taste and wearing them with originality. It settles in the haze of Indian summer and paints its dream on liquid canvas. The anglers who never say "die" return in the golden flame of the autumn for one more cast – just one more.

Meadow, cloud, and chilling air loosen the shortening days, preparing the river for a long season of meditation and mending, anticipating the first deep frost and perhaps an overcoat of snow. Now the river seems to slow in its tracks, as though looking backward to its birthplace and to friends across the years, pioneers in past centuries, vacationers last month. Then, seemingly aware of the dependence of all life upon its progress and purity, the river rolls on to an appointment with another springtime.*

**Outdoor
Recreation
in America**

24

*Part of the phraseology was taken from the narration of the film *Wild Rivers*, U.S. Department of the Interior.

Chapter 3 Significant Social and Economic Forces

The previous chapters, largely philosophical, were designed to introduce the topic of outdoor recreation and establish some basic concepts and meanings. The present chapter is essentially factual in character. It contains pertinent information about social and economic forces which have had, and will continue to have, significant impact on the lives of people, and particularly on their outdoor recreation. Although there is general agreement on the direction and extent of most of the changes discussed here, some experts disagree on the influence that the changes may have on people's lives. In view of this, the information in this chapter is limited to that which is supported by the best facts available.

The society in which we live is in precarious balance, threatened on one side by forces of potential destruction, and counterbalanced on the other side by a vision of a nation without material want. Occasionally we get a glimpse of a possible utopia. Holding us in this precarious position are the hopes and also the threats which accompany a highly automated and fast-moving society in which the watchword is "change." In our society change follows change with bewildering rapidity and of course influences the lives of people. In particular it affects our time, leisure, and recreational patterns.

Living in the presence of constant change is difficult, to say the least. In the past most people were able to go through life with the set of attitudes and beliefs appropriate to the age in which they were born. The rate of change in science, art, education, technology, and beliefs and ideals was slow enough to make them relatively **25**

> We are now living through the second great divide in human history, comparable in magnitude only with that first break in historic continuity — the shift from barbarism to civilization... — Alvin Toffler

constant throughout one's lifetime. Even then each generation expressed its frustration with the common phrase, "What is the world coming to?"

There are more well-qualified scientists in the world today than lived throughout all history prior to 1920, and they are revolutionizing our world in almost every respect. Never before has a competing individual had to be so versatile, knowledgeable, and perceptive as today.

In order to discuss the many important points of change which relate to the theme of this book, the remainder of this chapter is organized under the following headings: *population, urbanization, mobility, work and leisure time, income, automation and technology, education, and changing philosophy.* These headings are not totally satisfactory because they infer that they cover the only important changes. This is not true, but they do seem to be the most pertinent to the future planning for outdoor recreation.

Population

The number of people living in a given land area strongly influences their living patterns. This factor especially influences the use of natural resources. Resource management specialists are currently very concerned about people's extensive use of resources, and an increase in population implies still more extensive use. Moreover, an increase means more residential, commercial, industrial, and other such areas — therefore less natural resources. There is a point of population beyond which resources are unable to satisfy the demand for outdoor recreation, at least of the kind and quality to which we are accustomed.

If people did not exist in great numbers the problem of providing recreational programs, space, and facilities would be less difficult, but we do exist in great numbers and, according to demographers (predictors of population trends), the

Population is increasing faster than ever before. It spurts upward in geometric progression.

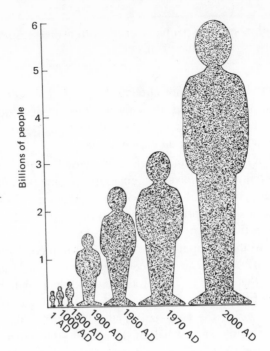

Figure 1. World population growth.

population growth will continue. It is estimated that from the year A.D. 1 until the year 1930 (nineteen hundred and thirty years) the world population doubled. It increased from .75 billion to 1.50 billion. Then during the next 35 years (1930-1965) it redoubled, increasing to 3 billion. The U.S. Commission on Population has stated that in the subsequent thirty-year period (1965-1995) it will redouble again, thus reaching 6 billion people (the 4 billion mark was reached in 1976). It has been calculated that if the present rate of world population growth (a little less than 2 percent per year) had existed since the beginning of the Christian era, we would now have an average of one square yard of earth for each living person. That would be hardly enough for mountain climbing, skiing, and long golf drives. Furthermore, it has been calculated that if the present rate of increase continues, in 650 years — less than the time back to the Renaissance — there will be standing room only on this earth. Figure 1 shows the trend of increase in world population.

Each minute 220 babies are born, while during that same minute about 140 people die. If your heart rate is normal, slightly more than one person is added to the world population every time your heart throbs. This results in 1.25 million additional people each week. Human multiplication is self-accelerating, like compound interest. It spurts upward in geometrical progression: 2-4-8-16-32-64-128. Because of the rapid population increase, some believe that in the future a large portion of the world will be run over by starving hordes, grabbing for a mouthful of rice or corn. They say our cities will engulf the suburbs and much of the countryside in a flood of brick and concrete structures. In such a world, democracy as we know it may become impossible, and people may become reduced to robots scuttling about in an antlike society.

Most of the world's population is in underdeveloped countries or countries where

> With respect to people, our most treasured resource, quality not quantity must be the theme of this era.

the natural resources are already depleted. This contributes to social unrest and political instability, and it smothers efforts to develop better lives for millions of people who are ill-fed, ill-clothed, ill-housed, poorly educated, and who lack the basic opportunities for an enriched life.

Currently North America and Western Europe have about 17 percent of the world's population and 64 percent of the income, as measured in goods and services produced. Asia has 56 percent of the population and 14 percent of the income. The deprived and underprivileged portion of the population is increasing more rapidly than the affluent portion.

It is especially important for Americans to recognize that the population problem is not confined to faraway places; our own predicted rate of increase is only slightly less than that of the world in total. In 1800 the population of the United States was less than five million. Fifty years later (1850) it had increased by five times, to 25 million. During the next half century (to 1900), the population increased to 85 million. During the first half of the nineteenth century (1900-1950), it almost doubled to reach 151 million, and during the next 27 years (1950-1977) 68 million people were added to bring the total to 219 million. Currently the U.S. is growing at a rate of about 3 million people per year. Even though the percentage of increase is less than a decade ago, never before has the population increased so rapidly in number — not even during the peak of the immigration flood just prior to World War I, when 1 million immigrants per year were added to the normal population growth. The U.S. Commission on Population has predicted that by the year 2000 the population will reach 300 million, approximately twice what it was in 1950.

The population explosion is a matter of simple mathematics, and it is well illustrated by this true story of John Eli Miller, who personally experienced his own population explosion. This illustration is an excerpt from a bulletin published by the Population Reference Bureau, Inc.[1]

Recently, on the eve of his 95th birthday, John Eli Miller died in Middlefield, Ohio, leaving to mourn his passing a very large number of living descendants. He was survived by five of his seven children, 61 grandchildren, 338 great-grandchildren, and six great-great-grandchildren, a total of 410 descendants.

John Miller actually had seen with his own eyes a population explosion. His data were not statistics on a graph or chart, but the scores of children at every family gathering who ran up to kiss Grandpa, so many that it confused him. His confusion can be forgiven, for there were among them 15 John Millers, all named in his honor. And what man could remember the names of 61 grandchildren and 338 great-grandchildren?

The remarkable thing about this large clan was that it started with a family of only seven children. John Miller's family was not unusually large. It is just that he lived long enough to find out what simple multiplication can do.

Outdoor Recreation in America

[1]*Population Profile*, U.S. Government Printing Office, Washington, D.C., 1964.

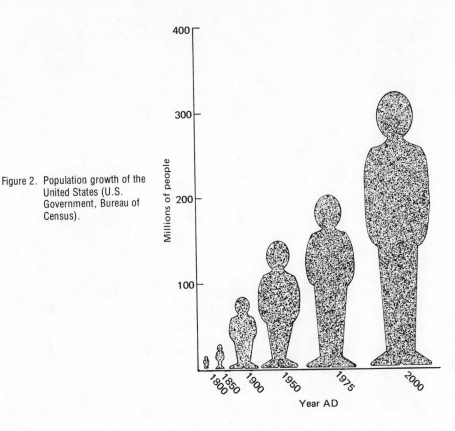

Figure 2. Population growth of the United States (U.S. Government, Bureau of Census).

At the time of John Miller's death, 61 of his 63 grandchildren were still living. Of the 341 great-grandchildren, only three had died. All six of his great-great-grandchildren were born during the last year of his life and were healthy infants. Thus, a major factor in the world-wide population crisis was vividly evident in John Miller's family; the fact that a very high percentage of children born in the twentieth century, who enjoy the benefits of modern medicine, are growing up to become adults and to have families of their own.

It was calculated that if John Miller had lived 10 more years he would have seen more descendants born to him than in all of his 95 years of life. He would have had at least 1000 living descendants. By that time he would have been receiving notice of a new descendant on the average of once every second day.

What did John Miller think about his family? Did it worry him to see it growing so large? Indeed it did. His concerns were the very ones that the demographers, economists, sociologists, and other serious students of world population have been voicing. He was not an educated man, but John Miller summarized it in one simple question he constantly repeated, "Where will they all find good farms?"

The total population increase is simply an expression of the ratio between birth and death rate. In 1900 the death rate was 17.2 per 1000 Americans. By 1976 it had been reduced to 9.2 per 1000. A male child born in 1900 could expect to live 46 years, whereas one born in 1977 has a life expectancy of 68.5 years. For females the

Too many people in one outdoor recreation spot detracts immensely from the pleasure of all of them.

gain has been even greater, from 48 years in 1900 to 75 years in 1977. What will life expectancy be in 1990 and 2000?

Another interesting factor of population is age distribution. In 1940, 25 percent of the population were age 15 and under. In 1977, that percentage had increased to 30 percent. In 1940, 10 percent of the population were age 60 or more. By 1977 the percentage had increased to 18. The proportion of both young and old members of the population is increasing, while the proportion of working age is decreasing. (It is important to note that during the mid and late 1970s the proportion of working age will increase because of the large number of babies born during the post World War II years who have entered or will soon enter the job market.)

In addition to total population and age distribution, the population density in particular geographic locations is another important factor which influences the living patterns of people. This factor leads us to the topic of urbanization.

Urbanization

For most Americans the days are gone when the benefits of inspiring natural beauty could be found around the corner of the next block. In recent decades there has been a mass move from the rural environment. As a result, the accessibility of outdoor areas has become greatly restricted to a major portion of the population.

First came villages, then towns, then cities, and finally sprawling metropolitan areas. Like inflating balloons, the small communities founded a century or two ago have grown larger and more complex, and as they have grown, problems that the founding fathers never foresaw have been generated — problems of decent housing, pleasant surroundings, and some attachment to nature.

The American society was originally an agrarian one. In fact, some of our institutions are still geared to seasons and harvests. But due to startling advances in the field of agriculture, the average farm worker today can produce enough food for 30 more persons. To show a comparison, at the time of the Revolutionary War 92 percent of our population were farmers, while today this figure is less than 10 percent, and some economic experts predict that by the year 2000 fewer than 5 percent of our population will produce a surplus of farm products. Because of increased population, combined with mechanized farming, a large number of people leave the rural environment every year and go to cities to live and work. At the time of the first U.S. census (1790) only 5 percent of the 4 million population lived in cities of 2500 or more, and all of these were small cities by today's standards. By the time of the Civil War we were 20 percent urban; by World War I we had become 45 percent urban; and in the year 1930 the population changed from predominantly rural to predominantly urban. In 1950 the census showed that 60 percent of the population lived in urban environments; by 1960 this had increased to 68 percent, and in 1977 it exceeded 75 percent of the population. Our larger cities have grown fastest, and our giants are now very large indeed.

In the past, most of the growth of cities has been due to migration either of foreigners who came to the United States to live and usually to settle in the cities, or our own native country youth who have gone to the cities to work and to live. This rural-urban migration is still going on.

In recent decades cities have begun to grow from their own excess of births over deaths. In the future, they will continue to grow more from this source rather than from migration. The migration both from the country to the city and from foreign countries to the United States will be proportionately less in the future.

While these large movements of people from rural to urban locations have been under way, there have also occurred some major changes within the urban complexes and these changes will continue. The old and central portions of the cities have grown little in recent decades and some have lost population. In contrast, the surrounding suburbs have expanded rapidly. Almost everyone in the United States has firsthand experience with some area of land which was in a farm or a forest a decade ago and which today is covered with suburbs, a shopping center, or an industrial complex. These population shifts from country to city and from central city to suburb have been highly selective as far as race, age, income, education, and other personal characteristics are concerned.

> Experimental studies with animal species have revealed that excessive crowding results in several forms of behavioral disturbances, ranging from cannibalism to social unresponsiveness.

Urban dwellers are currently divided about equally between the suburbs and the central cities. Because of the large and sprawling suburban developments, some metropolitan areas are taking on dimensions of 100 miles or more. These are known as megalopolis areas, a term used to define a region where several metropolitan districts have grown together. In the foreseeable future the Atlantic Seaboard, the Great Lakes region, and the Pacific Coast area extending from San Francisco to San Diego will take on strong megalopolis characteristics.

In spite of many advantages enjoyed by city dwellers, there is much criticism of the large cities as places to live and to work. They are often attacked for their ugliness, lack of order and unity, congestion, conditions of poor sanitation, and *lack of open space*. In many of our larger cities the central core suffers from blight. They are often breeding places of disaffection and violence. Furthermore, movement into the city for work and away from it for recreation and other qualities of good living causes severe transportation problems.

The number of people living in urban areas is expected to double during the next 30 years. The open spaces currently surrounding cities will turn into suburban developments, with greater emphasis on condominium and apartment complexes. Some of the present suburbs will be built into high-rise apartments. Single family units will become very costly. Nature and its inspiring environment will become more remote from people's day-to-day lives. As this trend develops, the great migration to the country during weekends and vacation periods will continue to demonstrate our struggle to keep in touch with nature. Increasing numbers will own two homes — one in the city and one in the country. In spite of strong efforts to cling to

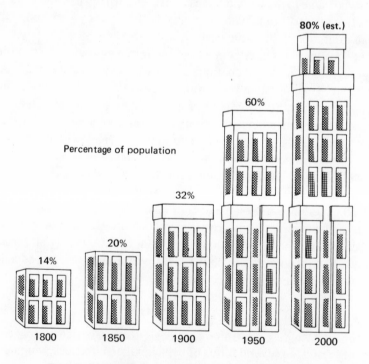

Percentage of population

80% (est.)

60%

32%

20%

14%

1800   1850   1900   1950   2000

Figure 3. Percentage of United States population living in urban environments.

All of the world is gradually becoming a city.

our rural heritage, urban living will dominate the lives of a great majority of people, and urban values will strongly prevail.

A very significant feature of the metropolitan pattern up to the present is its low density. This applies not only to residential areas, but also to industries, business, schools, and other types of facilities. Business, schools, and factories have tended toward the rambling type structure surrounded by large areas for parking. A century ago when a city increased by 1000 people it urbanized only about 10 acres. Thirty years ago 30 acres were needed. Today nearly 200 acres are required in metropolitan areas to absorb 1000 additional population. It is not implied that this sprawling type of suburban development is undesirable, but it does require a tremendous amount of land, and it puts many miles between the urban dwellers and the natural areas they use for outdoor recreation. However, the problem of many miles is partly offset by our great mobility. And this leads to the next important factor which influences outdoor recreation.

Mobility

Some say the most distinctive feature about life in America is its mobility. Never before has a nation of people been able to travel as far and as fast with such ease. Whether we choose to travel by land, air, or sea, and whether we travel long or short distances, comfortable and rapid modes of transportation are available to us. Our current rate of travel for both business and pleasure is unprecedented in the history of the world. The American people currently spend more than $28 billion per year for travel. Of this, $20 billion are spent for domestic tourist travel, $6 billion for business travel, and $2 billion for travel abroad.

During the early development of our nation modes of travel were very meager, but as the nation increased in size the transportation system grew with it, until finally the day came when travel by post roads and rivers was considered to be a

The most common carrier is the automobile. In the near future Americans will own over 100 million cars.

highly developed system affording extraordinary convenience. We still enjoy the stories of the old post roads and stirring sagas of the river steamers. During the latter half of the nineteenth century the iron horse came into being, and before long it dominated the transportation of both goods and people. Railroad travel was so successful that many of the larger railroads built resorts and other vacation facilities to meet the interests and needs of the travel-minded public.

By the late 1920s a new look in travel was beginning to take shape. Many people owned automobiles and, even though there were no transcontinental highways, people were beginning to do much of their travel by car. As this trend continued, many picnic, camp, and municipal tourist areas sprang up in all parts of the country. Extensive highway systems began to develop, and the way was literally paved for the automobile to become king of travel in America.

Today our most common carrier by far, as measured by passenger miles, is the automobile, followed respectively by air, train, and boat travel. Automobiles, like people, are appearing in great numbers. In America alone about 10 million cars are produced each year, and the number of privately owned cars now exceeds 90 million. If all of the currently owned cars were placed end to end on all of the paved highways in the United States, there would be one car every 200 yards. At the present time the entire United States population could be comfortably seated in these cars and they would average only 2.4 persons per car.

Proportionately the rate of increase in car ownership in recent years has been greater than the population increase. Four out of five families now own cars, and one of every four families owns two or more cars. In suburban and rural areas nearly nine out of ten families own cars.

The rapid increase in use of automobiles has demanded accelerated development of a vast network of highways and has greatly increased space needed for parking. Within the United States there are currently over 3,500,000 miles of highways, roads, and streets. This system connects in many places to extensive networks in Canada and Mexico. But even with this extensive system traffic is often slowed to a snail's pace. In order to relieve tourists and other highway travelers from passing through cities, a vast interstate highway system was initiated, and it now provides over 50,000 miles of interstate freeways. Surely the pressures resulting from the rapidly increasing use of automobiles will test the resourcefulness and skills of the nation's road builders and traffic experts.

Even though the automobile is the king of travel in the United States, other modern modes of travel have become increasingly important. Airplane passengers in the United States increased from 2.5 million in 1940 to over 80 million in 1977. The 600 mile-per-hour jet liner has revolutionized air travel in all parts of the nation and the world. It has put major cities within a few hours of each other and made almost every geographic area in the United States less than a day's travel away. But the best is yet to come. Aeronautic experts claim that during the next decade, planes traveling twice the speed of sound will become routine, and short route helicopter systems will become popular within large metropolitan areas. In a sense, the nation will take to the air.

Automation experts predict that some of us will live to see airliners cross the continent in 90 minutes, trains travel at 200 miles per hour over an air cushion, and ships skim through the water at 75 knots. In the future our great mobility will afford people in large numbers the opportunity to test their skills and interests against exciting leisure-time challenges in every geographic area of the world. Our highly developed system of transportation will deliver large numbers of people to the doorsteps of every outdoor recreation area in the world. This will have significant effects on natural resources, and the supply of outdoor recreation.

Work and Leisure Time

The line between leisure and labor has always been tenuous and shifting. Nevertheless, since the beginning of early civilizations there has been a certain stability, in that leisure time has always been available at least to a portion of society. Leisure and work are two sides of our shield, and they both protect us. The one side, labor, enables us to live while the other side, leisure, makes living more meaningful. "We labor in order to have leisure," said Aristotle. Work can ennoble a person, but leisure provides an opportunity to develop perfection and enrichment of character.

In the well-established societies throughout history, such as those of Mesopotamia, China, Egypt, India, Greece, and Rome, leisure and labor became

Leisure is the blessing and could be the curse of a progressive, successful civilization. Most Americans face the prospect of more leisure time in the future and, thus, the challenge of learning to use it well.

sharply defined, and both had increasing importance. Labor produced material wealth, and the wealth became concentrated in the hands of a few. Leisure became the grand prize of those few who possessed the wealth, while labor remained the lot of the great majority. Those individuals comprising the classes which controlled the wealth put their leisure time to use in a variety of sportive activities and in the pursuit of the aesthetic and the intellectual. As a result, cultural trends were established and civilizations were advanced.

In America the trends of work and leisure have not been very much different from those of other highly developed societies. Through the course of our development to the status of a prominent society, we have undergone many changes. Among the most dramatic during recent years are (a) what we do for a living, (b) how much time we devote to doing it, and (c) how much we are paid for it.

Americans are an enterprising people engaged in an endless number of jobs and creating many new ones each year. The kind of work that we do has changed greatly from the time of our early history. Currently more than one of every three Americans, a total of about 76 million, are employed in regular jobs. About 85 percent of these are on somebody else's payroll, while the other 15 percent are self-employed in such fields as farming, business, law, and medicine.

Currently the white-collar workers outnumber all other occupational groups in the United States, being about 43 percent of the working population. About 35 percent are engaged in the blue-collar occupations, while 10 percent work on farms and the remaining 12 percent are engaged in the professions.

Not only has our kind of work changed greatly, but the amount of time spent on it has also undergone a revolution. Among nonfarm workers, the average work week in 1850 was almost 70 hours, in 1900 it was 55 hours, and in 1950 it was 40 hours. Some occupational groups are now moving to a 36-hour work week, and a few specialized labor unions are pressing for a 32-hour week. Economic and labor specialists predict that by 1985 the work week among nonfarm workers in America will average 36 hours, and that by the year 2000 it will range between 28 and 32 hours.

While the work week becomes shorter, vacation periods become longer. Two-week vacations were once a rare privilege, but now the trend is toward vacations extending from three to five weeks. At the same time people are retiring at an earlier age. When we sum up the shorter work week, increased length of vacations, and earlier retirement, it is apparent that Americans today spend significantly less time on the job and more time at leisure than they spent 25, 50, or 100 years ago. Furthermore, off-the-job hours for the average American will increase even more as our highly automated society continues to develop.

The total amount of leisure time that people have does not tell the whole story. The *distribution of leisure* and the *size of its increments* are other factors which influence the uses made of it. Leisure time can occur on a daily, weekly, monthly, or annual basis.

Daily leisure is usually broken into small segments of an hour here and an hour there, but most of it is available in the evenings after the termination of the work day. This allows participation in only short-duration activities and leaves much to be desired with respect to new experiences and adventure.

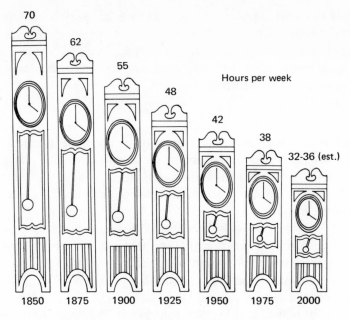

Figure 4. Changes in average work week in America among nonfarm workers.

Weekly leisure is usually defined in terms of weekends. Currently we think of this as two whole days, a large enough block of time to engage in long-term projects or to take a short trip away from home. However, weekend leisure is often interrupted by daily chores postponed during the week, and therefore often the large block becomes subdivided. Nevertheless, weekends do permit many pursuits that are impossible during the week.

Vacation leisure is of an entirely different kind. It represents the large block of time given annually which workers feel they have earned by a year of labor and which, therefore, they have the right to use in some unusual and often adventurous pursuit. To most working Americans the vacation period represents a segment of the year when time is not the greatest limitation. This period affords time to travel or become involved in some extensive project. Vacation leisure doubled from 1900 to 1950 and then doubled again by the early 1960s and doubled still again by the mid 1970s.

Retirement leisure is where the greatest changes have occurred. It increased four-fold from 1900 to 1950, and is expected to more than double by the year 2000. For many people retirement leisure represents an extended period where time is more

In a sense, when work is reduced, as it almost certainly will be, there is a very real crisis of values for people generally. Great groups of people have been trained by nothing in their whole culture, background, religion and philosophic conceptions, for anything other than work as a meaningful activity.

— Leo Cherne

abundant than any other commodity. They can therefore pursue whatever interests are within their means.

The amount of leisure, length of the leisure time periods, and how often they occur have great influence on the kinds of recreation people pursue and are important in planning for outdoor recreation.

Income

There are few aspects of life in this country more impressive than the tremendous amount of goods and services produced by our people. The total market value of these goods and services for a particular year is referred to as the "gross national product" (GNP). The GNP is generally accepted as an indication of the economic well-being of the nation.

In 1929, the first year it was calculated, the GNP was estimated to be $104 billion. At the darkest year in the depression (1933) it was only $56 billion, and it did not recover to its previous high (1929) until eight years later (1941). With the spending brought on by World War II, the GNP soared to $214 billion in 1945. It has increased consistently since that time except for slight setbacks in 1949 and 1954. The GNP for 1951 was $329 billion, and by 1965 it had more than doubled, to reach $675 billion. In 1970 it exceeded $900 billion, and in 1976 it exceeded $1100 billion.

A comparison of GNP from one year to another can serve as a general indication of the economic well-being of the nation, and of the individuals comprising the nation. But it must be recognized that, unless the GNP is interpreted in light of *inflation* and *increased population,* it does not truly represent the purchasing power of the people. Therefore, only when the GNP for all years is converted to a constant dollar value does it take on comparative meaning. (This conversion eliminates the effects of inflation.) For example, between 1940 and 1976 the GNP increased 1100 percent. But when the GNP for both years is expressed in 1976 dollar values (actual purchasing power), then the increase was only 280 percent. This equals a compound rate of increase of about 4.6 percent per year, which is still a significant gain.

Population is an important consideration in interpreting GNP because if, during a particular period, the GNP is doubled and the population is also doubled, then the goods and services produced per capita have remained unchanged. Therefore, the best comparison of GNP is the GNP per person in constant dollars. This eliminates the effects of both inflation and population increase. When expressed in these terms, the increase was 162 percent between 1940 and 1976, or a compound annual increase of 3.2 percent.

All of this simply means that in terms of purchasing power per capita, today's consumer is more than two and one-half times as well off as the consumer in the mid 1930s, and 18 percent better off than the consumer in the best economic years during World War II.

In order to relate the increased economy more closely to the individual American

It has always been difficult for a person to enjoy the fine things of life unless the means to provide the essentials are first available.

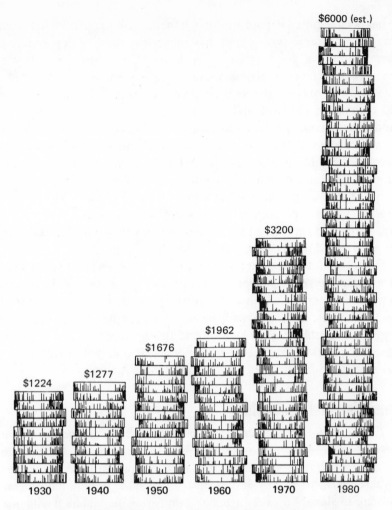

$6000 (est.)

$3200

$1962

$1676

$1277

$1224

1930   1940   1950   1960   1970   1980

Figure 5. Changes in per capita income of Americans. (This graph is based on actual
dollar amounts, and does not portray the effects of inflation.)

citizen, a comparison of annual per capita income is presented. In 1930 average income per person was $1224, and by 1940 it had increased only $53 to a total of $1277. By 1950 per capita income had reached $1676; in 1962 it was $2016; by 1965 it had increased to $2300; in 1970 it reached $3200; and in 1976 it was $5400.

Fifty percent of all nonfarm families in America currently enjoy annual incomes in excess of $12,000, and 25 percent of the families have incomes of $15,000 or more. However, there are also those on the lower end of the income scale. In 1976 an estimated 10 million families received incomes of $4000 or less. These families represented about one-fifth of the total population. For all nonfarm families the average income in 1976 was slightly more than $9200.

An interesting fact is that the nation's productivity, and therefore the individual income, could probably be higher than it is if it were not that beyond a certain point people choose free time over increased production. Throughout history most of our time has been required to produce enough food, clothing, and shelter to sustain life, but as our economic productivity has improved, there is opportunity to choose between additional goods or increased leisure time. After the salary earner has reached a certain level of income, the tendency is apparently to choose free hours in preference over increased salary because they contribute more to people's true wants than additional work and money.

Additional income per individual and per family has resulted in greater expenditure in all phases of life. But the greatest increase in spending has been on the nonessential goods (luxuries) as opposed to the necessities of food, clothing, and shelter. Only so much money is required for food and clothing, and this amount does not change a great deal as the average salary increases. However, as income increases, a greater proportion of it is spent on nonessentials.

It is difficult to know all of the influences that will result from additional income along with the additional time that we shall have in the future. Nevertheless, from past experience it is safe to predict that people will spend more on hobbies, sports, adventure, and other recreations which provide increased satisfaction. Many will own two homes, one of which will be in a resort area. Two-car families will become three-car families, and the cars will be used more for pleasure than necessity. Boats, ski equipment, athletic gear, hunting and fishing supplies, and other recreational goods will appear in ever increasing amounts. People will travel more miles and spend more time in activities which require these luxury goods.

Automation and Technology

In *The Republic,* Plato blueprinted his ideal society composed of thousands of slaves to perform the work, so that a few at the peak of the social structure could develop their spiritual, intellectual, and physical qualities and thereby improve the cultural status of the society. It is estimated that at the peak of the Athenian culture there were 15 slaves for each citizen. In comparing our situation with that of previous societies, automation experts estimate that at the present time the average American has at her or his disposal the equivalent of 500 human slaves. Our slaves are in the form of electricity, engines, computers, and various other mechanical devices. Visualize, for example, the number of human slaves that would be needed to equal the thrust of four jet engines as they carry a super airliner through space at 600 miles per hour, or the slaves that would be needed to transport the load of a freight train a distance of 300 miles, or to do the calculations that can be accomplished on a large computer in one hour.

In our society, mechanical devices perform an increasing number of functions with unmatched precision and rapidity. For example, computers can be used to

One thing that is new is the prevalence of newness, the changing scale and scope of change itself, so that the world alters as we walk in it, so that the years of a man's life measure not some small growth or rearrangement or moderation of what he learned in childhood, but a great upheaval.
— Robert Oppenheimer

analyze stock-market portfolios, determine the best combination of crops and live-stock for certain farm conditions, translate one language to another, and for many other tasks heretofore performed by human beings unaided. There is no basis for determining where this process of automation will be halted. The capacities and potentialities of these devices seem almost unlimited, and they contain extraordinary implications for the future of mankind.

Producing an automated system does not merely mean replacing people by having machines to do the task that people once did. Diebold,[2] a pioneer in automative techniques, points out that the system is a way of thinking just as much as a way of doing. He states that in America it is no longer necessary to think in terms of individual machines, or even in terms of groups of machines. Instead, it is practical to look at an entire production as an integrated system and not as a series of individual steps.

Walter Reuther,[3] one of our well-known labor leaders, stated:

> We shall make more technological progress in the next 25 years than was made in the last 250 years. A new generation of computers is coming on fast and strong without waiting for us to deal with the wholesale threat to job security already posed by automation, or to think through the revolutionary process of transforming a society based on work into a society which, if it is to remain democratic, must increasingly be given over to meaningful leisure.... We are now flying blindly into this new era. The new computers may shake us out of our complacency. They will be fast enough to do a decade's work in a coffee break, and their impact will be felt not by blue-collar workers alone, but by skillful technicians as well.

Probably the most severe problem to be coped with as a result of automation is unemployment. The automated system under which we live usually replaces personnel. The rapid increase of our work force while jobs are being eliminated by automation concerns economists. If these problems are coped with and the benefits derived from automation are retained, then men of the future will truly have the opportunity to live creatively. What they do with their time and resources will depend to a large extent on what they voluntarily choose to do. In turn, their choices will be based on what they think they should gain in life and how they view its purposes.

In the past, society has claimed that its members were entitled to a living only if they carried out a task for which society was willing to pay. The creation of a society of abundance will make it possible to relax this requirement some. People may be allowed to follow an interest they find vital even when society does not totally support it through the price mechanism.

In reviewing automation and technology and their effects on society, some people are overly pessimistic, while others lean toward extreme optimism. But it is obvious that we are in the midst of the most automated society in history and that we are rapidly becoming more automated. Automation and technology influence almost every phase of our lives, even what we eat and under what conditions we eat it. Automation and technology influence our economy, our political and social struc-

[2]John Diebold, *Automation: Its Impact on Business and Labor*, National Planning Association, Planning Pamphlet No. 106, Washington, D.C., May, 1969.
[3]Walter Reuther, "Freedom's Time of Testing," *Saturday Review*, August 29, 1964.

tures, our individual habits and practices, and even our physical fitness and mental health, and especially the types and amount of uses we make of our natural resources.

Needless to say, the new mode influences what we do for outdoor recreation, where we go for it, and how much time we spend doing it. In some respects technology has made outdoor living almost as convenient as staying at home and has opened new avenues in recreation pursuits. For example, some of the popular outdoor recreation activities now enhanced are speed boating, water skiing, camping, hunting and fishing, and snow skiing. Without the modern devices our outdoor recreation patterns would be quite different from what they are now.

Education

The purpose of an educational system such as ours is to prepare people to live effectively in their society and to help them contribute to the improvement of society. This means there is no end to the need for useful education.

Economic prosperity seems always to strengthen the demand for education. An example of this in our own industrial society is that of a middle class that has established its economic position and now seeks to broaden its political and social influence in order to further its advance to "the good life." Never before has it been so necessary for the average person to understand the effects and implications of modern science, as well as the economic and political system. Never before has it been so necessary to possess adequate communication skills and to develop the appreciations essential to a well-rounded individual. In the United States, the realization that such knowledge, skill, and appreciation are essential has created tremendous social pressure for more education. Primarily, two factors have influenced this new look: (a) the *population boom,* and (b) the *sudden awakening* of citizens Jane and John Doe to the fact that a high level of education is essential if they are to live effectively in our technicalized and complex society.

The population boom of the early 1940s and 1950s sent a stream of millions of additional people to our schools, causing overcrowding first in elementary schools, then later in the secondary schools and colleges. As a result of the postwar baby boom, the enrollment in elementary schools increased from 5.7 million in 1950 to 10.1 million in 1962, a gain of 77 percent. This tremendous increase carried over to the secondary schools and colleges, causing crowding in our schools at every level.

Not only has the total number of students greatly increased, so has the average level of education. For example, in 1910 only 63 percent of school-age children (5 to 18 years) were enrolled in school. By 1930 this percentage was 72; in 1950, 78; in 1960, 84; and by 1970, 86. It is presently at 87 percent.

A greater number of students are going on to college. College enrollments have increased from 1.5 million in 1940 to 3.2 million in 1960. The current college enrollments exceed 6.5 million. The great move toward a college education is further demonstrated by the fact that in 1950 only 27 percent of college-age students enrolled in college. This percentage increased to 39 in 1965 and is presently at about 45 percent. Following is a list of the percentage of school-age youth enrolled in schools in the U.S. at different years since 1930.

Year	Elem. and Sec. Schools (Age 5-18)	Colleges and Universities (Age 18-21)
1930	72%	—
1950	78%	27%
1960	84%	35%
1970	86%	43%
1975	87%	45%

All of this increased attention to education has two startling effects on our planning for outdoor recreation. *First,* education is the key to higher personal income, and higher income influences what people do for recreation and where they go to do it. The result of a recent survey reported in the *American Economic Review* showed that people who completed only elementary school had an average income of $4700, compared with $6800 for high school graduates and $11,700 for college graduates. *Second,* education's effect on recreation is due to the positive relationship between level of education and diversification of interests. As people further their education, they tend to broaden their horizon of interests, appreciations, and skills in recreational pursuits. Therefore, more highly educated people tend not only to have more interests, but also to have more means with which to pursue their interests. Increased education means greater participation per citizen in recreational activities and greater expenditure on recreation-related pursuits. In the future people will make greater demands for areas, facilities, and programs to satisfy their increased interests, appreciations, and skills.

Changing Philosophy

At present Americans are experiencing rapid changes in the structure of their lives in relation to time, work, leisure, pace, and basic values. These changes are prompted by a unique cooperation of scientific research, engineering skill, technological advancements, and mass production, which all contribute to automation. Despite many urgent problems, automation has brought with it a leisure mode that is taking its position in the usual evolution of events that occur in the development of a highly structured society. We have progressed from *feudalism,* based on a stable agricultural society, through *industrialism,* based on a system of mass production, to a *highly livable era* characterized by freely disposable time and materials. The additional free time and materials offer new potential for creativity and the further advance of civilization.

The realization of the potential, however, depends primarily upon the development of our system of values, and the extent to which we are able, in mass, to effectively integrate them into life. In order for the average American to effectively do this some basic changes in his philosophy must occur. According to Lewis Mumford:

> The role of work is to make man a master of the conditions of life: hence its constant discipline is essential to his grasp of the real world. The function of work is to provide man with a living: not for the purpose of enlarging his capacities to consume, but of liberating his capacity to create.[4]

[4]Lewis Mumford, *The Condition of Man*, Harcourt, Brace & Co., New York, 1944, p. 5.

> Bigger is not better; slower may be faster; less may well mean more.
> — Stewart Udall

Philosopher George Santayana expressed the idea that release from excessive work affords man the opportunity "to become." But he further said that "only he who has enlarged his mind and tamed his heart can profit from the free life which material competence is making possible in increasing abundance."[5]

As human beings are liberated from the totally utilitarian process that for ages has impoverished their cultural and creative development, they find themselves in an environment of new opportunity for personal enrichment and service to society. They find themselves more free to think, feel, and exercise their compulsions without keeping too sharp an eye on the bare necessities of survival. Thus leisure time may possess a value of its own, values which "avail for life."

But Karl Mannheim casts another light on the potentials of leisure time with this statement:

> Comparative studies in the use of leisure show at first glance that a higher position, larger income, and increased security do not necessarily lead to culture. Unless material advancement is combined with personal example and the persuasion exercised by the presence of intelligent standards for the use of leisure, it may end in boredom, neurosis, and general decadence . . . . Security alone is no guarantee that surplus energies will be turned in any particular direction, unless they are guided by personal influence and education . . . . The average citizen is unable to invent new uses for his leisure.[6]

This view strongly implies that in order to use leisure time effectively, people must be purposely prepared. This further implies that basic philosophical concepts, appreciations, and skills *must be taught*. This idea emphasizes the need for planned education which leads to the worthy use of leisure time, along with the development within our society of a sound philosophy about the use of time.

Leisure and recreation have traditionally been regarded with suspicion, sometimes with disgust, and often with condemnation, while work has always been held as one of the highest values of American life. We have, through the values passed to us, learned to regard work with great respect. Most of all, we have been influenced by the Protestant ethic, "that through work man serves God and gains the essential values of the good life." Moreover, work has traditionally been associated with more than material accomplishment or economics; it has been a source of social and moral recognition.

Even though modern concepts do not and should not minimize the values of work, they do indicate a greater appreciation for leisure and participation in worthwhile recreational pursuits. Many people now realize that wholesome recreation may contribute to a well-rounded personality, and add to life a spirit of adventure, creativity, and enrichment. Even though people have traditionally made their marks

[5]George Santayana, *The Philosophy of Santayana,* edited by Paul A. Schilpp, Northwestern University Press, Chicago, 1940, p. 332.

[6]Willard C. Sutherland, "A Philosophy of Leisure," *The Annals of the American Academy of Political and Social Science* (Philadelphia), Vol. 313, September, 1957, p. 2.

on society through long hours of work, they have done so with the "traveling hopefully" concept that there is something better still to come. This "something better" resides in the idea that leisure time affords the opportunity to create and to achieve in pursuits of one's own choosing, and that these pursuits will elevate the individual and society.

It is a fundamental truth that at least a moderate amount of wholesome recreation is essential to our cultural, moral, and spiritual well-being. The challenge to use leisure time effectively and constructively demands full development of our national, state, and local recreational resources.

The "new philosophy" is in essence a recognition that leisure time will become increasingly abundant, and that as it does so, it will afford additional opportunity to ordinary people to lift themselves to an elevated position, thereby improving themselves and society. For this *there must be adequate leadership,* part of which must be furnished in the form of connoisseurs who create and mold tastes, communicate purposes, skills, and appreciations, encourage the installation of adequate facilities, and accept the responsibility for cultural initiative and development of cultural traditions. The demand will emphasize the importance of leaders in the recreation and park field who have insight into "the good life," who know the needs of people and society, and who have the initiative and creativity to help large numbers of people achieve the qualities that contribute toward enrichment and happiness.

What Can Be Done?

The aforementioned trends indicate that the demand for outdoor recreation will continue at an ever increasing rate, while the supply of resources will steadily diminish. Because of this, we must more seriously analyze what it is we want in terms of outdoor recreation opportunities, and what kinds of opportunities we want for our children and grandchildren. Are the outdoor pleasures which we have enjoyed so much in the past really worth holding onto? If the answer is yes, then we had better act more wisely and with dispatch. We cannot afford to continue observing and discussing the problems while they roll over us. If acceptable quality and quantity of outdoor recreation opportunities are to be retained, the following actions are essential:

1. Natural resource management agencies must become more geared toward people management. They must accept that the resources are going to be heavily used by people, and the only way the resources can be properly conserved or preserved is by effective management of both the resources and the people who use them. People management as it relates to natural resources involves several aspects, such as the understanding of the needs and wants of people, the implementation of certain necessary controls, orientation toward basic conservation principles, and the development of appreciation for a clean and attractive natural environment.

2. Desirable outdoor recreation areas must be identified and reserved for that purpose. In many cases, other uses will have to give way to recreation.

3. Multiple use of resources must become more prevalent, with recreation as one of the prominent uses.

4. Local, state, and federal resource management programs will need to receive additional impetus from persons who recognize that the purpose of these programs is to provide an abundance of useable resources for the good and enjoyment of the people and not simply to protect a piece of natural real estate.

5. Privately owned lands with recreational potential will have to be more fully utilized by the public. Public agencies and individuals will need to work closely with private land owners to bring this about.

6. Americans will have to take a more intelligent approach to population increase and distribution. Circumstances in other countries have clearly proved that there is a point at which quantity of people seriously threatens the quality of life. Americans must be wise enough to learn from the experiences of other nations and to apply reason in population growth and distribution.

7. Some of the "great doers" in our society who want to turn all of nature into man-made structures for utility purposes must be strictly controlled, and people must learn that some resources are more valuable in their natural state than in any other form.

8. Finally, regardless of efforts to retain present patterns of outdoor recreation, our changing society and diminishing resources will dictate that recreation take new forms. Whether we can replace the vanishing opportunities with equally satisfying activities depends on our creativity and ingenuity combined with our ability to utilize resources effectively and efficiently.

Each year the gap between outdoor recreation demand and opportunity grows wider, and that between potential demand and potential opportunity grows still wider. The problem has become immense, and it has crept up on us so silently that many leaders in responsible positions do not even recognize its seriousness. It is a problem which deserves the attention of some of our best qualified leaders, but more important, it requires the individual attention of each responsible American citizen who believes that people have the right to fill their hearts with the joys of nature and to return occasionally to the beauty and gratification inherent in their natural environment.

Chapter 4 Historical Development of Outdoor Recreation

It is true that throughout the development of the recreation and park movement in America there has been a generalized distinction between the two broad categories of outdoor (resource-oriented) recreation and community (activity-oriented) recreation. Fortunately in recent years some melting together of these categories has occurred, resulting in more pronounced coordination and cooperation now than in the past. This melting effect can be partially attributed to the fact that during the past two decades leaders at all levels and in various walks of life have given increased attention to the importance of recreation to both the individual and society. This has resulted in greater attention to the total field with limited regard for categorization. Emphasis has been placed on the idea that the kind of leadership that is needed can be furnished best by those having a substantial base of information, a sound philosophy, and a broad scope of the total field of leisure-time pursuits.

Even though this chapter deals primarily with the historical development of outdoor recreation, it should not be interpreted as an effort to perpetuate the categorization of the total field. But this book deals with the outdoor phase of the total field and is not all-inclusive.

As we search far back into history, it is difficult to distinguish between some forms of outdoor recreation and occupational or survival activities. For example, hunting and fishing of different forms have always been done by people for various reasons. Further, people have consistently responded to such adventurous challenges as sailing, mountain climbing, and snow skiing. But even in early history there were some distinctions between people's pleasurable participation in these activities and their involvement for necessity. As civilization has developed, participation in outdoor activities has gradually become more recreational and less occupational or survival-oriented. Outdoor activities now represent one of the major aspects of recreation in this country and in certain other areas of the world.

Marie Luise Gothein in her monumental book *A History of Garden Art* credits the Asiatics with being the real inventors of parks. She traces the western Asiatic parks from the vineyards and fish ponds of the Sumerian king, Gudea, about 2340 B.C., down through the Hanging Gardens of Babylon about the ninth or tenth century B.C., past the introduction of flowers in the parks in the seventh century B.C.[1]

Centuries later Greek writers told of the parks and gardens of Persia. Gothein reports this in the following paragraph:

> ...The Persians were also familiar with the chase in open country. A grand hunting-ground was given to the young Cyrus by his grandfather, in the hope that it would keep him at home, but he despised it, and, fired with longing, summoned his companions and went off, for in this park there were so many animals that he felt as though he was only shooting captive creatures.

Wealthy and influential Romans were noted for having one or more large villas, and many of these had characteristics of parks with special emphasis on hunting. To quote again from Gothein:

> ...Quintus Hortensius had already made a park of fifty yokes of land, and enclosed it with a wall, and on this estate he had set up on the higher ground a shooting-box where he entertained his friends in a peculiar way. He had a slave dressed like Orpheus who sang before them, and then sounded a horn, whereupon a whole crowd of stags and boars and other quadrupeds came up, so that to him who told the tale the spectacle seemed more delightful than the hunt itself.

Generally speaking, throughout the Roman Empire the villas were on the outskirts of the towns or in the country. But in Rome itself they invaded the city so that the city was spotted with gardens. Here was the first significant move to bring the country to the city. Also, the Romans seemed to be the original inventors of the floral greenhouse, using mica for windowpanes. During the first century of the Christian era the Romans expanded their empire northward and their great villas and hunting parks began to appear in what is now France and Germany — some of them even as far north as Great Britain.

Because of space limitations no attempt will be made here to present a history of outdoor recreation between the time of the Roman Empire and the early development of our own country — this topic is adequately covered in the literature. In this book a summary of developments in the United States from 1776 to the present day will have to suffice.

[1]Marie Luise Gothein, *A History of Garden Art*, 2 volumes. Edited by Walter P. Wright, J. M. Dent & Sons, Ltd., Publishers, London, 1913. Quoted in Charles B. Doell and Louis F. Twardzik, *Elements of Park and Recreation Administration*, 3rd edition, Burgess Publishing Company, Minneapolis, 1973.

Early Developments in the United States

The conservation movement, which has had a significant impact on resource-oriented recreation, was prompted by the romantic and artistic efforts of poets, writers, artists, photographers, explorers, and mountain climbers. Certainly the writings of George Catlin, William Cullin Bryant, James Fenimore Cooper, and John Muir were influential in initiating a feeling for protecting areas of pristine beauty. Also, Emerson and Thoreau provided a philosophy toward nature which enhanced the saving of aesthetic resources.

Conservation of natural resources started in the United States as early as 1626 when the colony of Plymouth passed an ordinance that prohibited cutting timber on the colony land without official consent. In 1710 the town of Newington, New Hampshire, acquired a 110-acre community forest to be used by the townspeople for acquiring lumber for public buildings. In 1799 the U.S. Congress appropriated $200,000 to purchase timber lands. These early beginnings of forest management were based primarily upon economic supply and demand — the need for ready access to lumber to build public buildings and ships. But these actions automatically set the stage for a large number of other acts of conservation and preservation which have had a tremendous effect on the availability and use of natural resources for recreational purposes.

By the time of the Revolutionary War the American colonies were beginning to realize the need to control the shooting of game, and prior to 1775 twelve of the thirteen colonies had enacted closed seasons on certain game. In 1844 the first association for the protection of game was formed in the state of New York. In 1871 Congress passed a much needed bill for the protection of bison. The next year a law was passed in New York naming a seven-member commission to study the advisability of reserving wild lands for watershed preservation. By 1873 the state of New York had purchased 40,000 acres of forest land. This is accepted as the first substantial purchase of state forest reserves, which now total more than 2½ million acres in that state, mostly in the Adirondack and Catskill mountains.

On April 10, 1872, in Nebraska, Arbor Day was declared to create an awareness of the need for trees in metropolitan areas. In that same year Yellowstone National Park was reserved as a "pleasuring ground," and this marked the beginning of the national park system in the United States (and in the world). In 1874, Dr. Franklin D. Hough presented a paper at a meeting of the American Association for the Advancement of Science on "The Duty of Government in the Preservation of Parks."

The decade from 1875 to 1885 brought increased emphasis to conservation, which was highlighted by the writings and efforts of Theodore Roosevelt. Much of his conservation philosophy was expressed in his book *The Wilderness Hunter,* and he along with Gifford Pinchot gave significant national leadership during the late 1800s.

Also during the late 1800s increased attention began to generate for wildlife management. California and New Hampshire established state game commissions in 1878. And in 1883 the American Ornithologists Union was organized.

President Harrison created the first national forest reserve in 1891 — the Yellowstone Timberland Reserve, now part of the Shoshone National Forest. Before his term expired he had set aside other forest reserves totaling 13 million acres.

On March 31, 1891 the Park Protection Act was passed. It provided protection for wildlife in the national parks. In 1898 Gifford Pinchot was named head of the Federal Government Forest Division, and the forest conservation movement began to expand greatly under his leadership. He brought the word "conservation" into popular usage in application to natural resources. In 1899 Congress passed a law that allowed the recreational use of forest reserves. This was the first law to officially recognize the recreation value of forests.

The states began to take a more active role as Niagara Falls, New York, was set aside as a public reservation in 1885. In the same year Fort Mackinac was transferred from the federal government to the state of Michigan to mark the beginning of that state's system of recreation areas. In 1885 New York State instituted the first comprehensive administrative forestry act in America, and that same year California, Colorado, and Ohio created state boards of forestry.

The Early Part of the Present Century

The conservation movement progressed significantly in the first decade of the twentieth century. The passage of the Reclamation Act in 1902 provided for government aid to help develop water resources, and the Morris Act of 1902 established the great Minnesota forest. The first national wildlife refuge was established in 1902 on Pelican Island off the coast of Florida. In 1905 the Bureau of Biological Survey, the predecessor of the U.S. Fish and Wildlife Service, was established. The Division of Forestry in the Department of Agriculture was changed to the U.S. Forest Service, and the forest reserves that the General Land Office of the Department of the Interior had administered were turned over to the Forest Service.

The Antiquities Act of 1906 paved the way for setting aside national monuments by presidential proclamation. Also in 1906 President Theodore Roosevelt signed 33 proclamations that added more than 15.6 million acres to the forest reserve. In 1908 Roosevelt appointed a national conservation commission, with Gifford Pinchot as chairman, to study ways to save the country's natural resources. In 1909 the commission published an inventory of natural resources in the United States.

By 1916 several national parks and monuments had been set aside under the preservation concept, and during that year the National Park Service was established to administer these areas. The purpose of the NPS was "to promote and regulate the usual federal areas known as national parks, monuments, and reservations, to conserve the scenery and natural and historic objects and the wildlife, and to provide for the enjoyment of the same in such manner and by such means as will leave them unimpaired for their enjoyment for future generations."

Other noteworthy developments of the early 1900s were: (1) the passage by Congress of the Term-Lease Law of 1915 which authorized issuance of long-term permits for summer homes, motels, and other structures needed for recreation and for public convenience on national forest lands; (2) the establishment of the Rocky Mountain National Park in Colorado; and (3) the establishment of the Gila Wilderness in New Mexico in 1924 to protect wilderness values of the national forests.

An early hunting, fishing, and forest scene.

Central Park ice skating in the 1800s.

Aldo Leopold, a noted conservationist and an enthusiast of wilderness, was largely responsible for this action.

During the 1920s the U.S. Forest Service and the National Park Service gave increased emphasis to outdoor recreation. Stephen Mather, the first director of the National Park Service, claimed that recreation at the federal level was a function of the National Park Service. Forester William Greely wrote in *Outlook* (1925), "Outdoor recreation ranks today as one of the major resources of the national forests."

The depression years of the 1930s were boom years for outdoor recreation. The emergency conservation work programs of the federal government, debatable as they were, fulfilled certain definite needs. They created a demand for trained personnel through the work projects of the PWA, WPA, and CCC. Needed outdoor recreation facilities were constructed, and federally funded positions for 26,500 recreation leaders were made available through work programs. In addition to the direct effects of these programs on outdoor recreation, the aftereffects, as the men returned to their hometowns, brought recreation to communities that previously had not experienced organized programs under leadership. The principle of recreation as a community responsibility was greatly advanced.

Also in the 1930s wildlife management began to gain recognition as a science. Aldo Leopold's book *Game Management* was published during that decade, and it continued for a long time to serve as an important guide to wildlife management personnel.

The Migratory Bird Hunting Stamp Act of 1934 provided for acquiring lands for national wildlife refuges. Congress established an advisory board on national parks, historic sites, and monuments. The Soil Conservation Service was established during the early 1930s. The Forest Service continued to establish wilderness areas within the national forest reserve. The Natural Resources Committee was appointed in 1935 to investigate the country's natural resources, and to plan for their development and use. Also in that year, Congress passed the Fullmer Act which established federal aid to the states to acquire state forest lands.

In 1940 the Bureau of Biological Survey and the Bureau of Fisheries merged and became the U.S. Fish and Wildlife Service, located within the Department of the Interior. In 1941 several states passed enabling legislation for the establishment of state, city, town, and school forests. A few states already had state forests. In 1943 comprehensive interagency river basin planning began with the establishment of the Federal Interagency River Committee.

The Post World War II Years

Following World War II the growing public demand for resource-oriented recreation and sharpening competition for the various uses of natural resources became a matter of increasing national concern. The Dingle-Johnson Act of 1951 provided federal aid to state fisheries, and the Watershed Protection and Flood Prevention Act of 1954 authorized the Department of Agriculture to cooperate with state and local agencies in planning and carrying out improvements on small watersheds. The Recreation and Public Purposes Act of 1954 authorized state and local governments and nonprofit organizations to acquire certain federal lands for recreation use and for other public purposes. Congress amended the Coordination Act of 1958 to specify that wildlife and fishery conservation should receive equal consideration and should be coordinated with other features of water resource development. Also of major significance was the initiation in 1956 of the ten-year Mission 66 facility improvement program of the National Park Service. In 1957 the U.S. Forest Service launched a five-year special improvement program called Operation Outdoors.

Recognizing the need for a nationwide study of these problems, Congress in 1958 established the Outdoor Recreation Resources Review Commission (ORRRC) for the purpose of surveying the outdoor recreation needs of the people for the next 40 years, and to recommend actions to meet those needs. The report of the Commission consisted of 27 informative volumes. Several significant legislative acts and nationwide programs have resulted from the Commission's report.

The Multiple-Use Sustained Shield Act of 1960 made outdoor recreation an official function of the National Forest Service on the same basis as the other four identified functions. This was really more a formality than a significant official action because the national forests had been managed under the multiple-use concept for many years prior.

The establishment of the Bureau of Outdoor Recreation within the Department of the Interior was a major development in the year 1962. In 1964 the Land and Water Conservation Fund Act was passed, with the provisions of the act to be administered by the Bureau of Outdoor Recreation. This act provides matching grant-in-aid funds to the states and their political subdivisions for planning, acquiring, and developing outdoor recreational areas. It has added much by way of leadership and financial support to governmental efforts in outdoor recreation.

The 1960s and the early 1970s was an era of tremendous concern and action on behalf of outdoor recreation. The federal government was more active during this period in terms of new legislation and new programs than at any other time. The concern at the national level had a filtering-down effect into state and local government agencies and into the private sector. The more significant government acts and programs of that era are described in Chapter 6, Recent Legislation and Special Government Programs, and that information need not be repeated here. Descriptions of other recent developments in this field are explained in portions of several subsequent chapters.

Outdoor Recreation Organizations

The first association representing the natural resource interests of the nation was the American Forestry Association organized in Chicago in 1875. This association has exerted a strong influence in forest land management during the past century. A second influential conservation group that has developed strong interests in recreation is the Sierra Club founded in 1892 by John Muir, its director for two decades. The club was most influential in having Yosemite established as a national park. The dedicated members of this group frequently join forces with other associations, magazines, and newspapers to further their cause. For example, Mount Rainer became a national park in 1899 through the combined efforts of the Sierra Club, the National Geographic Society, the American Association for the Advancement of Science, the Geographical Society of America, and the Appalachian Club. Other organizations which have provided significant support to the park movement, especially national parks, are the American Museum of Natural History, established in New York in 1869; the National Audubon Society, established in 1905; and the Wilderness Society, established in 1935.

The first professional organization for persons directly involved in the park movement was formed by a group of municipal park superintendents in New England. The New England Association of Park Superintendents first convened in Boston in 1898 upon the invitation of George A. Parker, then the superintendent of Keney Park, Boston. By 1904 this group had become a national association, and changed its name to the American Association of Park Superintendents. Park superintendents revitalized the association in 1921 with a broader constitution, recognizing that parks were not only places to be viewed but also places where people should have the opportunity to participate in various recreational pursuits. The reorganization also included a change of title to the American Institute of Park Executives.

Other organizations which have left their mark on the outdoor recreation movement are the Boy Scouts of America and the Campfire Girls, organized in 1910, the Girl Scouts, 1911, the American Society of Landscape Architectures, 1916, and the American Camping Association, 1924.

The National Parks Association was formed in 1919 to promote the system of federal parks. This association became the National Park and Conservation Association in 1968.

The Izaac Walton League was established in 1922 as a national citizen-conservation organization working for the wise use and conservation of natural resources. The League has consistently spoken out for the preservation of resources for recreational use.

The National Conference on State Parks was formally organized in 1928, and it has served traditionally as the professional association for both state park professionals and federal park employees. Park and recreation professionals at the local and regional levels with a natural resource orientation are also attracted to this association.

During the 1930s the American Wildlife Institute and the American Wildlife Society were founded. Also the National Wildlife Federation was formed, and the first North American Wildlife Conference was held during that decade. Many students of the cooperative wildlife unit schools were employed in the federally aided wildlife restoration program which became effective in 1938.

Other organizations that have consistently spoken out for improved outdoor recreation opportunities are the Conservation Foundation, established in 1948, and Resources for the Future, organized in 1952 under a grant from the Ford Foundation.

The International Recreation Association was established in 1956, and in 1973 it changed its name to the World Leisure and Recreation Association. In 1958 the Association of Interpretive Naturalists was formed.

The National Recreation and Park Association (NRPA) was created in 1965 by the merger of six national professional and service organizations: the American Association of Zoological Parks and Aquariums, the American Institute of Park Executives, the American Recreation Society, the National Association of State

Park Directors, the National Conference on State Parks, and the National Recreation Association. This was a milestone in the history of the movement, and part of its significance was explained in the following statement by Alfred LaGasse:

> The broad park and recreation field has moved through three phases: (1) the stage of unity, when recreation was pursued on the estates of large land holders without thoughts of whether it dealt with parks; planning and design; recreation; or forestry, wildlife, and related national resources; (2) the stage of separation when those in organized recreation, parks, and forestry, pursued their individual fields of endeavor with little thought for the others; and (3) the stage of moving the three streams of development toward unity.[2]

Growth of Leadership Preparation Programs

The emphasis on resource management and conservation resulted in demands for more knowledgeable personnel. As a result universities began to offer instruction in resource management. Colleges of forestry were established at Yale University in 1873 and at Cornell University in 1874. By 1910, 19 colleges and universities had established schools of forestry. But none of them had curricula specifically in the field of outdoor recreation management. At that time, park superintendent positions were mostly filled by people with experience in planning and design or horticulture.

Beginning in 1915 there was a series of annual American game conferences held under the auspices of the American Game Protective and Propagation Association. In 1919 the American School of Wildlife Protection was established in McGregor, Iowa. The school initially consisted of a five-day session which later developed into two sessions. In 1924 the first national conference on outdoor recreation was held in Washington, D.C., with 309 delegates representing 128 national organizations.

During the 1930s several institutions began educating people in the management of natural resources for recreational use. The landscape architecture department of the University of Massachusetts played a leading role in this regard, and by the mid-1930s the forest management department of Utah State University offered three classes in recreation. A course in national park management was introduced in the College of Forestry at Colorado State University. Also courses having to do with wildlife management were added in colleges of forestry. In 1935 a recreation major was started in the Department of Forestry at Michigan State University, and in 1936 a four-year undergraduate curriculum in wildlife management was established in the Department of Forestry and Wildlife Management at the University of Massachusetts.

Immediately after World War II a number of colleges and universities established recreation curricula. North Carolina State University established an option in park administration, Colorado State University organized a department of forest recreation and wildlife conservation, and the Great Lakes Park and Recreation Training Institute was established. In the early 1950s the Southeastern Park and Recreation Training Institute and the Southwest Park and Recreation Institute were added. Subsequently numerous other such regional institutes have been established.

[2]Alfred B. LaGasse and Walter L. Cook, *History of Parks and Recreation*, Management Bulletin No. 56, National Recreation and Parks Association, 1965, p. 33.

During the 1950s noticeable changes took place in the underlying philosophy of recreation curricula. It was during this time that it became increasingly apparent that those managing natural resources had to be better informed and more oriented toward people's use of the resources, while those who were prepared in municipal recreation had to become more knowledgeable and more concerned about the planning and use of natural resources. As a result the base of many of the curricula began to broaden and the preparation of those enrolled was intensified.

In the mid-1950s a park management and municipal forestry curriculum was organized in the Department of Land and Water Conservation at Michigan State University, replacing a similar program established at that university in the Department of Forestry in 1935. A curriculum in park management was started in the Department of Horticulture and Park Management at Texas Tech University. Also a park management curriculum was started at Sacramento State College in 1959.

In 1953 the American Association for Health, Physical Education, and Recreation started an Outdoor Education Project, and the Association also sponsored national conferences on professional preparation in 1954, 1956, and 1958. Additional AAHPER-sponsored national recreation conferences included one on Education for Leisure in 1957 and one on Leadership for Leisure in 1963.

In 1968 the American Association for Health, Physical Education, and Recreation co-sponsored with the National Recreation and Park Association a national conference in Washington, D.C., on outdoor recreation in America. It was attended by 250 invited educators, government officials, and recreation professionals. In 1973 the AAHPER and the NRPA jointly published a booklet listing more than 300 colleges and universities that offer curricula in the park and recreation field. A portion of these include options or specialities in outdoor recreation. In 1976 the present author prepared for AAHPER a booklet entitled "Recreation and Leisure Time Careers" which includes much valuable information about professional preparation in outdoor recreation.

A later chapter in this text titled "Education for Outdoor Recreation" contains additional information that relates to the recent history of the educational aspects of this field.

Chapter 5 Federal Government Involvement

The involvement of the federal government in public recreation dates back to the Civil War period. The principal justification for involvement is contained in the Preamble and Article I, Section 8 of the Constitution, where to "promote the general welfare" is listed as one of the purposes of the government. For a long time the Congress of the United States has supported the recreation activities of federal agencies by means of enabling legislation and appropriations.

Federal functions in outdoor recreation include (a) the management of federally owned properties such as parks, forests, wildlife preserves, and reservoir areas, and (b) technical and financial assistance to state and local agencies, and private citizens.

The recreational activities of the federal government, which originally centered around the use of federal land and water areas for recreation, date back to June 3, 1864, when an Act of Congress granted Yosemite Valley and the Mariposa Big Tree Grove to the State of California for recreational purposes. Then in 1872 President Grant signed a bill creating the Yellowstone National Park — the first national park in the world. Subsequently the federal government steadily expanded its involvements in recreation-related activities, until now almost every major division of federal government contributes to outdoor recreation to some extent. This chapter is designed to give insight into the manner in which the different federal agencies are involved in outdoor recreation.

Major Outdoor Recreation
Resource Management Agencies

Several agencies of the federal government manage land and water resources which contribute significantly to outdoor recreation, while several other agencies perform a different kind of function.

National Park Service

The National Park System of the United States comprises nearly 300 areas covering some 31 million acres in 49 states, the District of Columbia, Puerto Rico, and the Virgin Islands. These areas are of such national significance as to justify special recognition and protection in accordance with various Acts of Congress.

The National Park System is in the early years of its second century. In the Act of March 1, 1872, Congress established Yellowstone National Park in the Territories of Montana and Wyoming "as a public park or pleasuring ground for the benefit and enjoyment of the people" and placed it "under exclusive control of the Secretary of the Interior." The founding of Yellowstone National Park began a worldwide national park movement. Today more than 100 nations contain some 1200 national parks or equivalent preserves.

In the years following Yellowstone, the United States authorized several additional national parks and monuments, most of them carved from the federal lands of the West.

Until 1916, the national parks and some national monuments were administered by the Department of the Interior, while other monuments and kindred natural and historical areas were administered as separate units by the War Department and the Forest Service of the Department of Agriculture. No single agency provided unified management of the varied federal parklands.

In an Act signed on August 25, 1916, Congress established in the Department of the Interior the National Park Service to provide cohesive administration of such areas. The Act states in part:

> The service thus established shall promote and regulate the use of the Federal areas known as national parks, monuments and reservations...by such means and measures as conform to the fundamental purpose of the said parks, monuments and reservations, which purpose is to conserve the scenery and the natural and historic objects and the wildlife therein and to provide for the enjoyment of the same in such manner and by such means as will leave them unimpaired for the enjoyment of future generations.

In 1933, a presidential executive order transferred 63 national monuments and military sites from the Forest Service and the War Department to the Park Service. This action was a major step in the development of today's truly national system of parks which covers all regions of the nation and includes areas of historical as well as scenic and scientific importance.

In 1964 the areas of the National Park System were classified into *natural, historical,* and *recreational area* categories for administrative convenience and to clarify park purposes for the public.

Congress declared in the General Authorities Act of 1970 that the National Park

> In a fruitful new partnership with the states and cities the next decade
> should be a conservation milestone. We must make a massive effort to
> establish — as a green legacy for tomorrow — more large and small parks,
> more seashores and open spaces than have been created during any period
> in our history.
>
> — Lyndon B. Johnson

System "began with the establishment of Yellowstone National Park in 1872... and that it is the purpose of this Act to include all such (natural, historical and recreational) areas in the System."

Additions to the National Park System are now generally made through Acts of Congress, and national parks can be created only through such Acts. But the President has authority, under the Antiquities Act of 1906, to proclaim national monuments on lands already under federal jurisdiction. The Secretary of the Interior is usually asked by Congress to make recommendations on proposed additions to the System. The Secretary is counseled on possible additions to the System and policies for its management by the Advisory Board composed of private citizens, on National Parks, Historic Sites, Buildings and Monuments.

Nomenclature. The diversity of the parks is reflected in the varied titles given to them. These include such designations as national park, national monument, national memorial, national historic site, national seashore, and national battlefield park.

Although some titles are self-explanatory, others have been used in many different ways. For example, the title "national monument" has been used for great natural reservations, historic military fortifications, prehistoric ruins, fossil sites, and the Statue of Liberty.

In recent years, the Congress and the National Park Service have attempted, with some success, to simplify the nomenclature and establish basic criteria for the use of the different official titles. Brief definitions of the most common titles are included in this section in the explanations preceding the park listings under *Natural, Historical,* and *Recreational* Areas. Most areas now conform to these definitions.

Natural Areas. Natural areas are unspoiled examples of the primeval heritage of the nation. To be a part of the National Park System a natural area must be an expanse or feature of land or water of such scenic and scientific value and quality as to be worthy of preservation as a national park, national monument, or national preserve.

Natural areas contain one or more distinctive attributes such as forest, grassland, tundra, desert, estuary, or river systems. They may contain "windows" on the past of geological history, imposing landforms such as mountains, mesas, thermal areas, and caverns, and habitats of abundant or rare wildlife and plant life.

Generally, a national park is large in size. It contains a variety of resources and encompasses sufficient land or water to ensure adequate protection of the resources. Chosen primarily for scenic and scientific values, all the national parks but one are natural areas.*

*The exception is Mesa Verde National Park, Colo., which is an historical area.

Point Reyes National
Seashore.

Recreational use of a water project constructed primarily for other purposes. Lake Powell National Recreation Area, Utah.

A national monument, usually smaller than a national park, is intended to preserve at least one nationally significant resource. It generally lacks the diversity of attractions found in a national park.

In 1974, Big Cypress and Big Thicket were authorized as the first *national preserves*. This is a new category of natural areas established for protection of resources and in which activities such as extraction of minerals, gas, and oil, and hunting may be permitted where they do not conflict with a preserve's purpose.

Historical Areas. Although best known for its great scenic parks, the National Park System contains more than twice as many historical areas as natural areas. These historical areas preserve places and commemorate persons, events, and activities important in the nation's past. They range from archeological sites associated with prehistoric Indian civilizations to sites related to the lives of modern Americans. Historical areas are customarily preserved or restored to reflect their appearance during their periods of greatest historical significance.

In recent years, "national historic site" has been the title most commonly applied by Congress in authorizing the addition of historical areas to the Park System. A variety of titles — national military park, national battlefield park, national battlefield site, and national battlefield — have been used for areas associated with American military history. But other areas, including national monuments and national historical parks, may include features associated with military history. National historical parks are usually areas of greater physical extent and complexity than national historic sites.

The title "national memorials" has customarily been reserved for areas which are predominantly commemorative in nature. These need not be sites or structures directly related to the subject's historical contribution. For example, the Springfield, Illinois, home of Abraham Lincoln is a national historic site, but the Lincoln Memorial in the District of Columbia is a national memorial.

Recreation Areas. Units of the National Park System in the recreational area category have been set aside primarily to provide opportunities for outdoor recreation. Natural and historical features worthy of careful preservation are often found within these units, but the areas are subject to more intensive public use and more development than those in the natural or historical categories.

National Recreation Areas. Originally, national recreation areas in the Park System were units surrounding reservoirs impounded by dams built by other federal agencies. The National Park Service manages many of these areas under cooperative agreements; other national recreation areas have been established by Acts of Congress.

There are also national recreation areas outside the National Park System administered by the Forest Service and the U.S. Army Corps of Engineers.

Wild and Scenic Rivers. National scenic riverways and national rivers preserve ribbons of land bordering on free-flowing streams which have not been dammed, channelized, or otherwise altered by man. In addition to preserving rivers in their natural state, these areas provide opportunities for outdoor pursuits such as hiking, canoeing, and hunting.

Performing Arts. Two areas of the National Park System have been set aside primarily as sites for the performing arts. These are Wolf Trap Farm Park, Va.,

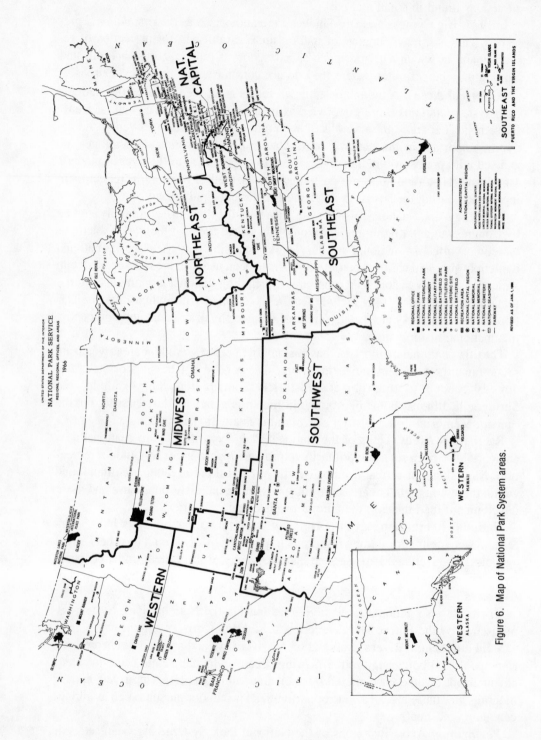

Figure 6. Map of National Park System areas.

America's first national park for the performing arts, and the John F. Kennedy Center for the Performing Arts, Washington, D.C. Two historical areas, Ford's Theatre National Historic Site, Washington, D.C., and Chamizal National Memorial, Texas, also provide performing arts entertainment.

National Lakeshores and Seashores. Preserving shoreline areas and offshore islands, the national lakeshores and seashores focus on preservation of natural values and provision of water-oriented recreation. Although national lakeshores can be established on any natural freshwater lake, the existing four are all located on the Great Lakes. The national seashores can be found on the Atlantic, Gulf, and Pacific coasts.

National Parkways. The parkways encompass ribbons of land flanking roadways and offer an opportunity for leisurely driving through areas of scenic interest. The parkways are not designed for high speed point-to-point travel. In addition to the areas set aside as parkways, other units of the National Park System include parkways within their boundaries.

The National Park Service currently administers 286 separate areas of different kinds which receive more than 215 million visitors per year. Following is a list of the kinds of areas administered by the NPS and the number and acreage of each kind.

Classification	Number	Total Acres
National Parks	38	15,618,891
National Monuments	81	9,851,306
National Battlefield Parks	3	6,661
National Battlefields	7	7,197
National Battlefield Sites	2	1,801
National Cemeteries	...	218
National Military Parks	11	34,623
National Historical Parks	16	61,952
National Historic Sites	51	13,554
National Memorials	22	5,935
National Memorial Parks	1	70,408
National Seashores	10	604,726
National Lakeshores	4	190,365
National Scenic Riverways	3	150,479
National Rivers	1	94,146
National Recreation Areas	16	3,495,625
National Parkways	4	168,427
National Scenic Trails	1	50,000
Parks (Other)	9	31,669
National Preserves	2	669,550
White House	1	18
National Mall	1	146
National Visitor Center	1	18
National Capital Parks	1	7,495
Total	286	31,135,219

Some of the strong preservationists have criticized the National Park Service for being too much recreation oriented, while at the same time some recreationists and resource-user groups have objected to the strong preservation concept exercised by the National Park Service. The essence of the whole preservation-use idea seems to

Federal Government Involvement

> ...the size of a park is directly related to the manner in which you use it. If you are in a canoe traveling at three miles an hour, the lake on which you are paddling is ten times as long and ten times as broad as it is to the man in a speedboat going thirty...Every road that replaces a footpath, every outboard motor that replaces a canoe paddle, shrinks the area of the park.
>
> — Paul Brooks

be "Eat as much of the cake as we can, but be sure we still have it to eat in the future."

It must be remembered that many of the resources in areas of the National Park System are nonrenewable, and others are renewable only after a long period of time. For instance, the ruins of Mesa Verde and the geysers at Yellowstone are not renewable, and they are prone to easy destruction with use. Also many of the wonders of Grand Canyon and Glacier National Park are not renewable, but these are not prone to easy destruction. Trees, such as those found in Sequoia National Park, and stalactites and stalagmites found in many of our national park caves are renewable but only after many centuries of work by nature. Because of lack of renewability of almost all the resources that are significant in our National Park System, the aspect of preservation must remain dominant while the use is governed by the limits dictated by the preservation concept.

United States Forest Service

National forests, administered under the Department of Agriculture, are based fundamentally upon the Act of March 3, 1891, which authorized the President to reserve, by proclamation, certain lands from the public domain and to designate such lands as forest reserves. The Act stated:

> That the President of the United States may from time to time set apart and reserve, in any State or Territory having public lands, wholly or in part covered with timber or undergrowth, whether of commercial value or not, as public reservations, and the President shall, by public proclamation, declare the establishment of such reservations and the limits thereof.

The first Forest Reserve, established under the Act in 1891, was originally known as the Yellowstone Park Timberland Reserve. It was later named the Shoshone National Forest (Wyoming). After its initiation, the Forest Reserve System grew rapidly. Two years after the passage of the Act, more than 13 million acres of forest land had been placed in reserve. Through the years, suitable land has been identified, and piece by piece it has been added to the system, until now more than 187 million acres are included in 124 different national forests in 44 states and Puerto Rico. Because of its nature much of the national forest system has high outdoor-recreational value.

The United States Forest Service, which is the administrator of the National Forest Reserve, was created by the Act of March 3, 1905. (The forest reserves were under the General Land Office of the U.S. Department of Interior until 1905.) When the 1905 Act became effective, "the Secretary of Agriculture, 'Tama Jim' Wilson, issued a set of instructions which laid the basis for Forest Service policy since that

Multiple-use forest land is one of America's most valuable resources.

time. Among these instructions were: (a) 'All the resources of forest reserves are for use and this use must be brought about . . . under such restrictions only as will assure the permanence of these resources . . .'; (b) 'In the management of each reserve local questions will be decided upon local grounds . . .'; and (c) '. . . the dominant industry will be decided first, but with as little restrictions to minor industries as may be possible.' . . . Where conflicting interests must be reconciled the question will always be decided from the standpoint of the greatest good to the greatest number in the long run." The instructions given by Mr. Wilson have since remained the watchword for the United States Forest Service Administration. The concepts of conservative use, multiple use, and decentralized administration still form the foundation of Forest Service policy.

In studying the past trends in Forest Service administration, it appears that the Forest Service was originally pushed into recreational activities in self-defense. People gradually discovered the recreational values of the forests and began to use them accordingly. The Forest Service found itself attempting to manage recreation in order to minimize fire hazards, stream pollution, and hazards to the recreationists themselves. Once having become involved, the Forest Service personnel apparently adapted themselves to the situation. In so doing they caused the official policy of the U.S. Forest Service to become one of encouraging recreational use of the forests. It even prepares posters, movies, pamphlets, and other media to carry the message, "The National Forests, America's Playground." Because of the particu-

> The kings of England formerly had their forests "to hold the king's game" for sport or food...Why should not we...have ours or shall we, like villains, grub them (game) all up, poaching on our own national domain?
> — Henry David Thoreau

lar kind of land managed by the Forest Service, and because of public demand for recreational use of that land, the Forest Service is presently very much in the recreational business. This is indicated by the fact that about 200 million visitors go to national forests for recreational purposes each year. This figure represents a tremendous increase over the 46 million visitors received in 1955.

The national forests are used for many different outdoor recreational activities. Probably the most common of these are pleasure driving and sightseeing, but consider the variety and extent of other forms of recreation involved from the following facts: One-third of the big game animals in the U.S. live all or part of the time in the national forests. This includes four-fifths of the moose, elk, and grizzly bear, and nearly two-thirds of the mule deer, black bear, and bighorned sheep. In 1976, about 17,000,000 visitor days of fishing occurred in the 81,000 miles of streams and in 2,000,000 acres of lakes of the national forests. There are approximately 5,500 developed camp and picnic areas on national forest land; 203 developed ski areas; over 400 recreational resorts; approximately 18,500 summer homes; 96,000 miles of hiking and riding trails; 152,000 miles of scenic roads; and 104 wilderness and primitive areas. The theme, "The National Forests are America's Playgrounds," has become appropriate.

In order to effectively accomplish its objectives relative to outdoor recreation, the Forest Service has established some significant guidelines: (a) recreation resources are to be made available to the public insofar as it is consistent with overall management of the forest; (b) within reason all measures are taken to assure the safety of users; (c) care is taken to prevent unsanitary conditions, pollution, and forest fires; (d) provision is made for the best possible wildlife habitat and best possible hunting and fishing consistent with all other uses; (e) only those facilities suitable to the forest environment are provided; (f) operation of service facilities such as resorts, motels, ski lifts, filling stations, and the like by concessionaires is under supervision of the Forest Service; (g) lands that are mainly valuable for their wilderness qualities are protected; (h) preferential private uses, e.g., summer homes, are allowed only where lands are not needed or are not suitable for public use.

The great increase in recreational visits to national forests has created problems in fire control, the providing of clean water and adequate sanitary facilities, the protection of people from hazards, and the protection of the recreation resources *themselves* from destruction by the users. In order to overcome these problems the Forest Service has in recent years received increases in appropriations for recreational purposes. But these increases must be interpreted in view of (a) inflation, (b) the great increase in the cost for developing facilities, and (c) the fact that visitors' expectations are considerably higher than they used to be.

The Forest Service has generally followed the multiple use concept since 1905, when Secretary of Agriculture Wilson directed that "all the resources of forest reserves are for use" and "the dominant industry will be decided first but with as little restrictions to minor industries as may be possible." The Multiple Purpose Act, passed in June of 1960, simply bestowed congressional approval on existing Forest Service policy. The intended meaning of multiple use is shown in this quotation from the 1960 Act:

"Multiple Use" means: The management of all the various renewable surface resources of the national forests so that they are utilized in the combination that will best meet the needs of the American people; making the most judicious use of the land for some or all of these resources or related services over areas large enough to provide sufficient latitude for periodic adjustments in use to conform to changing needs and conditions; that some land will be used for less than all of the resources; and harmonious and coordinated management of the various resources, each with the other, without impairment of the productivity of the land, with consideration being given to the relative values of the various resources, and not necessarily the combination of uses that will give the greatest dollar return or the greatest unit output.

The Act further provides "that it is the policy of the Congress that the national forests are established and shall be administered for *outdoor recreation, timber, range, watersheds,* and *wildlife and fish* purposes." These five basic uses are supposedly of equal importance, although any one of them may be emphasized over the others in a particular area, depending on the suitability of the specific resources in that area. Some specific areas may be administered primarily for timber production, while others may be primarily for grazing, while still others may be administered primarily for outdoor recreational use. Recent large increases in appropriations for recreation further indicate acceptance by Congress of recreation as one of the principal uses of national forests.

The national forests contain 85 wildernesses and 19 primitive areas totaling some 15.4 million acres. In 1924, the Forest Service established the first wilderness, the Gila Wilderness, in southern New Mexico. From 1924 until 1964 the Forest Service established administratively some 88 acres which they managed in a natural state. These included wildernesses, wild areas, primitive areas, and one canoe area in northern Minnesota. In 1964, the Congress passed the Wilderness Act which created a National Wilderness System. The Act immediately designated all wilderness, wild areas, and the canoe area as wilderness under the act and directed the study of the 34 primitive areas to determine their suitability or nonsuitability as wilderness. These studies have been completed and submitted to the Congress. Sixteen of these have been designated wilderness and the remainder are still being considered by the Congress. Until such time as Congress changes the designation, primitive areas will be managed identical to wilderness.

The tendency nowadays to wander in wildernesses is delightful to see. Thousands of tired, nerve-shaken, over-civilized people are beginning to find out that going to the mountains is going home; that wilderness is a necessity; and that mountain parks and reservations are useful not only as fountains of timber and irrigating rivers, but as fountains of life.

— John Muir, 1901

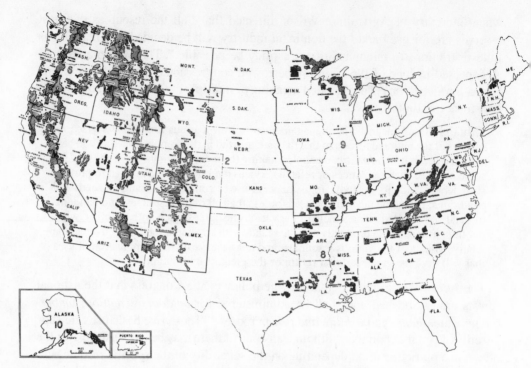

Figure 7. Map of United States Forest Service areas.

Under controlled conditions most of the wild and wilderness areas contain alpine-type timber growth of low commercial value and are so located as to make access difficult and too expensive for profitable logging operations. They have some value for summer grazing, and there are a considerable number of mining claims in wilderness-type areas.

Since recreation is the most recent, most rapidly growing, and probably the most politically volatile of national forest uses, the Forest Service has had to prove that its capabilities in recreation are equal to or better than its capabilities in other fields included under the multiple-use concept. The Forest Service has made significant efforts to establish a reputation for such capability through (a) the establishment of wilderness areas; (b) the administration of the Operation Outdoors Project (a five-year crash program aimed at constructing enough recreation facilities to meet the demand); (c) the Forest Service Recreation Resources Survey; (d) establishment of a recreation research center in Pennsylvania; and (e) the publication of a recreation-development program.

Indications are that the recreational use of the national forests will continue to increase at a rate of about 3 percent per year. If it does, the Forest Service personnel will be tested in their efforts to meet the demand and still allow the forests to adequately serve their other basic purposes.

The Corps of Engineers

The Corps of Engineers, an integral part of the United States Army, traces its origin to 1775 when the first Chief of Engineers fortified the Colonies' positions for the battle of Bunker Hill. In 1776, the Continental Congress authorized General Washington to "raise...a Corps of Engineers," which was constantly employed building fortifications, batteries, and siege works — and often fighting as infantry — during the remainder of the Revolutionary War. In 1783, as part of a general reduction of the Army, the Corps of Engineers was disbanded and its companies of "sappers and miners" were mustered out. In 1794, an Act of Congress provided for a Corps of Artillerists and Engineers to be raised for a period of three years, and established an engineer school at West Point. Subsequent Acts of Congress (March 3, 1795, and May 30, 1796) provided that the Corps of Artillerists and Engineers be continued indefinitely and that it become a permanent part of the military establishment. On March 16, 1802, Congress divided the Artillerists and Engineers into separate corps and provided for Corps of Engineers superintendence of the Military Academy at West Point.

Evolution of the mission of the Corps of Engineers from the early strictly military function to one including many-sided civil works began in 1824 with passage of the first River and Harbor Act. Following is a brief summary of the more significant events that have shaped the present civil works activities of the Corps of Engineers:

1824: Under authority of the commerce clause of the Constitution, Congress formalized the civil works function of the Corps of Engineers and authorized studies of canals, roads, and river and harbor improvements.

1836: Improvement of the Ohio River was authorized under the superintendence of the Corps of Engineers.

1863: The Corps of Topographical Engineers, which traces its origin to 1777, was merged with the Corps of Engineers.

1879: The Mississippi River Commission with an Army Engineer as president was created to supervise the program for controlling the river and developing its Alluvial Valley.

1893: Participation by the Corps in the regulating of hydraulic mining and flood control in the Central Valley of California extended the Corps' interests west of the Mississippi River Valley.

1917: Congress adopted the first major flood control legislation, which authorized Corps of Engineers improvements on the Mississippi and Sacramento Rivers.

1927: Congress directed the Corps of Engineers to make comprehensive surveys of United States rivers for navigation, flood control, hydroelectric power, and irrigation. Basic data were collected and analyzed and plans of development prepared for 191 rivers.

1932: The authority of the Corps of Engineers was extended to provide for consideration of recreational boating as well as commercial waterborne commerce in planning navigation improvements.

1936: The 1936 Flood Control Act established a national flood control policy and assigned responsibility for planning and construction of flood control projects to the Corps of Engineers.

1944: The 1944 Flood Control Act greatly expanded Corps of Engineers responsibilities in providing recreational facilities at civil works projects.

Other legislation enacted at various times since 1944 provides the Corps of Engineers with continuing authority to plan and construct certain small flood control, small navigation, and small beach-erosion and shore-protection projects; develop domestic, municipal, and industrial water supplies; prepare flood-plain information studies; engage in emergency flood control and flood damage rehabilitation work; and administer certain laws providing for the preservation and protection of navigable waters.

The 1944 Flood Control Act authorized the Corps of Engineers "to construct, maintain, and operate public park and recreational facilities in reservoir areas" as part of multiple-purpose projects. The Act also specified: "The water areas of all such reservoirs shall be open to public use generally, without charge...and ready access to and exit from such water areas...shall be maintained for general public use."

The Corps interprets that act to authorize the installation of basic facilities for recreationists. These facilities include overlook stations for viewing the project, public sanitary facilities, parking areas, access roads, guardrails, fences, informational signs, camping and picnicking facilities, and boat-launching ramps. The Corps of Engineers encourages state or local governments to assume responsibility for additional construction and maintenance of recreation facilities.

The Land and Water Conservation Fund Act authorizes the establishment of entrance, admission, and user fees at designated federal recreation areas. Some Corps of Engineers areas fall into the group of designated areas.

The 1965 Federal Water Projects Recreation Act provides for federal participation in all federal projects in which recreation and fish and wildlife are project purposes, to the extent of repaying 50 percent of the separable cost assigned to recreation and fish and wildlife, and maintenance and operation of all recreation facilities.

The various functions of the Corps of Engineers, as dictated by the various Acts, are now carried on under a multi-use concept when feasible, with the objective of maximizing various uses of water resources.

In 1962, the President approved Senate Document No. 97, 87th Congress, Second Session, entitled *Policies, Standards, and Procedures in the Formulation, Evaluation, and Review of Plans for Use and Development of Water and Related Land Resources*. This document was prepared for use by federal agencies engaged in water-resources development. It specified that full consideration be given to the opportunity and need for outdoor recreation and fish and wildlife enhancement in planning for water and related land use and development.

The recreation use of Corps of Engineers projects has experienced a phenomenal increase since World War II. In 1946, visits to these projects totaled only 5 million. And then came the boats! By 1959, the number of visits exceeded 100 million per year, and in 1964 they exceeded 155 million. In 1976 over 250 million people visited Corps of Engineers projects, mostly for boating, fishing, picnicking, and sightseeing. Guardrails, overlooks, and scenic turnouts were no longer adequate when the Corps was confronted with the task of accommodating such vast numbers of recreationists at all reservoir projects. In addition to the millions of acres of water surface, and thousands of miles of shorelines within Corps of Engineers projects,

Corps of Engineers and Bureau of Reclamation projects have created numerous lakes that provide a variety of new recreation opportunities.

the following special facilities and areas are provided: reservoir-access areas, boat-launching lanes, picnic areas, camp areas, swimming beaches, guest rental units, and boat rentals.

The 1954 Flood Control Act authorized the Corps to issue licenses to federal, state, and local governments without monetary consideration to develop and maintain recreational areas at Corps of Engineers projects. Leases may be granted for commercial concession developments, and to nonprofit organizations such as the Izaak Walton League, Boy Scouts of America, and church organizations at reduced or nominal rentals. Under certain conditions, and when lands are available, the Corps may lease lands for private recreational purposes or cottage sites.

The Corps of Engineers' policy on recreation in project planning and the evaluation of recreation benefits is indicated by the following statement:

The current (1966) Corps of Engineers' policy on recreation is to consider it a project purpose except when the project is not expected to produce a significant increase in recreation. However, to insure against overemphasis of recreation, the Corps does not recommend federal construction of projects which include recreation, unless the sum of all benefits other than recreation is sufficient to cover at least 50 percent of the total project costs. Further, in plan formulation, each purpose (including recreation) must produce benefits at least equal to the incremental cost of adding that purpose to the plan. Also, when recreation is a project purpose, the recreational benefits must be evaluated and taken into account in the economic analysis in the same manner as other benefits. At the present time, pending the development of more refined methods, the procedure is to use a monetary value per visitor-day. In determining this monetary value, the views of the National Park Service, the U.S. Fish and Wildlife Service, and other agencies concerned therewith are considered.

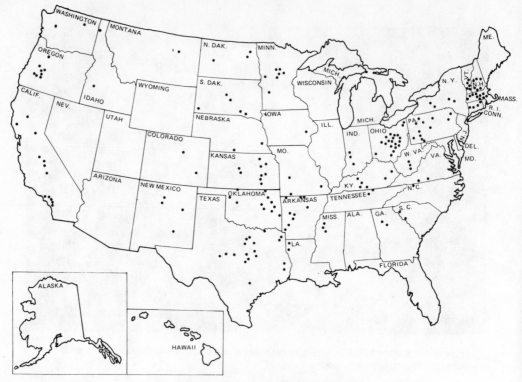

Figure 8. Map of Corps of Engineers areas.

The rapid growth in outdoor recreation facilities by the Corps of Engineers is evidenced by the fact that it played host to more visitors (285 million) in 1976 than did any other federal agency, and the rate of increase of recreational use of Corps of Engineers' projects during the past two decades has exceeded that of any other federal agency. In the future, many more people will require and demand more outdoor recreation opportunities, and this will require the Corps to continue to adjust to outdoor recreational needs and demands of the public. In so doing, the Corps must continually evaluate policies on recreation in order to meet the recreational demands and at the same time accomplish its other responsibilities.

Bureau of Reclamation

The Bureau of Reclamation, which is within the Department of the Interior, was established in 1902 for the major purpose of applying the receipts from the sale and disposal of public lands in certain states and territories to the construction of irrigation works for the reclamation of arid lands.

Early Bureau of Reclamation reservoirs were constructed for a single purpose — storage of irrigation water. Gradually, other purposes were added: power, municipal and industrial water, flood control, and, most recently, recreation and fish and wildlife. The early projects received no appropriation of federal funds for recreation or fish and wildlife facilities, and therefore no official attention was given to recreation. The Forest Service established some recreation facilities at a few Bureau of Reclamation reservoirs within national forests.

More recently, Congress has recognized the need for minimum basic recreation facilities at federally constructed reservoirs. Beginning in 1949, the Weber Basin (Utah) Project Act provided for certain basic recreation facilities, including access roads, parking area, picnic areas, water supply, sanitation, and boat-launching ramps.

Besides, the Colorado River Storage Act of April 11, 1956, authorized and directed the Secretary of the Interior to investigate, plan, construct, operate, and maintain (a) public recreational facilities on lands withdrawn or acquired for the development of that project or of the participating projects, to conserve the scenery, the natural, historic, and archeologic objects, and the wildlife on said lands, and to provide for public use and enjoyment of the same and of waters created by these projects by such means as are consistent with the primary purposes of said projects; and (b) facilities to mitigate losses of, and improve conditions for, the propagation of fish and wildlife.

Other projects have been recently authorized with similar special instructions for the establishment of basic recreational facilities at specific reservoirs.

Subsequently, statutory authority was sought to provide for future coordinated planning and construction of recreational facilities at all reclamation projects. Such authority was granted with the passage of the Federal Water Project Recreation Act on July 9, 1965, as Public Law 89-72. This Act provides that in the investigating and planning of any federal navigation, flood control, reclamation, hydroelectric, or multiple-purpose water resource project, full consideration shall be given to the opportunities, if any, which the project affords for outdoor recreation and for fish and wildlife enhancement and that, wherever any such project can reasonably serve either or both of these purposes within the provisions of this Act, it shall be constructed, operated, and maintained accordingly. There is a definite need for facilities to be established around some of the older reclamation projects, which were authorized and constructed before recreation was considered as a purpose. The Federal Water Project Recreation Act, Public Law 89-72, provides that as much as $100,000 of federal funds may be expended on each project for recreation purposes if the administering agency participates on a 50:50 basis. When administering agencies get in position to take advantage of this legislation, the serious lack of facilities at these older projects may be partially alleviated.

The Bureau of Outdoor Recreation cooperates with the Bureau of Reclamation in preparing plans for recreational developments on Bureau projects. It also assists the Bureau in arranging for the operation of recreational areas by state or local agencies. The Bureau of Reclamation also cooperates with the Bureau of Sport Fisheries and Wildlife in the planning of facilities to mitigate damages to and for the enhancement of fish and wildlife resources whenever possible in the development of reclamation projects. When reservoirs are within forest boundaries, the Bureau cooperates with the U.S. Forest Service in the development and operation of recreational facilities.

It is, and will probably continue to be, Bureau of Reclamation policy to transfer reservoir areas whenever possible to local, state, or other federal agencies for administration and further development of recreational resources. If an area has national recreation significance, it is designated a National Recreation Area and

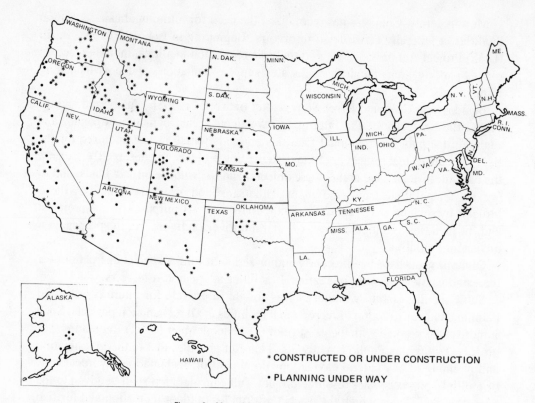

* CONSTRUCTED OR UNDER CONSTRUCTION

• PLANNING UNDER WAY

Figure 9. Map of Bureau of Reclamation areas.

administered by the National Park Service; if it is located within a forest boundary, it is administered by the Forest Service. If a reservoir area has less than national significance, its recreational potential is usually administered by a state or local agency. In some instances, the Bureau administers the reservoir area until a suitable agency becomes available.

The agencies that were responsible for the administration of recreation on reclamation projects in 1976 and the number of areas administered by each are as follows:

Agency	Number of Areas
State agencies	68
U.S. Forest Service	38
Water-user organizations	32
U.S. Fish and Wildlife Service	13
Counties	15
National Park Service	10
Local recreation districts	10
Bureau of Indian Affairs	3
Bureau of Reclamation	42
Total:	231

The Bureau of Reclamation takes pride in the amount of recreation use provided by its reservoir areas. By 1976 the Bureau had constructed 219 reservoirs with over

> How we Americans spend leisure time might seem to have little bearing on
> the strength of our nation or the worth and prestige of our free society. Yet
> we certainly cannot thrive as a strong and vigorous free people unless we
> understand and use creatively one of our greatest resources — our leisure.
> — John F. Kennedy

9,700 miles of shoreline. These areas support over 45 million recreation visitor
days per year. This represents a significant increase over the 6.6 million visitor days
in 1950. The future offers little hope of relief from the demands placed on the
Bureau to arrange for provisions for outdoor recreation on their project areas. In
fact, it seems apparent that in the future demands for recreation on their projects will
soar at an increasing rate.

Bureau of Land Management

The Bureau of Land Management, under the Department of the Interior, was
created in 1946 through the combining of the General Land Office and the Grazing
Service. The BLM is the manager of the "public domain," the great federal land
reserve. The public domain is that part of the original public lands of the United
States still under federal ownership which has not been set aside for other uses, such
as national forests, parks, etc.

One-fifth of our nation's land (approximately 460 million acres) is under the
jurisdiction of the BLM. Of this, 290 million acres are in Alaska, and most of the
remaining 170 million acres are in the 11 western states. A few small land parcels are
located in other states. A storehouse of resources for the future, these lands produce
forage, fiber, forests, water and wildlife, plus space for outdoor recreation.

The Bureau of Land Management manages the public lands under many public
land laws. Some of the principal ones are the Taylor Grazing Act of June 28, 1934,
the Soil Conservation and Domestic Allotment Act of 1935, and the Classification
and Multiple-Use Act of 1964. Under these laws, the BLM seeks to balance the uses
of the public domain to the best interests of the public.

The use of the public domain for outdoor recreation is increasing rapidly. Recreation is becoming an important partner with livestock grazing, mining, timber production, and the other traditional uses of the land. The recognition of recreation as a
primary objective has resulted in the opening of a number of recreation areas on
BLM lands. These areas now include over 170 camp-picnic sites, 1000 family picnic units, 1300 family camping units, 298 trailer spaces, 46 swimming beaches, and
26 boat-launching ramps. Also, more than 115 areas of unusual natural attractions
have been identified on public domain lands. These are in the form of massive land
slides, rare forest species, arcades, and other significant features.

To help promote the best recreational use of the land for long-term public benefits, the BLM is encouraging state and local governments to lease or purchase
suitable tracts of land and to develop them for outdoor recreation.

In 1954 Congress amended the Recreation and Public Purposes Act of June 4,
1926, authorizing the Secretary of the Interior, under specified conditions, to sell or
lease public domain lands to state and local governments for recreation and other

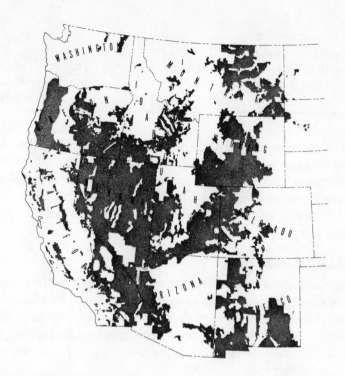

Figure 10. Map of Bureau of Land Management areas (excluding Alaska, where a high percentage of the land belongs to BLM).

public purposes and to qualified nonprofit organizations for public and quasipublic purposes, including recreation, education, and health. The purchase price for states and other governmental agencies is $2.50 per acre for education, health, and recreation purposes, while the lease of such land is 25¢ an acre per year. This Act applies to all lands administered by the Bureau of Land Management. Leases in force for recreation and wildlife purposes in 1976 involved 69 leases for 6,463 acres to states, 128 leases for 96,880 acres to cities and counties, and 46 leases for 8,340 acres to nonprofit organizations.

The BLM is currently cooperating with other federal agencies and with state governments in a program designed to achieve coordinated wildlife, recreation, and other resource-management activities on substantial portions of the public domain.

Visitor days recorded annually on public land are approximately 45 million, compared with 14.5 million in 1964. The highest number of visits was recorded for sightseeing, followed in order by hunting, fishing, picnicking, and camping.

U.S. Fish and Wildlife Service

The United States Fish and Wildlife Service in the Department of the Interior is the principal agency through which the federal government carries out its responsibilities for conserving the nation's fish and wildlife resources for the enjoyment of all the people.

The agency's national responsibilities reach back over 100 years to the establishment in 1871 of a predecessor agency, the Bureau of Fisheries. A second predecessor agency, the Bureau of Biological Survey, was established in 1885. The two agencies were consolidated in 1940 and named the Fish and Wildlife Service. This agency in turn was reorganized in 1956 and two federal bureaus were added to it: the Bureau of Commercial Fisheries and the Bureau of Sport Fisheries and Wildlife. The Bureau of Commercial Fisheries was transferred to the Department of Commerce in 1970.

Several Acts of Congress have authorized funds to be administered by the FWS for the establishment of national wildlife refuges and research programs: Migratory Bird Hunting Stamp Act (48 Stat. 451 as amended), the Pittman-Robertson Act (50 Stat. 917 as amended), the Dingell-Johnson Act (64 Stat. 430 as amended), and the Fish and Wildlife Coordination Act (48 Stat. 401, as amended).

The Migratory Bird Hunting Stamp (or the "Duck Stamp") Act requires a $5 fee for all persons over age 16 who hunt wild ducks, geese, or brant. The proceeds from the sale of duck stamps are used to acquire refuge properties for migratory waterfowl.

Under the Pittman-Robertson Act, an 11 percent manufacturer's excise tax is levied on sporting arms and ammunition, the proceeds going to state wildlife agencies as grants-in-aid for wildlife management.

The Dingell-Johnson Act provides benefits to states for sports fishery management from revenues derived from a 10 percent manufacturer's excise tax on fishing equipment.

The Fish and Wildlife Coordination Act (48 Stat. 401, as amended) of 1958 provides that "wildlife conservation shall receive equal consideration and be coordinated with other features of water-resource development programs." It requires that federal agencies constructing or licensing water-development projects shall consult with the U.S. Fish and Wildlife Service and the comparable state agency prior to the construction or licensing of such projects, for the purpose of protecting fish and wildlife resources. In carrying out this requirement, the Fish and Wildlife Service studies all federal water construction projects and those requiring a federal license (a) to determine the effects of the project on fish and wildlife resources, and (b) to formulate measures to mitigate adverse effects on these resources and to take advantage of the construction to enhance their usefulness.

This Act requires not only that the director of any water-resource development financed in whole or in part with federal funds, or constructed under federal license, must consider fish and wildlife, but it also has the effect of equating fish and wildlife values with other water-development benefits.

The responsibilities of the FWS include the managing of wildlife refuges and fish hatcheries, the controlling of predators and rodents, the coordinating with state governments to administer the Dingell-Johnson and Pittman-Robertson Acts, the conducting of studies of water-development projects and the submitting of recom-

---

Support is required not just for a battle here, or a rearguard action there, but for a fundamental and continuing program to make our country a better place in which to live, a cherished place of beauty passed on with pride from one generation to the next.

— Henry M. Jackson

mendations thereon, the making of efforts to save rare and endangered species, and the promoting of federal or state research on a wide variety of matters relating to fish and wildlife management.

While almost all the activities of the FWS contribute to outdoor recreation, the fish hatcheries and wildlife refuges constitute a substantial recreation resource. In 1976, 26 million visits were made to the 326 national wildlife refuges, and more than 1.7 million persons visited the 98 national fish hatcheries. These refuges and hatcheries cover a land and water area of over 30 million acres.

The FWS tries to enhance the opportunities of our population. In attempting to accomplish this the Service is constantly faced with several difficult problems, such as (a) preservation of wildlife habitat; (b) inadequate public access to water areas; (c) water pollution; (d) misuse of insecticides; (e) inadequate visitor facilities; (f) control of predators; (g) coordination with the many agencies involved; and (h) promotion of public hunting and fishing on private lands.

The problem of preserving habitat is increasing for all wildlife agencies. Along with a rising population and the expectation of high living standards have come advances in engineering techniques which allow extensive and rapid exploitation of natural resources, possibly destroying favorable wildlife environment. At the same time a greater proportion of the increasing population wants to hunt and fish. During recent years the number of hunting licenses has increased faster than the population. Wildlife is therefore caught in a squeeze from two directions: diminishing habitat and increasing demand.

Water quality is a major determinant in the maintenance of fish populations. The Service has become active in reviewing the applications to EPA for permits to discharge waste materials into the waters of the United States (Sec. 402 of the Federal Water Pollution Control Act) as well as applications for permits from the Corps of Engineers for disposal of dredge spoil in such waters under Sec. 404 of the Act. These actions, in conjunction with other functions exercised under the Fish and Wildlife Coordination Act, will go far in ensuring a healthy aquatic environment.

The FWS contends that insecticides are being marketed and used in quantities before they have been adequately tested to determine their effect on human beings, domestic animals, and wildlife. It also claims that insecticides with known harmful effects to fish and wildlife are being used in excessive quantities indiscriminately over areas with varying degrees of insect concentration. In its concern over these matters it sometimes finds itself opposing the work of the Plant Pest Control Division of the Agricultural Research Service.

Federal agencies need to coordinate their efforts to accomplish acceptable results. The FWS operations must be concomitant with the Bureau of Reclamation, the Bureau of Land Management, the U.S. Forest Service, the Soil Conservation Service, the TVA, the Corps of Engineers, and the Environmental Protection

The survival of wildlife in a fast-changing world serves as a barometer of the health of man. If wild creatures can thrive, it is a good bet that humankind will find the environment livable too.

One more cast, just one more.

For each thing there is a time and a season.

In the short history of our country, 47 wildlife species have been driven over the brink of extinction. More than 120 species have disappeared throughout the world since A.D. 1600. Today hundreds of others face a similar fate.

Agency. The FWS continually cooperates with state fish and game departments or conservation agencies and frequently with state, highway, park, forestry, and land departments.

A large portion of the hunting and fishing now takes place on privately owned lands. The FWS can contribute to the resolution of the basic problem of diminishing habitat and increasing demand by encouraging increased fish and game production on private lands and by developing methods for the creation of better rapport between sportsmen and landowners. The development of game management plans, plus possible assistance in stocking farms and private forests, should result in increased wildlife.

With the steady increase in population, combined with increased interest in fish and wildlife activities, it seems certain that the FWS will be under ever increasing demands. Many of their problems, which are fundamentally related to increased population and a decrease in suitable fish and wildlife habitat, will continue to escalate. In the future the FWS and the corresponding state agencies will find it difficult to maintain adequate populations of fish and wildlife to meet the need and interests of the people.

Tennessee Valley Authority

The Tennessee Valley Authority is a U.S. government corporation created in 1933 as a regional resource development agency, under the TVA Act, based on the concept that all the resources of a river basin are interrelated and should be developed under one unified plan for maximum effectiveness. To put the Tennessee River to work, TVA built a system of multipurpose dams with primary goals of flood control, navigation, and electric power production.

The original TVA Act made no specific reference to recreation. But it did authorize surveys, plans, and demonstrations for fostering an orderly and proper physical, economic, and social development of the Tennessee basin and adjoining territory. TVA officials apparently interpreted this to include planning and development of recreation and scenic potentials, because these have been seriously planned for since the beginning of the TVA projects.

Recognition of the lakes' recreation potential resulted in a decision to acquire such lands as might be necessary to guarantee public access to the project, and the Authority never departed from the principle of including lands for public access.

The lakes created under the TVA cover over a half million acres and have shorelines totaling over 10,000 miles. These man-made lakes attracted 68.8 million recreation visits in 1976. Recently recreation visits there have increased by an average of 3.2 million per year. Much of the popularity of the TVA projects can be attributed to the fact that they combine scenic beauty with water resources. They are in a climatic setting which is suitable to outdoor recreation most of the year and is within two days of automobile travel to more than half the people in the United States.

By 1976, 526 public access areas, 19 state parks, and 92 county and municipal parks had been created on the shores of the TVA lakes. In addition, TVA had transferred about 125,000 acres to the National Park Service, the U.S. Fish and Wildlife Service, and the U.S. Forest Service. Some 340 fishing camps, boat docks, and resorts were operated by private businesses on TVA lakeshores, and about 13,000 privately owned vacation homes had been built on lakefront sites. Campsites and marinas have also been sold to private clubs and to service organizations such as the YMCA and the Boy Scouts. Properties sold for recreation are subject to repossession by TVA should they no longer be used for recreation purposes.

While flood control, navigation, and power development remain the primary purposes, recreation values have been given high priority by TVA board members ever since the inception of the project. The foresight of early planners, the imaginative and resourceful administration, and the favorable attitudes of TVA board members, coupled with the natural endowments and location of the area, have made the Tennessee Valley one of America's foremost playgrounds. TVA's policy with respect to recreational use of the reservoirs has always been to treat them as regional and national assets. Inasmuch as the people living near the reservoirs are the primary economic beneficiaries, it is right that they should share in the responsibilities of development and management. Thus TVA has endeavored to stimulate local and regional initiative by making appropriate lands available to the local agencies and organizations and private groups or individuals for the development of recreation facilities and by providing needed technical assistance.

At the same time TVA broadened the effect of these reservoirs by conveying extensive lands to other federal agencies for national parks, national forests, and wildlife refuges. It has also transferred and otherwise made available substantial areas to the states for development as state parks and state wildlife-management areas.

TVA was the first federal water resources agency to plan for recreational use of impounded waters and shoreline, and the other resource-managing agencies benefit from its experience. TVA policies have produced highly successful results in the past, but increasing recreation-use pressures will call for more attention to recreation planning on a broader scale than in the past.

TVA's concern with recreation, as with other resources of the Tennessee Valley, is not limited to its lakes. Its responsibility is *regional resource development,* and in recreation it operates through a program of direct action as well as providing technical assistance to other agencies and organizations throughout the region.

In addition to providing special water releases from some of its dams to accommodate fishing and boating interests on the rivers, TVA has purchased land to provide public access to scenic rivers and other streams. The agency also works with state organizations to purchase and protect certain natural and scenic points not associated with reservoir lands, and sets aside small areas of natural or scenic interest on its own lands.

TVA's technical assistance programs range from identification, planning, development, and programming use of community recreation projects to market

Water skiing is a popular sport on TVA waters.

analysis for potential resort operations or historic site evaluation. Over the years the agency has also undertaken a number of demonstration projects in recreation aimed at stimulating activity in keeping up with the changing and diversifying recreational demand within the Valley.

Land Between The Lakes National Program. At Land Between The Lakes in west Kentucky and Tennessee, TVA is carrying out a major national demonstration program in outdoor recreation and environmental education. The 170,000-acre wooded peninsula is located between Kentucky Lake and Lake Barkley, two of the largest man-made lakes in America.

Land Between The Lakes is being developed under a multiple-use concept to show how submarginal land can be restored and utilized to provide recreational and educational benefits for the public, while upgrading the forest and open lands to provide greater wildlife benefits. The area is being managed as a year-round public use area where people can have a wholesome outdoor experience and at the same time maintain or regain an appreciation of our natural environment and the importance of proper conservation and utilization of our resources. Camping, fishing, boating, hiking, hunting, and nature study are among the favorite recreational activities in Land Between The Lakes.

Bureau of Indian Affairs

Indian lands total some 51 million acres — an area slightly larger than the state of Kansas. These lands are held in trust or restricted status for the Indians and are, therefore, in that sense private property. Nevertheless, a significant number of them are used by the general public for outdoor recreation. The lands are administered jointly by the Indian tribes and the Bureau of Indian Affairs, a branch of the Department of the Interior.

Most Indian lands are located west of the Mississippi, except for reservations of considerable size in Minnesota and Wisconsin and smaller reservations in Florida, Michigan, Mississippi, North Carolina, and South Carolina. Arizona contains the most Indian land, 21.5 million acres; New Mexico is second, with 6.4 million acres; Montana is third, with 5.2 million; and South Dakota is fourth, with 4.9 million.

Indian reservations contain more than 3600 ponds and lakes with a water surface area of approximately 750,000 acres. There are 6600 miles of rivers and streams — some of which have high fishing values. About one-half of the total of Indian land has been classified as hunting areas. During 1976, about 700,000 visitor-days were spent in fishing and 290,000 visitor-days in hunting on Indian reservations. In the same year, recreation visits for all purposes (including ceremonials and calls at museums) exceeded 2,800,000.

As a general rule, even in the absence of treaty provisions, Indians may hunt or fish on the Indian reservations in accordance with their own tribal regulations or customs and are not subject to state laws. Non-Indians may not hunt or fish on Indian reservations without the permission of the Indians, regardless of state fish and game laws. Other recreational uses of Indian lands are also dependent upon permission from the Indians.

Until recently the Indians have generally declined to share the recreation potentials of their reservations with non-Indians, especially as regards hunting and fishing. But in recent years some Indian tribes have recognized the income potential of recreational use of the reservations. This is exemplified by many tribal recreational projects that have been and are currently being developed.

Federal Highway Administration

The Federal Highway Administration, which is within the Department of Transportation, has three principal functions: (1) the administration of federal aid to the states for highway construction, (2) highway planning and research, and (3) road-building on federal domain.

As the roadbuilding agency for the federal government, the Federal Highway Administration administers funds for roads on federal lands or directly handles the engineering and construction. These roads include forest highways, park roads and parkways, logging and development roads for the Forest Service and Bureau of Land Management, and access roads to national fish hatchery sites and game management areas.

Highways link together and make more accessible to the public, recreational, historic, scientific, and other similar areas of scenic interest and cultural importance. The tremendous increase in the use of federally owned recreation resources during the past years has been possible because of their accessibility via the public road system. It is estimated that over 95 percent of the visitors to Yellowstone, Glacier, Grand Canyon, and Great Smoky Mountains National Parks come by private automobile or private recreational vehicle.

While they are usually considered as a means to an end, highways also provide opportunities for recreational experience in and of themselves, just in the traveling.

Federal Agencies Providing Technical and Financial Assistance in Outdoor Recreation

In addition to the resource-management agencies already discussed, a number of other federal agencies contribute significantly to outdoor recreation by providing technical and financial assistance. These agencies are not necessarily more or less important to outdoor recreation than the resource-management agencies. They simply perform a different kind of function.

Bureau of Outdoor Recreation

The Bureau of Outdoor Recreation was created in April, 1962, by the Secretary of the Interior as an outgrowth of studies by the Outdoor Recreation Resources Review Commission (ORRRC). The Bureau serves as the federal focal point to assure prompt and coordinated action at all levels of government for (1) coordinating, planning, and financing public recreation, and (2) encouraging and assisting all governmental and private interests to conserve, develop, and utilize outdoor recreation resources for the benefit and enjoyment of present and future generations.

In brief, the Bureau of Outdoor Recreation is:

(1) Banker of the Land and Water Conservation Fund. The Land and Water Conservation Fund, currently authorized at $300 million annually, provides matching grants to states for the planning, purchase, and development of public outdoor recreation areas, and money to federal agencies for acquisition of nationally significant recreation lands and waters.

(2) Departmental Coordinator of the National Wild and Scenic Rivers System and National Trails Program. The Bureau studies rivers assigned to the Department under Public Law 90-542, which established the National Wild and Scenic Rivers System. BOR studies determine whether rivers qualify for the National System, what lands are needed to preserve their free-flowing character and provide for maximum public use, and the most appropriate federal or state agency to handle administration.

The 1968 National Trails System Act, Public Law 90-543, established a National Trails System of National Scenic Trails, National Recreation Trails, and connecting or side trails. The Act placed two "instant" National Scenic Trails in the System — the Appalachian and Pacific Crest — and named 14 more routes for study. The Bureau studies proposed trail routes and reviews applications for National Recreation Trail designation.

A truly splendid environment doesn't just "happen" except in untouched wilderness. Wherever there are People, constant care is needed to guard — against People. Only by being our own sternest taskmaster can we keep from being our own worst enemy.

A scene from Mammoth Mountain trail, in the Inyo National Forest, California.

Everywhere, water attracts people for recreation.

(3) Land and Water Resources Planner. The Bureau is a leader in land use planning through Statewide Comprehensive Outdoor Recreation Plans (which are required of states for participation in the Land and Water Conservation Fund program); water and related land resource project proposals; special resource area studies; and transportation project proposals. The Bureau also serves as chairman of the Department of the Interior's Land Planning Group which reviews studies and proposals involving use of the federal "side" of the Land and Water Conservation Fund.

(4) Nationwide Outdoor Recreation Planner. In December, 1973, the Bureau published the first nationwide outdoor recreation plan, "Outdoor Recreation — A Legacy for America." The plan is a mandate for action by the federal government to ensure better management of recreation resources and to increase the availability of those resources. It also presents actions for state and local governments and private interests to increase opportunities for outdoor enjoyment. By law, the plan must be updated every five years.

(5) Coordinator of Federal Outdoor Recreation Programs. As the federal focal point for outdoor recreation operations, the Bureau evaluates and monitors over 290 federal programs in 16 different agencies contributing to or affecting outdoor recreation.

(6) Conveyor of Federal Surplus Property for Parks. Working with the Federal Property Council and the General Services Administration, the Bureau transfers surplus federal real property to state and local governments for public park use.

(7) Source of Recreation Technical Assistance. The Bureau provides broad-based technical assistance to recreation suppliers and users; publishes technical papers and booklets; maintains a clearinghouse of recreation-related information and a referral system to other sources of expertise; and conducts nationwide workshops or seminars on recreation problems and opportunities.

(8) Environmental Reviewer. The Bureau prepares BOR environmental impact statements and reviews recreation-related statements of other federal agencies to ensure that proposed actions will not degrade or destroy existing or potential outdoor recreation opportunities.

The Bureau was given a broad charter and a basic mission with passage by Congress of Public Law 88-29 on May 29, 1963. Subsequent laws that have affected the BOR are listed below.

Land and Water Conservation Fund Act of 1965 (Public Law 88-578; 78 Stat. 897), as amended

Section 6(a) of the Federal Water Project Recreation Act (Public Law 89-72; 79 Stat. 213)

Section 4(f) of the Department of Transportation Act of 1966 (Public Law 89-670; 80 Stat. 931), as amended

Wild and Scenic Rivers Act (Public Law 90-542; 82 Stat. 906), as amended

National Trails System Act (Public Law 90-543; 82 Stat. 919)

The Sikes Act (Public Law 86-797; 74 Stat. 1053), as amended

Redwood National Park Act (Public Law 90-545; 82 Stat. 931)

National Environmental Policy Act (Public Law 91-190; 83 Stat. 852)

"Federal Lands for Parks and Recreation" (Public Law 91-485; 84 Stat. 1084)

Alaska Native Claims Settlement Act (Public Law 92-203; 85 Stat. 688)

The BOR headquarters office is in the Interior Building, Washington, D.C., and there are the following seven regional offices:

NORTHWEST
Regional Director
915 Second Avenue, Room 990
Seattle, Washington 98174

Alaska, Idaho, Oregon, Washington.

PACIFIC SOUTHWEST
Regional Director
Box 36062
450 Golden Gate Avenue
San Francisco, California 94102

American Samoa, Arizona, California, Guam, Hawaii, Nevada.

MID-CONTINENT
Regional Director
P.O. Box 25387
Denver Federal Center
Denver, Colorado 80225

Colorado, Iowa, Kansas, Missouri, Montana, Nebraska, North Dakota, South Dakota, Utah, Wyoming.

SOUTH CENTRAL
Regional Director
5000 Marble Avenue, N.E.
Albuquerque, New Mexico 87110

Arkansas, Louisiana, New Mexico, Oklahoma, Texas.

LAKE CENTRAL
Regional Director
3853 Research Park Drive
Ann Arbor, Michigan 48104

Illinois, Indiana, Michigan, Minnesota, Ohio, Wisconsin.

SOUTHEAST
Regional Director
148 Cain Street
Atlanta, Georgia 30303

Alabama, Florida, Georgia, Kentucky, Mississippi, North Carolina, Puerto Rico, South Carolina, Tennessee, Virgin Islands.

NORTHEAST
Regional Director
Federal Office Building
600 Arch Street
Philadelphia, Pennsylvania 19106

Connecticut, Delaware, Maine, Maryland, Massachusetts, New Hampshire, New Jersey, New York, Pennsylvania, Rhode Island, Vermont, Virginia, West Virginia, and the District of Columbia.

Agricultural Stabilization and Conservation Service

The primary responsibilities of this agency are in agricultural production, conservation, and market stabilization; but the agency does participate in several programs related to outdoor recreation.

The *Agricultural Conservation Program* (ACP) was established by the Soil Conservation and Domestic Allotment Act of 1936. In brief, this Act authorizes payments to farmers for shifting acreage from soil-depleting to soil-building crops and for conservation practices.

According to ASCS, "many of these soil, water, and woodland conservation practices, established for their agricultural conservation benefits, contribute to outdoor recreation and provide recreational benefits ranging from incidental to substantial."

Until 1962, the ACP had not shared costs for any project that had benefits to recreation or wildlife as its primary purpose. The ACP Guidebook did, however, encourage the use of shrubs and trees that would enhance wildlife, and it also encouraged the use of private ponds for the production of fish. Then the Appropriations Act for 1962 (Public Law 87-112) specifically authorized cost-sharing payments to landowners when the primary benefit is wildlife conservation. This provision marked a definite change in policy and has caused expanded outdoor-recreation benefits from the Agricultural Conservation Program.

The farm ponds already constructed number about 3 million. Many are stocked with fish. The program has also produced many thousands of acres of improved wildlife habitat.

The Water Bank Act (Public Law 91-559), approved in 1970, provides for annual payments to owners of eligible wetlands along important migratory waterfowl flyways who agree under contract to maintain the wetlands for waterfowl nesting and brooding purposes.

Soil Conservation Service

The SCS is involved in outdoor recreation through three different approaches. Following are brief descriptions of these SCS programs.

Technical Assistance to Landowners and Operators. The Soil Conservation Service provides technical assistance to landowners and operators in planning and installing recreation enterprises. SCS also provides technical help on use of soil, water, and related resources for outdoor recreation on nonfederal lands owned or operated by local units of government, nonprofit organizations, and other community groups.

These services are made available through some 3,010 Soil and Water Conservation Districts which blanket the nation. Soil and Water Conservation Districts are units of local government, organized by landowners and operators under state-enabling laws, and administered by local leaders.

Resource Conservation and Development Projects. The assistance of the Department in carrying out Resource Conservation and Development Projects is available to local public bodies, associations, and others in areas where local leadership assumes responsibility and initiates action necessary to promote conservation and development of an area usually multicounty in size. Resource Conservation and Development Projects call for stepped-up community programs to increase economic opportunities.

The Soil Conservation Service is responsible for providing Department of Agriculture leadership and guidance in Resource Conservation and Development Projects. It works through local Soil and Water Conservation Districts and with other local sponsoring groups. USDA technical, educational, credit, and cost-sharing assistance is coordinated through the project approach.

Small Watershed Projects. Under provisions of Public Law 566 — The Watershed Protection and Flood Prevention (Small Watershed) Act of 1954, as amended — the Soil Conservation Service may share with state and local government agencies up to half the cost of construction, land rights, and basic facilities needed for public health and safety, access to and enjoyment of public recreation, and fish and wildlife developments in small watershed projects.

State park and fish and game agencies are eligible to sponsor watershed projects. So are counties, municipalities, special purpose districts, and other units or agencies of government. Sponsors own all structures and facilities that are built and are responsible for their operation and maintenance.

Qualified local organizations are eligible to obtain watershed loans through the Farmers Home Administration to finance the local share of project costs set forth in approved watershed work plans.

This same assistance is available to project sponsors in eleven watersheds where work is authorized under the Flood Control Act of 1944.

Extension Service, USDA

The Extension Service is the educational branch of the Department of Agriculture. It cooperates with the various states and most of the counties within the states in an effort to take education to the people. In addition to carrying on many specific programs relating to recreation through the 4-H Clubs, the Extension Service also provides advisory service to states and political subdivisions on outdoor-recreation matters.

Information on recreation enterprises, costs and returns, demand, and other considerations is available through most county extension offices. The state Cooperative Extension Services now have approximately 100 recreation specialists and 26 wildlife specialists working full time throughout the country in outdoor-recreation and related activities.

Other Federal Agencies

In addition to those agencies already discussed, a number of other agencies within the several departments of the federal government contribute in a secondary or indirect way to outdoor recreation. Following are brief statements about how they are involved.

Department of Agriculture

Four agencies under the Department of Agriculture have already been discussed (U.S. Forest Service, Agricultural Stabilization and Conservation Service, Soil Conservation Service, and Extension Service). In addition, the *Economic Research Service* performs studies related to supply and demand and the economic effect of outdoor recreation. The *Farmers Home Administration* provides loans and management assistance to farmers in rural groups. The FHA program has been expanded to include income-producing outdoor-recreation projects. Through the *Agricultural Experiment Station* valuable information is distributed on land uses, supply and demand, population, recreation planning, etc.

Department of Commerce

The Bureau of Census furnishes population statistics and projections needed for recreation planning and surveys. For instance, special studies by the Bureau were conducted recently for the Bureau of Outdoor Recreation and the Bureau of Sports, Fisheries, and Wildlife. The Bureau of Domestic Commerce provides publications, study reports, and other materials useful to manufacturers of recreation equipment, operators of resorts, ski lifts, golf courses, sports arenas, and other recreation facilities. The Economic Development Administration can provide a maximum of 75 percent of the cost of parks and recreation projects to public or nonprofit private organizations that qualify under the Economic Development program. Economic development research devotes particular attention to the potential effects of recreation development on local economy. The Economic Development Administration appropriated 167 million dollars for public works and planning grants, loans, and other services relating to recreation since 1966. Within the National Oceanic and Atmospheric Administration is the Weather Bureau, which keeps the public informed of weather conditions that influence day-to-day recreational activities such as boating, snow skiing, camping, hunting, fishing, swimming, picnicking, etc. The U.S. Travel Service carries out a comprehensive program designed to stimulate travel to the U.S. by residents of foreign countries for the purpose of study, culture, recreation, business, and other activities.

Department of Defense

Approximately 27 million acres of land are administered by the Department of Defense. Active programs concerned with natural beauty and outdoor recreation are administered by 220 military installations, of which 180 are open to the public. Outdoor-recreation use on military installations exceeds 2 million visits per year.

Department of Health, Education, and Welfare

Within this department the *Office of Education* provides programs involving consultation and financial assistance, publications and research studies, some of which relate to outdoor recreation. Title I of the Higher Education Act (1965) provides grants to states to enable colleges and universities to strengthen community-service programs, including recreation and land-use programs. The Elementary and Secondary Education Act (1965) provides for grants to states for supplemental educational centers and services, some of which may be in the area of outdoor recreation. The *Public Health Service* provides technical assistance in environmental and sanitation aspects of recreation areas and facilities. Community and environmental health training is provided through conferences held annually and attended by park and recreation personnel and other community leaders. As a result of grants through the Public Health Service, the National Recreation and Park Association has conducted training programs to update knowledge of professionals working with the ill and handicapped in the field of recreation. The *Rehabilitation Services Administration* provides training grants concerned with recreation for the ill and disabled, including mentally retarded. The *Welfare Administration* has within it the Children's Bureau, which provides consultation services designed to encourage the extension of recreational opportunities for youth, cooperating with national, state, and local organizations and for disseminating useful materials and information.

The Bureau of Education for the Handicapped, a division of HEW, provides grants to institutions for the training of physical education teachers and recreation leaders for the handicapped; the Bureau will also make small amounts available for research grants in these fields.

Grants to improve and extend community schools, ordinarily including strong recreational components, are authorized under the Special Projects portion of the education Amendments of 1974 (Sections 402 and 405 of PL 93-380).

Department of Housing and Urban Development

The U.S. Department of Housing and Urban Development (HUD) administers the Community Development Block Grants Program which provides open space and recreation facilities that may be used by local communities.

Authorized in 1974 by the Housing Community Development Act, the block grant program consolidates into a single program the seven previous categorical programs of urban renewal, Model Cities, water and sewer facilities, open space, neighborhood facilities, rehabilitation loans, and public facilities. Activities eligible under these former categorical programs can be carried out under the block grant formula, with the important difference that the latter allows a community to choose among all of the permissible uses and determine how to allocate its block grant funds. In sum, under the block grant program, a community maps out its own approach to meeting the needs of the community: it assesses its development needs, establishes its own priorities, and allocates its resources accordingly.

Block grant funds go directly to the general local government, as the body which is most responsive to the electorate and has the broadest authority to deal with community development. All cities of over 50,000 population and most counties of over 200,000 are entitled to a certain amount of funds. Distribution of the funds to the communities is based on a formula that takes account of need as indicated by objective census data on population, housing overcrowding, and poverty.

The community's application for block grant funds — which maps its strategy for meeting its needs over a three-year period — is reviewed by the Department of Housing and Urban Development which must (within 75 days) approve the application unless it is plainly inconsistent with generally available facts, plainly inappropriate to the needs identified by the community itself, or not in compliance with law. HUD is also assigned the role of monitoring the community's performance in carrying out its stated program.

The 1974 Act marks a major redirection in the way that federal assistance for housing and community development is provided to local communities: it transfers major responsibility and decison making to local elected governments; and it contemplates a new kind of partnership between the federal government and local governments by limiting the federal role to one of assisting rather than directing local development programs.

Thus, available federal block grant funds may be used to meet a need for local open space facilities, but the community, working through its local government, must initiate and carry out an open space program.

Department of the Interior

Six agencies of the Department of the Interior have already been discussed (National Park Service, Bureau of Reclamation, Bureau of Land Management, U.S. Fish and Wildlife Service, Bureau of Indian Affairs, and Bureau of Outdoor Recreation). Three other agencies in that department contribute to outdoor recreation. The *Federal Water Pollution Control Administration* helps to assure an adequate and continuous supply of clean water for all uses. Consideration is given to the conservation of pure waters for recreational purposes. Programs to accomplish this are carried out in cooperation with states, municipalities, and industries. Financial assistance for research development is available for projects which demonstrate improved methods for water pollution control. The *Geological Survey* develops and provides geographic and topographic maps which are very useful in recreation-resource planning and to recreation participants such as hikers, boaters, and others making trips away from familiar areas. This agency makes geological maps of national parks and other areas of national significance. It frequently collaborates in studies of proposed parks. The *Office of Water Resources Research* administers financial aid programs authorized by the Water Resources Research Act of 1964. Some of these programs include the use of water for recreation facilities, wildlife, and other similar purposes.

Department of Transportation

In addition to the Federal Highway Administration, which has already been discussed, the Department of Transportation has two other agencies involved in outdoor recreation. The *Federal Aviation Agency* administers a federal grant-in-aid program designed to assist public agencies in developing a nationwide system of airports, including facilities to provide access to out-of-the-way recreation areas. The *United States Coast Guard* is responsible to (a) develop and administer a maritime safety program, (b) furnish aids for navigation, (c) enforce all applicable federal laws on the high seas and various federal impoundments. The Coast Guard cooperates with the various states in the numbering of small recreation boats, as required by the 1958 Federal Boating Act. It also patrols regattas and marine parades, conducts boating-accident studies, provides public training for safe boating, helps prevent the pollution of navigable waters, and conducts courtesy examinations of motor boats.

Independent Agencies

In addition to the Tennessee Valley Authority, which has already been discussed, there are several other independent federal agencies that contribute to outdoor recreation.

The *Appalachian Regional Commission* carries on a program of reclamation and restoration of mining areas to a condition of natural beauty. Besides, the commission is responsible for developing a network of highways totaling more than 2350 miles. Much of this highway system will contribute to the accessibility of recreation areas. An additional 1000 miles of accessible roads are authorized for specific recreational sites.

The *Atomic Energy Commission* controls 2.7 million acres of federally owned land. Some of this land has high recreation potential, although it is necessarily restricted to some extent for security reasons. The Commission's land and facilities disposal program provides for transfer of land suitable for parks and recreation facilities to local governments contiguous to the commission's installations.

The *Federal Power Commission,* through its licensing procedures, has administrative responsibility for important segments of the nation's water-based recreation opportunities and fish and wildlife habitat. The 377 hydroelectric projects, currently licensed by the FPC, contain about 900 reservoirs representing between 2 and 3 million acres of water surface, thousands of miles of shoreline. In 1965, in order to provide for more effective discharge of its administrative responsibilities, a recreation, fish, and wildlife section was created. Since that time the FPC has taken positive action requiring license applicants to assume primary responsibility for developing comprehensive plans for utilizing project property for outdoor-recreation purposes.

The *General Services Administration.* Under the Surplus Property Act of 1944, certain federal surplus real property can be acquired by state and local governments for public park and recreation purposes through the General Services Administration for 50 percent of fair market value. Surplus property may be transferred for historic preservation without cost. During the federal fiscal year 1966, approximately 10,600 acres of land and 400 buildings were conveyed for park, recreation, historic monument, or wildlife conservation purposes.

The *Office of Economic Opportunity* was created in 1964 to coordinate all antipoverty programs on the federal government level. These include the Job Corps, VISTA, and the Community Action Programs. The estimated value of the work related to recreation development by the Job Corps alone through 1966 totaled $34 million. The Community Action Program reported approximately $7 million were expended in 1965 for various recreation programs for the poor. Amendments to the Economic Opportunity Act of 1965 increased authorized appropriations for grants to include community beautification and other projects contributing to the management, conservation, or development of recreation sites.

The *Public Land Law Review Commission* has been recently formed and is still in the study stage. The Commission expects to report specific recommendations to Congress in the near future. Since recreation and park use of public land by local, state, and federal governments is a common policy, the recommendations of the Commission will cover these areas.

The *Small Business Administration* makes business loans for the following forms of recreation: golf, tennis, skiing, camping, boating and bathing, and skating. In addition to direct loans and loans in participation with banks, the Small Business Administration can provide funds for the expansion or modernization of facilities owned by recreation enterprises. About 3 percent of all loans approved by SBA is allocated to recreation enterprises. The Water Resources Council is responsible to the President for the comprehensive and coordinated planning of the nation's waterways. It works closely with other federal agencies at state and local governments and private enterprises. Matching grants to states for comprehensive water

A place where only a
few people have been.

resource planning are available. Much of the planning done under these grants is closely related to park and recreation development.

National Outdoor Recreation Plan

Early in its existence the Bureau of Outdoor Recreation was charged with the responsibility of developing and maintaining a national plan, and for coordinating the outdoor recreation effort at the national level in accordance with the plan. After much work with federal, state, and local government agencies and with non-government groups and individuals, the BOR produced the written form of the plan in 1973. Its title is *Outdoor Recreation – A Legacy for America.*

Authority for the Plan

Public Law 88-29 directs the Secretary of the Interior to: "Formulate and maintain a comprehensive nationwide outdoor recreation plan, taking into consideration the plans of the various federal agencies, states, and their political subdivisions. The Plan shall set forth the needs and demands of the public for outdoor recreation and the current and foreseeable availability in the future of outdoor recreation resources to meet those needs. The Plan shall identify critical outdoor recreation problems, recommend solutions, and recommend desirable actions to be taken at each level of government and by private interests." It further states that "federal departments and independent agencies... shall carry out such (recreation) responsibilities in general conformance with the nationwide (outdoor recreation) plan."

Scope of the Plan

The Plan explains how governmental and other public and private institutions manage resources to provide outdoor recreation opportunities for people. It provides a basis for establishing the roles and responsibilities of the various levels of government and the private sector in meeting outdoor recreation needs. It identifies the actions necessary to achieve effective and creative use of recreation resources and programs. Integral parts of this are the identification of means of preserving and improving outdoor recreation resources and of providing outdoor recreation opportunities. In some instances these actions may constitute only the initial step toward full realization of problem solutions. In these instances the actions are designed to focus on and catalyze further actions necessary to solve specific problems related to outdoor recreation and the associated recreation environment. The Plan looks at recreation as an important element in land use and land use planning and places outdoor recreation in context with this process.

Plan Objectives

The objectives of the Plan are:
1. More effective investment of public and private recreation funds in meeting high priority recreation demands;
2. A strengthened ability of state and local governments and the private sector to meet recreation needs;
3. Improved efficiency and effectiveness of present federal recreation efforts;
4. Achievement of maximum recreation potential of nonrecreation programs consistent with the primary purpose of such programs;
5. Expansion of efforts to protect and conserve the future resources that have special scenic, historic, and scientific, or recreation value;
6. Better coordination and cooperation between and among public and private recreation suppliers;
7. Maximum results by the private sector in meeting high priority outdoor recreation needs; and
8. Maximum citizen participation and education through involvement in recreation resource programs.

Committed Federal Actions

To increase the availability of recreation resources, the federal government will:
1. Complete a program of identification and selection and a plan for acquisition of those superlative areas needed to round out the federal recreation estate.
2. Continue to utilize the Land and Water Conservation Fund to acquire needed federal lands and assist the states in acquiring and developing recreation lands and facilities. As demands for federal acquisition are reduced, more of the Fund monies will be made available to the states.
3. Open to the public directly or through state and local entities those underutilized portions of federal properties or facilities having public recreation values compatible with the primary purposes, when such lands are not available for transfer under the "Legacy of Parks" program.

> There are rational arguments for altering this environment that appeal to a sense of enlightened self-interest. And there are other arguments that speak even more eloquently to the human heart.

4. Accelerate studies and evaluations of proposed trails, wild and scenic rivers, wilderness areas, wetlands, and historical properties to ensure that those unique lands are preserved by federal, state, or local governments or private interests for the benefit of the public; and accelerate the evaluation of federal land holdings to determine if beaches, shorelines, islands, and natural areas can be made available for increased public recreation use.

To improve the management and administration of recreation resources and programs, the federal government will:

1. Accelerate the identification and no-cost transfer of surplus and underutilized real property to state and local governments for park and recreation purposes.
2. When the land is not available for transfer, and direct federal management is not necessary or desirable, take necessary steps to transfer management responsibility for existing recreational units to state and local governments; legislation will be requested where needed to permit provision of federal operation and maintenance funds on a descending scale for a period not to exceed five years to a state or local government accepting management responsibility for a recreation complex currently operated by a federal agency.
3. Promote recreation facilities development on or adjacent to federal lands on the basis of regional land use plans. Whenever possible, private investment should be utilized for the provision of these services.
4. Undertake preparation of recreation land use plans for all management units and coordinate such planning with all interested federal, state, and local government agencies and private entities with full citizen participation. It is essential that these plans set forth the recreation carrying capacity of the lands involved and provide for institution of necessary user controls and development of new ways of managing the movement of people to ensure that use does not exceed the determined capacity.

Chapter 6 Recent Legislation and Special Government Programs

In recent years recreation has gained much support from federal and state governments. Legislation has been passed and programs initiated which are having, and will continue to have, significant influence on outdoor recreation. Great changes have occurred in the emphasis toward recreational use of land and water owned by federal and state agencies. To a large extent a new system of values toward recreational use of natural resources has taken place. Accordingly, new government policies and programs have been established.

The federal government has inaugurated a number of programs under which the states, their political subdivisions, individuals, and organizations may qualify for assistance in outdoor recreation. The assistance involves credit, cost-sharing, technical aid, educational services, and research. This chapter does not by any means include all of the recent legislation and special programs influencing outdoor recreation. It includes only selected information with broad application.

Outdoor Recreation Resources Review Commission

Traditionally, the outdoors has been an important part of American life — first as a wilderness to be conquered and then as a source of inspiration and recreation. In this latter sense its importance is still increasing.

During the 1950s the growing public demand for the outdoors and sharpening competition for outdoor-recreation resources became matters of increasing concern. Recognizing the need for a nationwide study of these problems, Congress in **97**

> The challenge of our age is whether we shall seize the opportunity to decide what kind of life, what kind of environment, and what kind of opportunities we want for ourselves and for our children.
>
> — Henry M. Jackson

1958 established the Outdoor Recreation Resources Review Commission (ORRRC), consisting of eight members of Congress and seven private citizens appointed by the President. Lawrence Rockefeller was first chairman of this Commission. Congress directed ORRRC to survey the outdoor-recreation needs of the people for the next 40 years and to recommend action to meet those needs.

The Commission took inventory of the nation's supply of outdoor-recreation spaces including parks, forests, and fishing and hunting areas. It questioned a large number of people in order to learn what the people do for recreation and what they are likely to do in the future. It estimated recreation demands through the year 2000, and made more than 50 specific recommendations intended to ensure that the benefits of outdoor recreation would be available to all Americans, now and in the future. The final report to the Congress, made in 1961, included 27 volumes, each volume written on a separate topic of special significance to outdoor recreation in America. Copies of the Commission's 27-volume report may be obtained from the Superintendent of Documents, Washington, D.C.

The Commission found that adequate provisions were not being made for the rapidly expanding outdoor-recreation needs. It found that the gap between demand and supply would widen over the coming years if effective action were not taken promptly. And it found a qualitative as well as a quantitative lag. Many existing programs were not aimed at providing what most people actually wanted and needed. Better-planned, bolder, and more imaginative efforts were required.

Several significant actions have resulted from the recommendations set forth by the Commission: (a) Several states have authorized and helped to finance recreation-land-acquisition programs. (b) The National Park System has been expanded significantly. (c) The Bureau of Outdoor Recreation was established. (d) A national wilderness system was officially established. (e) The Land and Water Conservation Fund Program was inaugurated. (Among other things this program has prompted the completion of a comprehensive outdoor-recreation-development plan for each of the 50 states.) (f) The Housing and Urban Development Open Space Program was established. (g) A wild rivers system was established. (h) A national trails system was started. (i) A national outdoor recreation plan was developed.

Since that time much additional action has taken place relative to improvement of our outdoor environment and opportunities for outdoor recreation now and in the future.

Specific Acts and Special Programs

The legislative Acts and programs described in this section have had, and will continue to have, significant influence on the preservation and conservation of our nation's resources for recreational purposes. For the most part, the actions described herein have been taken (a) to help safeguard the important recreational and inspirational features of our natural environment, and to protect and preserve these features in the future, or (b) to improve recreation use and practice of natural resources.

Land and Water Conservation Fund Program

The Land and Water Conservation Fund Act of 1965 (PL 88-578), amended in 1968 (PL 90-401) and amended again in 1974 (PL 93-303), provides for financial assistance to certain federal agencies with principal roles in outdoor recreation. It also provides for grants to states, and through them to political subdivisions of states, for planning, acquisition, and development of public outdoor-recreation areas and facilities. The grants usually cover 50 percent of the cost of the project.

The basic eligibility requirement for grants is that the state must develop a comprehensive statewide outdoor-recreation plan and update and refine the plan on a continuing basis. All 50 states have completed such plans that have been approved by the Bureau of Outdoor Recreation. To qualify for funds, an acquisition or development project must be in accord with the state plan; that is, it must meet high-priority public recreation needs identified in the plan.

Assistance is provided for acquisition and development projects in highly populated urban areas as well as in more primitive areas. Eligible projects may vary from bicycle paths to hiking trails, from roadside picnic stops to multipurpose recreation complexes, and from beautification to outdoor-sports facilities. Priority consideration is generally given to projects serving urban populations and the general public rather than limited groups, for basic rather than elaborate facilities, and for projects for which other adequate financing is not available.

Some of the funding for the Land and Water Conservation Program comes from money collected through the Golden Eagle Passport Program, amended in 1972 (PL 92-347). The passport, which costs $10 per year, admits the holder into identified National Park areas of the Department of the Interior and National Recreation areas of the Department of Agriculture. However, most of the revenue for the fund comes from mineral leases on outer continental shelf lands, as described in the 1974 amendment of the Conservation Fund Act.

Applications for local grants from the Land and Water Conservation Fund must be made through the state, which has the initial prerogative in determining which projects shall be supported. Each state has a liaison officer appointed by the governor to assist the Federal Bureau of Outdoor Recreation in administering the program. Besides, each state has an agency designated to process the grant applications. Current addresses of these contacts may be obtained by writing directly to the Bureau of Outdoor Recreation, or to the outdoor-recreation liaison officer, in care of the governor's office for the particular state.

Wilderness System

Humanity itself presents the greatest threat to nature. In one way or another its mark mars the countryside. Its ever-increasing expansion of its environment has a detrimental effect on the balance and survival of nature. In partial realization of this fact, the Wilderness Act (PL 88-577) was passed in 1964. The law is intended to preserve certain areas in their natural form and provide a natural habitat for the diminishing wildlife population. Upon signing the Act, President Lyndon Johnson commented, "The Wilderness Bill preserves for our posterity, for all time to come, 9 million acres of this vast continent in their original and unchanged beauty and wonder."

By definition from the Act itself, "A wilderness, in contrast with those areas where man and his own works dominate the landscapes, is hereby recognized as an area where the earth and its community of life are untrammeled by man, where man himself is a visitor who does not remain."

An area of wilderness is further defined in the Act as

An area of undeveloped federal land retaining its primeval character and influence, without permanent improvements or human habitation, which is protected and managed so as to preserve its natural conditions and which (a) generally appears to have been affected primarily by the forces of nature, with the imprint of man's works substantially unnoticeable; (b) has outstanding opportunities for solitude or a primitive and unconfined type of recreation; (c) is sufficient size as to make practicable its preservation and use in an unimpaired condition; and (d) may also contain ecological or other features of scientific, educational, scenic, or historical value.

The Act established 54 areas in the wilderness system, encompassing a total of 9.1 million acres contained in the U.S. National Forests. Numerous areas have been added to the wilderness system since the Act was passed in 1964, and undoubtedly many new additions will be made in the future.

Recreation and Public Purposes Act of 1954

The Recreation and Public Purposes Act of 1954 (PL 83-387) authorizes state and local governments, and qualified nonprofit organizations, to acquire certain federal lands for recreation use, and for other purposes. The Secretary of the Interior has established the purchase price to states and other governmental agencies at $2.50 an acre and the lease price at 25¢ an acre per year. The Act applies to all public domain lands administered by the Federal Bureau of Land Management. Under certain conditions it applies also to about 25 million acres of public land held by other federal agencies. Most of the 465 million acres of public domain in 28 states administered by the Bureau of Land Management are in the 11 western states and Alaska, although there are small acreages in some of the eastern states. Under the provisions of this Act, a large amount of land has been transferred into recreational use. Information about the amount of land which may be purchased in any one year, the conditions under which patents or leases are issued, and other procedures to be followed may be obtained from Bureau of Land Management offices.

Federal Water Projects Recreation Act of 1965

The Federal Water Projects Recreation Act (PL 89-72) has strong influence on the operation of three federal agencies: the Bureau of Reclamation, the Army Corps

...there must always be wilderness, a lovely someplace for young spirits to discover the wonder of nature and the dependence of man on other living things.

Somewhere in late September a mountain stream comes to a lonely, quiet time. Summer has slipped away like the wake of a canoe on a foggy day.

of Engineers, and the Bureau of Outdoor Recreation. It affects the amount and type of development that may occur on federal water projects, most of which are constructed by the Bureau of Reclamation and the Corps of Engineers, and it assigns several specific responsibilities. The law specifies that the recreation resources of *new* federal water projects are generally to be administered by nonfederal agencies on a cost-sharing basis. The federal government can assume up to 50 percent of the separable costs for developing the recreation potential of each project. But, to have the recreation potential of the project fully developed, a nonfederal agency must indicate its intent to assume one-half of the separable costs of recreation development and all costs of operation, maintenance, and replacement, and to administer the project lands and waters for recreation and fish and wildlife purposes. In the absence of such an expression of nonfederal intent, only minimum facilities for protection of public health and safety will be provided.

This law also fills a longstanding need for general authority for federal development of recreation facilities on *existing* projects. It provides for federal participation, on a cost-sharing basis, in the development of recreation and fish and wildlife enhancement facilities on such projects, on a nonreimbursable basis up to a maximum of $100,000 for each reservoir. Expenditures of more than $100,000 of federal funds must have additional congressional approval. This authority will assist in alleviating deficiencies in recreation and fish and wildlife enhancement facilities on existing projects.

Recent Legislation and Special Government Programs

101

Under this Act the Bureau of Outdoor Recreation carries out the following functions:

1. prepares a general plan for recreation development of the project and recommends its adoption by the construction agency;
2. coordinates recreation planning in project areas with existing and planned federal, state, and local public recreation development;
3. recommends federal or nonfederal administration for project areas;
4. determines the costs and benefits attributable to recreation and estimates costs of providing equivalent benefits elsewhere;
5. recommends fee schedules, requirements for minimum facilities needed, lands needed to be acquired to preserve recreation potential, and interagency transfer of project-recreation lands where appropriate; and
6. encourages nonfederal bodies to lease areas and facilities and administer recreation at existing projects, and to acquire, develop, and administer recreation resources where there are minimum or no recreation facilities; in such instances financial assistance could be available under the Land and Water Conservation Fund program.

Small Reclamation Projects Act

Under the Small Reclamation Projects Act (PL 84-984), certain types of public organizations can obtain loans, for projects not exceeding $10 million total cost, in the 17 western reclamation states and Hawaii.

In certain instances, grants up to $6.5 million for a single project may be made specifically for recreation and fish and wildlife purposes, when these are incorporated as functions of the total project and are in the general public interest. This Act has greatly enhanced the recreation development of small reclamation projects in the western states.

Watershed Protection and Flood Prevention (Small Watershed) Act of 1954

Under the provisions of this Act (PL 83-566), as amended by the Food and Agricultural Act of 1962, the Soil Conservation Service (Department of Agriculture) may share with state and local agencies up to half the cost of construction, land rights, and minimum basic facilities needed for recreation purposes. The areas are to be managed by state and local sponsors for public recreation. State fish, wildlife, and park agencies are eligible for assistance, as are counties, municipalities, and special purpose districts.

Funds may advance to local organizations for immediate purchase of land, easements, and rights-of-way to prevent encroachment of other developments. Such advances have to be repaid with interest before construction starts. Under provisions of this Act a large number of water projects with much recreation potential have been completed.

Water Resources Research Act of 1964

This Act (PL 88-379) authorized allotment of $75,000 to every state in fiscal year 1965, $87,500 in each of the second and third years, and $100,000 each year thereafter to assist every one of the 50 states and Puerto Rico in carrying out work of a competent and qualified water-resources research institute or center.

Also, under Title I of the Act, Congress authorized appropriations not to exceed $1 million in fiscal 1965, $2 million in 1966, $3 million in 1967, $4 million in 1968, and $5 million in 1969 and each succeeding year for matching, on a dollar-for-dollar basis, money made available to the institutes by states or other nonfederal sources. Research centers established under this Act will probably make some significant contributions to the suitability of water for recreation purposes in the future.

Water Quality Act of 1965

The Federal Water Pollution Control Administration, established by the Water Quality Act of 1965 (PL 89-234), has the responsibility of assuring an adequate supply of water suitable in quality for all legitimate uses — public, industrial, agricultural, recreational, propagation of fish, aquatic life, and wildlife. Recognizing that, without water of suitable quality, many outdoor-recreation activities would not be possible, the water pollution control program is deeply involved in provision of water of adequate quality for water-oriented, outdoor-recreation activities.

To achieve water of a quality suitable for all beneficial uses, including recreation, the Federal Water Pollution Control Administration does the following:

1. participates with the states in the establishment of water-quality standards for all interstate and coastal waters;
2. develops comprehensive water pollution control programs on a river-basin basis;
3. provides grants to municipalities for the construction of waste treatment works;
4. provides grants to state and interstate agencies to help strengthen their water pollution control programs;
5. provides grants to help state and local planning agencies develop effective comprehensive water-quality control and abatement plans for river basins;
6. provides grants to agencies, institutions, and individuals for research, training, fellowships, and demonstration projects in the field of water pollution control;
7. provides grants and contracts for research and development into (a) improved methods of controlling discharges of inadequately treated wastes from sewers, and (b) advanced waste treatment for municipal and industrial wastes;
8. assists in development of state and local training programs regarding water pollutions; and
9. conducts an enforcement program against pollution on interstate or navigable waters.

Natural Historic Preservation Act of 1966

This Act (PL 89-665) authorizes matching grants to states and to the National Trust for Historic Preservation in the United States. It authorizes grants up to 50 percent of the cost of acquiring or developing districts, sites, buildings, structures, or objects that are historically significant. The law also authorizes matching grants to states for 50 percent of the cost of preparing comprehensive statewide historic preservation plans, the results of which will guide the making of grants for specific projects. A project may include historic preservation work by a state or local government or other public body, or by private organizations and individuals. To be eligible for funds made available to the states, a project must be in accord with the comprehensive statewide historic preservation plan approved by the Secretary of the Interior. The program is administered under the Department of the Interior.

Greenspan Program

Greenspan is an assistance program of particular interest to rural areas. It is part of the Cropland Adjustment Program (PL 89-321) to help farmers divert cropland to conservation uses. This program also offers state and local government agencies financial assistance to acquire cropland for preserving open space and natural beauty, for developing wildlife or recreation facilities, or for preventing air or water pollution. In addition, it offers cost-sharing in establishing land conservation practices to protect open space, natural beauty, wildlife, or recreation resources. This program is administered under the Department of Agriculture.

Highway Beautification Act of 1965

This Act (PL 89-285) has three major provisions with regard to the beautification of federal-aid highway systems: (a) the control of advertising along interstate highways, (b) the control of junkyards and other such unattractive scenes along interstate highways, and (c) landscape and scenic enhancement along interstate highways. The Act provides that if the Secretary of Commerce determines that any state has not made adequate provisions for controlling advertisements within 660 feet of any highway partly financed by the federal government, the appropriations to the state may be reduced by 10 percent per annum until adequate provisions are made. The Act further provides that the same action should be taken (reduction of appropriations by 10 percent per annum) if the Secretary determines that the state has not made adequate provisions for the control of junkyards and other such unattractive scenes within 1000 feet of the highway. Further, the Secretary may approve as part of the construction of federal-aid highways the costs of landscape and roadside development, including acquisition and development of publicly owned and controlled rest and recreation areas and other facilities necessary to accommodate the traveling public. The amount appropriated for beautification shall not exceed 3 percent of the annual federal appropriations for the highways.

Air Quality Act of 1967

Recognizing that pollution of our air is a problem of national significance, the Congress passed the Air Quality Act (PL 90-148) on November 21, 1967. The purposes of the Act are:
1. to protect and enhance the quality of the nation's air resources so as to promote the public health and welfare and the productive capacity of its population;
2. to initiate and accelerate a national research and development program to achieve the prevention and control of air pollution.
3. to provide technical and financial assistance to state and local governments in

connection with the development and execution of their air-pollution-prevention and control programs; and

4. to encourage and assist the development and operation of regional air-pollution-control programs.

The Act provides that the Secretary of Health, Education, and Welfare shall establish a national research development program for the prevention and control of air pollution. It further provides for that department to work with and furnish financial assistance to national, state, and local agencies who plan and conduct air-pollution prevention and control programs.

Wild and Scenic Rivers Act of 1968

This Act (PL 90-542) established the policy that within the United States there are certain rivers of national significance which possess outstanding and remarkable scenic, recreational, geographic, fish and wildlife, historic, cultural, or other similar values, and that these rivers should be preserved in their free-flowing condition for the benefit and enjoyment of present and future generations.

The purpose of this Act is to implement the aforementioned policy by instituting a national Wild and Scenic Rivers System, designating the initial components of that system, and prescribing methods by which additional components may be added in the future.

Within the Wild and Scenic Rivers System are three categories of rivers: wild, scenic, and recreational. *Wild rivers* are those rivers or sections of rivers that are free of impoundments and generally inaccessible except by trail, with watersheds or shorelines essentially primitive and waters unpolluted. These represent vestiges of primitive America. *Scenic rivers* are those rivers or sections of rivers that are free of impoundments, with shorelines or watersheds still largely primitive and shorelines largely undeveloped, but accessible in places by roads. *Recreational rivers* are those rivers or sections of rivers that are readily accessible by road or railroad, that may have some development along their shorelines, and that may have undergone some impoundment or diversion in the past.

In this Act (as amended) 10 rivers or sections of rivers have been set aside as the initial wild and scenic river areas: Clearwater (Middle Fork), Idaho; Eleven Point, Missouri; Feather, California; Rio Grande, New Mexico; Rogue, Oregon; St. Croix, Minnesota and Wisconsin; Salmon (Middle Fork), Idaho; Wolf, Wisconsin.

The Wild and Scenic Rivers System will be managed under the jurisdiction of the Secretary of the Interior. Upon his approval in some instances, or by Act of Congress in other instances, additional rivers will be added to the system from time to time.

The real way to know a river is not to glance at it here or there in the course of a hasty journey, nor to become acquainted with it after it has been partly civilized and spoiled by too close contact with the works of man. You must go to its native haunts; you must see it in youth and freedom; you must accommodate yourself to its pace, and give yourself to its influence, and follow its meanderings whithersoever they may lead you.

— Henry Van Dyke

National Trails System Act of 1968

In this Act (PL 90-543) the policy is established that, in order to accommodate a rapidly increasing population that is becoming ever more enthusiastic about outdoor recreation, there is need for a system of national trails. The purpose of the Act is to preserve scenic and otherwise interesting trail routes through various parts of the U.S. for present and future use. The national system of trails shall be composed of three kinds of trails: (a) national recreation trails, (b) national scenic trails, and (c) connecting or side trails. The trails shall be under the jurisdiction of the Secretary of the Interior or the Secretary of Agriculture, depending upon the particular land over which the trails cross. National scenic trails shall be authorized and designated only by Act of Congress. Recreational trails and connecting and side trails may be established under authority of the Secretary of the Interior or the Secretary of Agriculture.

The present Act established two trails as the initial trails in the system. They are (a) the Appalachian Trail, which extends approximately 2000 miles along the Appalachian Mountains from Maine to Georgia, and (b) the Pacific Crest Trail, which extends approximately 2300 miles from the Mexico-California border generally along the mountain ranges of the West Coast to the Canadian-Washington border. Other trails that are receiving serious consideration are the Continental Divide Trail, Potomac Heritage Trail, Old Cattle Trails of the Southwest, Lewis and Clark Trail, Natchez Trace Trail, Northern Country Trail in the Appalachian Mountains of Vermont, Kittanning Trail, Oregon Trail, Santa Fe Trail, Long Trail, Mormon Trail, Mormon Battalion Trail, El Camino Real Trail.

Environmental Education Act of 1970

The purpose of this Act (PL 91-516) is to encourage and support the development of new and improved curricula which will encourage understanding of policies and support of activities designed to enhance environmental quality and maintain ecological balance, to demonstrate the use of such curricula in model educational programs, and to evaluate their effectiveness. Its purpose is also to provide support for the initiation and maintenance of programs in environmental education at the elementary and secondary school levels and to disseminate curricular materials. The Act provides for training programs for people associated with environmental education, and for the planning of outdoor ecological study centers.

The Act established within the U.S. Office of Education an office of environmental education. The administrator in charge of the new office is responsible for administering the programs described under the purposes of the Act, and coordinating all of the activities of the U.S. Office of Education which relate to environmental education. Included in the Act are provisions for a citizen's advisory council to work directly with the administrator.

Funds may be appropriated in the form of grants and contracts to state and local

Wilderness Areas... are great reservoirs in the serene order of nature.
— Donald Culross Peattie

educational agencies for the following purposes: (a) the development of curricula; (b) dissemination of information relating to the curricula; (c) support of environmental education programs at the elementary and secondary levels; (d) preservice and inservice training for adult personnel; (e) planning of outdoor ecological study centers; (f) community education programs; and (g) preparation and distribution of materials for mass media use. In addition to the grants to public education agencies, small grants, not to exceed $10,000 annually, may be made to public and private nonprofit agencies. Applications for grants and contracts must be made to the U.S. Commissioner of Education.

Water Quality Improvement Act of 1970

This Act (PL 91-224) is an amendment to the Federal Water Pollution Control Act (Water Quality Act of 1965) which was discussed earlier in this chapter. The Act provides for specific controls of the following: (a) pollution of water by oil; (b) pollution by other hazardous substances; (c) pollution by sewage from vessels; (d) pollution by acids and other chemicals; and (e) pollution of the Great Lakes. In addition to the specific controls which it enacts into law, the Act provides for training grants and contracts, scholarships, demonstration projects, etc. For detailed information about the controls contained in the Act and the programs enabled by it, it is necessary to refer to a copy of the Act which consists of 23 printed pages.

Environmental Quality Improvement Act of 1970

This Act consists of Title II of Public Law 91-224. The purposes of the Act are: (a) to assure that each federal department and agency conducting or supporting public works activities which affect the environment shall implement the policies established under existing law; and (b) to authorize an office of environmental quality which shall provide the professional and administrative staff for the council on environmental quality established by Public Law 91-190. The Act describes the duties of the office of environmental quality and states guidelines on the appropriations necessary to conduct the programs and business of the office.

National Environmental Policy Act of 1970

The purposes of this Act (PL 91-190) are: to declare national policies which will encourage productive and enjoyable harmony between man and his environment; to promote efforts which will prevent or eliminate damage to the environment and stimulate the health and welfare of man; to enrich the understanding of the ecological systems and natural resources important to the nation; and to establish a council on environmental quality.

In the Act, the Congress authorizes and directs that to the fullest extent possible, (a) the policies, regulations, and public laws of the United States shall be interpreted and administered in accordance with the policies set forth in the Act (the policies have to do with procedures and controls for the purpose of protecting and enhancing the environment), and (b) all agencies of the federal government shall conduct their programs as far as possible in manners which will protect and enhance the environment and shall not do otherwise.

The Act establishes in the executive office of the President of the United States a council on environmental quality. It is the responsibility of the council to (a) assist and advise the President in the preparation of the environmental quality report which he must deliver to Congress annually; (b) gather timely and pertinent information concerning the conditions and trends in the quality of the environment; (c) review and appraise the various programs and activities of the federal government in light of the policies set forth in the Act; (d) develop and recommend to the President national policies to foster and promote the improvement of the environment; (e) conduct studies and investigations having to do with improving the environment; (f) document and define changes in the natural environment; (g) report their information and findings at least once each year to the President, and (h) conduct studies and furnish such information as requested by the President and by the Congress.

Federal Boat Safety Act of 1971

The purpose of this Act (PL 92-75) is to improve boating safety and to foster greater development, use, and enjoyment of all the waters of the United States by encouraging and assisting participation by the several states, the boating industry, and the boating public in development of more comprehensive boating safety programs. It is intended that this will be accomplished by authorizing the establishment of national construction and performance standards for boats and associated equipment and by creating more flexible regulatory authority concerning the use of boats and equipment. Further, it is the purpose of the Act to encourage greater and con-

Boating of all kinds has become so popular that carefully planned use and safety regulations are necessary.

tinuing uniformity of boating laws and regulations among the several states and the federal government.

The Secretary of the department in which the Coast Guard operates is the one responsible for carrying out the provisions of the Act. In addition to conducting the various programs and enforcing the several controls described in the Act, the Secretary has the responsibility and authority to cooperate with state governments in the establishment of uniform regulations governing boat safety. Further, the Secretary has the authority and responsibility to enter into financial agreements with the several states and with certain nonprofit organizations in accordance with the provisions of the Act. These agreements will result in considerable financial assistance from the federal government to aid states in the development of more satisfactory boating safety programs. Applications by states or nonprofit organizations for either financial or technical assistance should be made directly to the Secretary of the department in which the Coast Guard is operating. More detail about the regulations included in the Act may be obtained by reading the Act, which consists of 16 printed pages.

Endangered Species Act of 1973

The purpose of this Act (PL 93-205) is to direct the Secretary of the Interior to establish and implement a program to conserve (1) fish or wildlife which are listed as endangered species or threatened species pursuant to section four of the Act, or (2) plants which are included in the provisions of the Act. To carry out such program the Secretary is directed to:

1. utilize the land acquisition and other authority under the Fish and Wildlife Act of 1956 as amended, the Fish and Wildlife Coordination Act as amended, and the Migratory Bird Conservation Act, and
2. acquire by purchase, donation, or otherwise lands, waters, or other areas necessary to implement the purposes of the Act.

Funds made available pursuant to the Land and Water Conservation Act of 1965 as amended may be used for the purpose of acquiring lands and waters as needed.

> No one can say that aimless hours of youth were wasted on the river. One can only make sure that the river is a fit companion. So it has been and so it should always be.

The Act directs the Secretary to cooperate to the maximum with state government agencies. Such cooperation shall include consultation with any state before acquiring land or water therein for the purpose of this Act. Further work and management agreements between the federal and state governments are to be made as needed for the implementation of the Act.

Water Resources Development Act of 1974

This Act (PL 93-251) authorizes the Secretary of the Army, acting through the Chief of Engineers (the administrator of the Army Corps of Engineers), to undertake the initial phase (Phase I) of the engineering and design plan of 17 multipurpose water resource development projects. These are extensive projects that will require long-term planning and development.

As in practically all other major water development projects, outdoor recreation will be a valuable benefit that will accrue, and it is one of the important aspects of planning and development. The projects are Mid-Atlantic Coastal Area (Virginia Beach, Virginia); James River Basin, Virginia; Salt River Basin, Kentucky; Pascagoula River Basin, Mississippi; Pearl River Basin, Mississippi; Upper Mississippi River Basin; Lower Mississippi River Basin; Pee Dee River Basin, North Carolina; Altanaha River Basin, Georgia; Coosa River Basin, Georgia; Guadalupe River Basin, Texas; Arkansas River Basin, Arkansas; Spring River Basin, Missouri; Columbia River Basin, Montana; Umpqua River Basin, Oregon; Delaware River Basin, Delaware and Pennsylvania; Charles River Watershed, Massachusetts.

Programs Affecting Planning and Urban Development

The legislative acts and programs described in this section are especially designed to encourage and enhance sound planning and development in urban areas. Some of these programs have been used extensively to plan and develop a better living environment in and near cities.

Section 701 of the Housing Act of 1954

Under this section of this Act (PL 83-560 as amended) grants may be made for two-thirds (up to three-fourths in certain instances) of the cost of all aspects of comprehensive urban planning, including recreation.

Section 702 of the Housing Act of 1954

Section 702 of this Act (PL 83-590) authorizes interest-free advances to state or local public bodies to assist in the planning of specific public works or facilities, including recreation projects. An advance is repayable when construction of the planned project commences. This is also administered under the Department of

Housing and Urban Development. Assistance may be provided for surveys, inventories, and analyses of existing conditions, as well as for the scheduling and location of future recreation and other facilities. Open-space and recreation planning supported by Section 701 funds must be undertaken as part of a comprehensive plan. State, interstate, metropolitan, and regional planning agencies are eligible for grants.

Assistance under the program has been provided for preparation of a large number of the state outdoor-recreation plans that are required for grant eligibility under the Land and Water Conservation Fund Program. In addition, much local and regional open-space and recreational planning is being supported under this Act as part of the comprehensive planning for counties, metropolitan areas, and cities throughout the country. The provisions of the Act are administered under the Department of Housing and Urban Development.

Section 704 of the Housing and Urban Development Act of 1965

Under Section 704 of this Act (PL 89-117), the Secretary of Housing and Urban Development is authorized to make grants to local public agencies to acquire sites needed for the future construction of public facilities, including recreation centers. Federal grants may include the cost of land to be acquired, as well as the costs of condemnation proceedings, appraisals, title evidence, documentary taxes, and recording fees.

Public Works and Economic Development Act of 1965

Through this Act (PL 89-136) urban areas with high unemployment, rural areas with low family income, certain Indian reservations, and those areas that have lost, or are about to lose, their major source of employment may obtain federal financial assistance to enable them to stabilize and diversify their economies and create new job opportunities. This assistance includes:

1. *grants and long-term loans* to communities for public works and facilities;
2. *long-term loans to applicants,* both public and private, to help finance the purchase of land, buildings, and equipment for industrial and commercial use;
3. *technical assistance and research* to find answers to economic problems; and
4. *job retraining,* under a special section of the Manpower Development and Training Act.

In many cases the development of the recreation potential of an area can be a boom to its economy. In such cases, recreation developments and retraining of personnel to perform recreation-type jobs will qualify under this Act.

Older Americans Act of 1965

Under this Act (PL 89-73) the Administration on Aging, in the Department of Health, Education, and Welfare, develops and conducts research and demonstration programs, and provides technical assistance to state and local governments. This administration can provide up to 75 percent in federal grants for community planning and coordination programs for existing centers conducting recreational and other leisure-time activities for older people. Construction costs are not included.

Housing and Community Development Act of 1974

This Act resulted in termination of several programs that were useful in certain ways for the development of recreation and parks. The programs terminated were Open Space Grants, Urban Beautification Grants, Historic Preservation Grants, Public Facilities Loans, Neighborhood Facilities Grants, Urban Renewal, and Model Cities Supplemental Grants. The primary purpose of the present program is to provide decent housing and a suitable living environment and to expand economic opportunities principally for persons of low and moderate income.

Communities can make applications to the Department of Housing and Urban Development for grants in support of various kinds of community improvements, among which are: (1) preservation or restoration of historic sites, (2) urban beautification, (3) conservation of open spaces, (4) preservation of natural resource areas or scenic areas, or (5) the provision of parks and recreation facilities.

From the standpoint of recreation, the Act has two main objectives:

1. The development and preservation of desirable surroundings of housing areas with emphasis on low income and moderate income residential areas. This objective includes the provision of sufficient open space and the development of neighborhood park and recreation areas.
2. The restoration and preservation of properties of special value for historic, architectural, and aesthetic reasons.

Detailed information about the program and how to apply for grants may be obtained by acquiring from the Department of Housing and Urban Development a pamphlet entitled, "Summary of the Housing and Community Development Act of 1974."

Education Programs Affecting Outdoor Recreation

The Acts discussed in this section were designed primarily to enhance education, but they have some significant side effects on outdoor recreation.

Economic Opportunity Act of 1964

Under Title 1-13 of this Act (PL 88-452), the Department of Labor carries out a *Neighborhood Youth Corps (NYC)* program. It enters into agreements with local sponsors to develop work programs for economically disadvantaged 16- to 22-year-olds in order to enable them to stay in school, resume their school attendance, or improve their employability.

The program includes projects that will contribute to the conservation, development, or management of a community's natural resources or recreation areas. Priority is given to projects having a high training potential for participants.

Projects must permit or contribute to an undertaking or service in the public interest, which otherwise would not be performed, and must not displace any workers or impair existing contracts for services.

Sponsors may be nonfederal government units or private nonprofit organizations. States, counties, municipalities, and authorized subdivisions, such as park commissions, boards of education, municipal hospitals, and state and public libraries, are generally eligible to enter into agreements. The federal government can pay up to 90 percent of the cost of approved Neighborhood Youth Corps projects.

The *Job Corps,* which is also administered under this Act, provides a complete environmental change for its enrollees, offers young men and women the opportunity to learn useful vocational skills, to acquire basic education, and to replace an attitude of futility and frustration with hope and encouragement. Job Corps Conservation Centers, comprising one part of this program, are operated in conjunction with agencies of the Departments of Agriculture and Interior. In addition to basic education, and prevocational and citizenship training, Corpsmen at conservation centers devote 50 percent of their time to work projects that preserve, expand, and beautify natural resources and public recreational facilities.

Under the Nelson Amendment of the Economic Opportunity Act, the Department of Labor receives money to administer *Operation Green Thumb.* To utilize the talents of the older people with low incomes and farming backgrounds, Operation Green Thumb provides employment opportunities in community-development and beautification projects. Operation Green Thumb is sponsored by the National Farmers Union and administered under the Department of Labor.

Higher Education Act of 1965

Title I of the Higher Education Act (PL 89-329) provides for grants to states to enable colleges and universities to strengthen community-service programs in the solution of community problems, including problems in recreation and land use. The Act defines a community-service program as "an educational program, activity, or service, including a research program and a university extension or continuing education offering, which is designed to assist in the solution of community problems in rural, urban, or suburban areas, with particular emphasis on urban and suburban problems." The Act is administered under the Department of Health, Education, and Welfare.

Elementary and Secondary Education Act of 1965

The United States Office of Education grant-in-aid programs authorized by this Act (PL 89-10) may be used in part to promote recreational purposes. For example, the grants made under Title I for improvement of educational programs for children of low-income families may involve recreational activities. The Act specifies recreation as one of the supplementary educational services to enrich school programs that can be supported through grants to local educational agencies (see Title III). Likewise, the grants to strengthen state departments of education can be used by such departments to develop or strengthen their technical assistance, consultation, and services to local educational agencies and schools in various aspects of education, specifically including recreation (see Title V). Grants for educational research and training (see Title IV) may also have application to recreation. The Act is administered under the Department of Health, Education, and Welfare.

Chapter 7 The Roles of State Agencies

A century ago state government was relatively simple and was concerned with only a few functions. Many of the present services, such as education, health, and welfare, were initiated and carried on for a long time by private agencies. As their need and value became more recognized they were gradually taken over by government authorities, and special agencies were created to provide and administer them. During a long period, recreation was considered of no public concern, and the early attempts to provide recreational opportunities were carried on by private initiative and funds. During the past century, recreation has changed from solely private support to a responsibility of government. Today recreation is — in fact, in law, and in public opinion — a recognized function of state government.

States' Authority to Provide Recreation

"The powers not delegated to the United States by the Constitution, nor prohibited by it to the States, are reserved to the States respectively, or to the people."

This Tenth Amendment to the Constitution of the United States gives the separate states authority to provide recreational services as the need for such services becomes evident. This amendment, commonly referred to as "the states' rights," is also the authority by which state governments provide public education, welfare, and health services.

In view of this right, every state has seen fit to become involved in selected recreational services. These services are not consistent throughout the states, nor is the type of organization for administering the services consistent. Each state government is somewhat unique in the services it offers and in organization for administering the services. Because of this situation the reader should keep in mind that, as a rule, the information herein is concerned with recreational services common to most of the states.

Development of State Recreation Services

"The state comes into existence that man may live. It continues that man may live well."

The state is the institution created by the people to enable them to do collectively what they would be unable to accomplish individually. It is the principal organization through which people have been able to promote education and health, improve living and working conditions, expand ways and means of communication and transportation, and achieve many other acts that contribute to an orderly and stable society.

The first clear-cut involvement of a state in the field of recreation was in 1864 when Congress granted to the state of California a large portion of public domain which included Yosemite Valley and the Mariposa Big Tree Grove, on condition that the areas "shall be held for public use, resort and recreation...for all time." In essence this became the first state park. Unfortunately California at the time was unable to manage those resources adequately. Later the federal government repossessed the areas, and in 1884 the Yosemite National Park was established. In 1872 the federal government declared Yellowstone a national park, providing 25,000 square miles of land which were placed under the supervision of the territory of Wyoming. This proved unsuccessful and subsequently Yellowstone was under the supervision of the military for 32 years.

The state of New York was actually the first state to make a clearly successful effort related to recreation when in 1885 New York established a state forest reserve in the Adirondacks. Later this preserve became Adirondack State Park. Also in 1885 Fort Macinack was given to the state of Michigan. It has since developed into a significant recreational attraction.

In 1894 the New York Constitution was amended to provide funds to purchase forest lands under the Forest Preservation Act of 1885. This resulted in enlargement of the preserves known today as the Adirondack and the Catskill Reserves. In 1898 Pennsylvania followed New York's lead and took measures to protect selected forest areas from exploitation. Subsequently other states became involved in recreation as the need arose to do so.

State governments have gradually developed recreation-oriented responsibilities along the same historical pattern as education, health, and other now well-established public services. The time has come when social, educational, and governmental leaders generally accept recreation as an important responsibility of state

> The state is created to enable people to do collectively what they could not accomplish individually. It is an instrument of the people and for the people.

Water comes in all shapes and sizes, from babbling brooks to the great sea. Sonoma Beach State Park, California.

government, and most states now provide a variety of recreational services and facilities. Forests, parks, game refuges, and other state-owned recreational areas now total more than 40 million acres.

Each of the 50 states has at least one agency with a principal responsibility in outdoor recreation. Several other departments in each state contribute to recreation on a limited basis. The table at the end of this chapter shows the agencies of state government having recognized outdoor recreation responsibilities. The agencies are classified into (a) those with principal outdoor-recreation responsibilities, and (b) those with limited outdoor-recreation responsibilities. Some agencies not listed contribute to outdoor recreation, but their contributions are difficult to define or are unauthorized by law. The information included is taken from a recent survey conducted by the author.

Enabling Legislation

Legal powers are needed for the acquisition, development, and maintenance of recreation areas; for the construction and operation of buildings and facilities; for the purchase of supplies; and for the employment of personnel for leadership and other services. Through enabling legislation, states permit local government authority to conduct recreation programs under the administrative arrangement considered most effective, and to cooperate with other local subdivisions in conducting joint programs.

The first enabling act of this kind was passed in 1915 in New Jersey, and by 1947, 34 states had such laws. The other states have passed recreation-enabling Acts since that year. Now all of the states allow local governments to sponsor recreation programs and manage areas and facilities. However, in many of the states enabling legislation is still inadequate. Periodic reviews of the enabling laws by the recreation and park professionals in each state are recommended.

When writing legislation, it is advisable that experts from the recreation profession as well as legal advisors who have had some training in drafting such legislation be selected. New laws must be consistent with other forms of legislation, and careful consideration must be given to objectives and basic principles. Recreation practices which are enacted into law should always be: (1) consistent with the spirit of the law, (2) consistent with other legal principles, (3) comprehensive or inclusive, (4) peaceably agreed to, and (5) neither obscured in meaning nor merely implied.

State Park Systems

All 50 states now have state park systems, which administer a combined total of approximately 3500 areas covering nearly 8 million acres. These parks are second only to municipal areas in number of visitors per year. Their patronage (over 450 million per year) is greater than the total for national parks and national forests. State park systems are best developed in states having large populations, with the most extensive systems in New York (205 areas), California (174 areas), and Pennsylvania (202 areas). State parks vary considerably in type, depending on the geographic features in the state and the philosophy and purpose on which the particular state park system is based. With few exceptions geographic location as it relates to population is vital in the selection of sites for state park areas.

At the time of the first national conference on state parks in 1921 at Des Moines, Iowa, 19 states had at least one park. This marked the beginning of an organized state park movement. National parks were proving successful, and the states and the public were asking the first director of the National Park System, Stephen T. Mather, for more national parks. Mather saw state administration as an alternative to protecting some areas until he could gather political and financial support to bring a few of these parcels into the national park system. As a result of these concerns Mather was a dynamic influence in organizing the Des Moines meeting.

Since its inception, the National Conference on State Parks has been the foremost professional group in the development of our present state park systems. This organization encourages states to seek suitable lands and funds to improve their state parks. The Conference has also been successful in encouraging cooperation among the states and the National Park Service.

A few states have been successful in finding wealthy philanthropists to help finance the state park systems, and the federal government has been helpful to states through the authorization of various programs whereby states have been able to acquire selected sites of public domain at a very low cost. Also, under certain programs the federal government has cooperated in the direct financing of areas and facilities. Nevertheless, financing has been a traditional problem for state park systems. One of the major solutions has turned out to be bond issues. In 1960 the state of New York passed a bond issue for $75 million to acquire state park and recreational lands. In succeeding years the total grew. California in 1964 approved bonds for $150 million, Michigan in 1968 for $100 million, and New Jersey in 1974 for $200 million. Several other states have passed bond issues for similar or lesser amounts, totaling approximately $300 billion since 1960.

State parks are primarily intermediate-type areas, usually being more remote than municipal areas but closer to the using population than national parks and forests. Typically, they contain significant natural features along with constructed improvements in the form of picnic areas and campsites, eating accommodations, and various sports facilities.

State parks are administered under a variety of organizational structures. In some states the park agency is a separate department of government as in Arizona, Georgia, Idaho, and Kentucky, where the park system is administered by the State Park Department. In many of the states the park system is a division within a larger department. For instance, in Alabama, New York, Illinois, Iowa, and several other states it is a division within the Department of Conservation. In Alaska, California, Hawaii, Indiana, Utah, Michigan, and other states, the park system is within the Department of Natural Resources. In Oregon it is a division of the Highway Department; in South Carolina and Arkansas it is combined with the Tourist and Publicity Agency; and in New Hampshire, New Jersey, and Oklahoma it is a part of the Department of Economic Development. In certain other states the administrative structure takes other forms than those mentioned (see Figure 11).

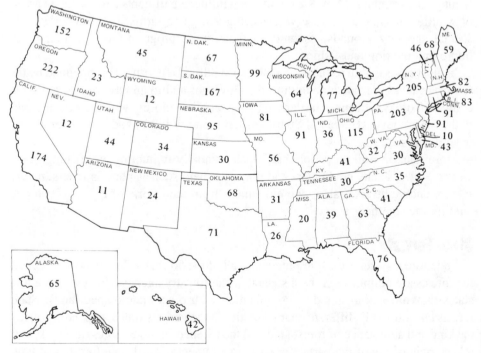

Figure 11. Map indicating the number of State Parks in each state.

The fighting leap of a silver king tarpon in Matanzas River exemplifies the exciting fishing action to be found in St. Augustine, Florida, the nation's oldest city.

Fish and Wildlife

Each of the 50 states has created either a separate department or a major division within a department to administer a program of fish and wildlife management. Generally speaking, the responsibilities of the State Fish and Wildlife Agency are to propagate, manage, and distribute game animals, fur-bearing animals, game birds, and game fish. It manages game land and fisheries and issues licenses for hunting, fishing, and trapping. Many state fish and wildlife departments administer a variety of wildlife areas, such as reserves, sanctuaries, game farms, fish hatcheries, and special shooting grounds, as units in their broad programs for regulating and improving hunting and fishing.

In most cases the director of the Fish and Wildlife Department is appointed by the Governor and is responsible both to the Governor and to an advisory commission composed of lay citizens. The departments work very closely with their counterpart at the federal level (Bureau of Sports Fisheries and Wildlife) and with several other federal and state agencies.

More than 35 million people participate annually in hunting and fishing in the United States. Many nonhunters and nonfishermen, such as photographers, nature hikers, and sightseers, also reap enjoyment from the efforts of the state fish and wildlife management agency.

State Forests

State forest systems exist in practically all of the 50 states. In a majority of cases the forests are administered by a separate state forestry agency. However, in a few states they are administered in combination with other state-owned lands. State forests take on vastly different characteristics in the various states, depending on (a) the kind and abundance of forest land, (b) the extent of national forest reserves, and (c) the philosophy of the particular state government toward state forests and how they should be used.

Typically, state forest systems are better developed in the eastern, southern, and midwestern states, where the forests are of high quality and make a significant contribution to outdoor recreation. State forests are of relatively low quality and are less developed in the great plains states and the western states, where they have rather limited potential for recreation. In the western states most of the top quality forest land is in the national forest reserve.

Public Education

Until recent decades education for leisure was entirely unplanned and not considered a responsibility of the schools. In light of vast changes in living conditions, education for leisure has now become recognized as an important function of the public schools. Worthy use of leisure time was one of the seven cardinal principles of education defined in 1917, and skills, attitudes, and abilities in desirable recreation activities are accepted as important results of modern education. The state has assumed a responsibility in education for leisure as part of its responsibility for education in general. More is said on this topic in Chapter 13.

Highways and Access Roads

In all 50 states the state highway departments are charged with the responsibility to construct roads into certain areas of recreational value. Also, they participate in maintaining such roads and often keep roads open to certain winter sports areas. Roadside parks and roadside historic markers are usually the responsibility of State Highway Departments. Roads inside state-owned recreation lands, such as state parks and state forests, are often constructed under the authority of this department. Many recreation areas would receive much less use if they were not readily accessible by good roads.

Travel itself has become a popular recreation activity. In fact, travel accounts for the greatest single recreation expenditure in America. State roads are used in a significant portion of this travel.

Colleges and Universities

Extension Services of the Land Grant Colleges were among the first state agencies to provide leadership in recreation. The Extension Services have for a long time conducted recreation training courses, sponsored statewide conferences, provided consultation services, and published resource materials.

Over 300 colleges and universities now offer specialization in outdoor recreation. More than 50 universities offer graduate degrees in fields of recreation. Some of the institutions conduct recreation surveys of various kinds and also offer consultation services to communities and private enterprise.

Other State Agencies

The other state agencies that contribute to outdoor recreation in a less direct manner than those already discussed are (a) the State Land Department, (b) the State Water and Power Department, (c) the State Tourist Department, and (d) the State Health Department.

State Outdoor Recreation Plans

In order to participate in the benefits accrued from the Land and Water Conservation Fund Act (see description on page 99) each state is required to develop and maintain a state outdoor recreation plan. Every state has developed a plan in close cooperation with the Federal Bureau of Outdoor Recreation. Each state plan contains outdoor recreation development guidelines for selected state agencies. These state plans correspond to the national plan which is described on pages 84 and 86-87. The national plan includes the following recommendations which were intended to influence the state plan and action within the state. A copy of the state plan for any particular state may be obtained from the State Outdoor Recreation Liaison Officer (see list at the end of this chapter).

Complementary Actions

To increase the availability of recreation resources, state and local governments and private interests should take actions which would:

1. Provide tax and/or financial incentives to encourage owners to open their lands to recreationists and limit the liability of landowners for injuries suffered on property which has been made available to the public.

State forests and other state-owned lands offer a variety of recreational opportunities.

2. Assure public access to existing but underused recreation resources such as beaches, shorelines, islands, and other unique natural areas.

3. Identify floodprone areas, surface-mined lands, and other unique areas with recreation potential and take steps, where appropriate, to make them available for open space and recreation purposes.

4. Encourage the donation of lands and facilities which have open space or recreation value.

5. Utilize the Land and Water Conservation Fund to acquire those lands which serve the dual purpose of providing outdoor recreation opportunities and preserving critical land resources.

To improve the management and administration of recreation resources and programs, state and local governments and private interests should take actions which would:

1. Coordinate the planning and management efforts of park and recreation agencies with school, municipal water supply, and other land-managing authorities to take full advantage of the recreation benefits to be derived from the multiple use of land and water resources.

2. Assist the federal government in the identification of and assumption of management responsibility for, through joint agreements or other cooperative devices, federal recreation units which would complement the recreation programs.

Sample State Organizational Plans

Following are descriptions of the way state agencies are involved in three different states. It should be recognized that the other 47 states are involved similarly, but not identically.

California

In California the majority of the state's responsibility for outdoor recreation is centered in the Resources Agency, one of the major divisions of the state government. The departments within the Resources Agency which have principal outdoor-recreation responsibilities are indicated in the organization chart which follows.

The head of the Resources Agency acts under the authority of the Governor and is responsible to the Governor for the efficient operation of the various departments, boards, and commissions within the Agency and for their formulation of policy and long-range programs. The administrator of the Resources Agency

1. reports to the Governor for the Agency and its departments and affiliated boards and commissions;
2. serves as the normal channel of communication between the Governor's office, the Agency, and its departments, boards, and commissions;
3. prescribes the working relationships among the parts of the Agency;
4. reviews all legislative, budgetary, and other administration programs of the departments, boards, and commissions in the Agency, and makes appropriation recommendations to the Governor;
5. reviews the broad effects of all the departmental programs within the Agency, and makes recommendations for improvements.

**State of California
Resources Agency
Organization Chart**

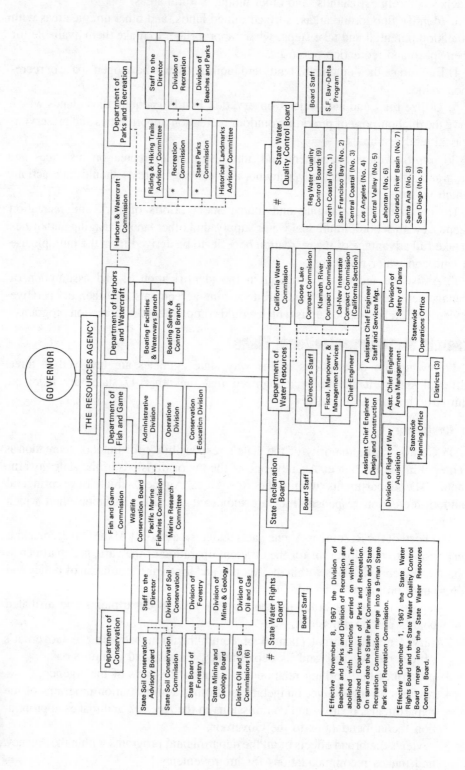

Planning and constructing the facilities for a state lakeside park in a large project.

Utah

Utah has four governmental units that are primarily concerned with outdoor recreation at the state level. They are the Division of Parks and Recreation, the Division of Wildlife Resources, the Outdoor Recreation Agency, and the Provo-Jordan River Parkway Authority. These units function as divisions of the State Department of Natural Resources, organized in July 1967, under authority of Chapter 176, Session Laws of Utah.

State agencies which make a secondary contribution in outdoor recreation are the Division of State Lands; the Utah Travel Council; the State Department of Transportation; the Utah National Guard; the Division of Water Resources; and the Division of State History.

Division of Parks and Recreation. The Division of Parks and Recreation functions under the direction of the Board of Parks and Recreation. The Division has responsibility for acquisition, planning, protection, development, operation, and maintenance of park areas and facilities in such manner as may be authorized by the policies and rules and regulations of the Board.

The Board is authorized to acquire, designate, establish, plan, operate, control, develop, and maintain all state parks, monuments, and state recreation areas; acquire, designate, develop, control, regulate, and maintain state roadside parks; acquire real and personal property in its name by all legal and proper means, including purchase, gifts, devise, eminent domain, lease, designation of state land, exchange, or otherwise; develop regulations for use of state parks and other areas administered by it, protect, care, and use the state park system; and make exchanges of state land wherever it can be done to advantage. It is also responsible for administration of the 1959 Boating Act and the Off-Road Vehicle Act.

The Board receives its income from user and entrance fees to state park facilities plus a state appropriation. The Utah State Board of Parks and Recreation has developed a long-range program with the full cooperation of all 29 counties, many independent organizations, and federal and state agencies. The initial request for suggested areas brought forth a list of 118 existing and potential areas to be considered for inclusion in the state park program. Proposals include historical sites and trails, areas of important scientific interest, and areas of unusual scenic and topographic attraction. These areas range from alpine peaks in the north to semidesert areas in the southern part of the state.

Division of Wildlife Resources. The Division of Wildlife Resources under the Department of Natural Resources is charged with the responsibility to protect, propagate, manage, and distribute game animals, game birds, and game fish. It manages game land and fisheries and issues licenses for hunting, fishing, and trapping. Policies of the Division are developed by the Wildlife Board and the Board of Big Game Control.

The Division is supported by fees and licenses, fines, sales (principally of beaver furs), state appropriations, and federal grants.

The Wildlife Board has the power to enter into cooperative agreements with federal agencies, sister states, educational institutions, municipalities, corporations, clubs, landowners, associations, and private individuals in the interest of game, fish, bird, or fur-bearing animal management.

Cooperative management of recreation areas is maintained with the State Forester. The State Division of Water Resources cooperates with the Division of Wildlife Resources by providing it with consulting services and maps. The State Road Commission provides maps and equipment and does road work for the Division. The Board of State Lands assists in retaining areas of state-owned land for fish and game purposes.

The Division owns 12 developed waterfowl marshes and four undeveloped areas in addition to several tracts maintained for upland game and big game purposes. There are 12 state fish hatcheries and two game bird farms. The Division owns or otherwise controls approximately 350,000 acres of land.

Utah Outdoor Recreation Agency. This agency was established in 1968 by executive sanction and is under direction of the State Department of Natural Resources. Its functions are to direct the state's comprehensive outdoor-recreation-planning effort and to administer provisions of the Federal Land and Water Conservation Fund Act at the state level.

An eight-member committee provides advisory services to the Agency. The Committee is composed of directors of the State Division of Wildlife Resources, Division of Parks and Recreation, Division of Industrial Promotion, Division of Travel Development, and State Department of Highways; State Planning Coordinator; Executive Director, Utah Association of Cities; and the Executive Director, Utah State Association of Counties.

Division of State Lands. This board, an agency of the State Department of Natural Resources, has responsibility for the direction, management, and control of

State of Michigan
Department of Natural Resources
Organization Chart

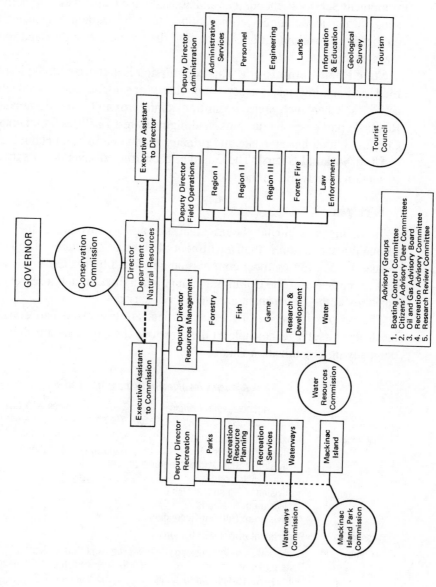

all lands granted to the state, except lands used or set apart for specific public purposes or occupied by public buildings, and may sell or lease same for the best interests of the state. It has the power to acquire land which it may transfer to the State Board of Parks and Recreation. There is reserved to the public the right to hunt, trap, and fish upon lands owned by the state.

Utah Travel Council. This division, an agency of the State Department of Development Services, encourages and assists in the coordination of activities of persons, firms, associations, corporations, and governmental agencies engaged in publicizing, developing, and promoting the scenic attractions and tourist advantages of the state.

State Road Commission. This commission is authorized to build and maintain roads and parking spaces to serve areas used for salt-flat races, ski meets, and other activities, when such areas are in immediate proximity to a designated highway. Roadside parks, scenic turnouts, and highway-rest facilities are maintained by the Commission along interstate and primary road systems throughout the state.

Utah National Guard. The Guard has constructed several roads that are used as recreation travelways in the state.

Michigan

In Michigan as in Utah the principal state agency involved in the administration of outdoor recreation is the Department of Natural Resources. The Department is headed by a seven-member commission appointed by the Governor with the consent of the Senate. The Commission appoints a director and a secretary. All other positions in the Department are under civil service.

The various functions of the Department are organized into divisions, whose heads are directly responsible to the director. The divisions are shown on the accompanying Organization Chart.

State Agencies Involved in Outdoor Recreation

State	Agencies with Principal Responsibilities in Outdoor Recreation	Agencies with Limited Responsibilities in Outdoor Recreation

Alabama	Department of Conservation
	  Division of Water
	  Division of State Parks, Monuments, and Historical Sites
	  Division of Game and Fish
	  Division of Seafoods
	  Division of Outdoor Recreation
		Mound State Monument
		Department of Highways

Alaska	Department of Natural Resources	
Arizona	Game and Fish Commission State Parks Board Outdoor Recreation Coordinating Commission	Highway Commission Office of Economic Planning and Development
Arkansas	Game and Fish Commission Department of Local Services Department of Parks and Tourism	Ozarks Regional Commission (joint federal-state agency) Geological Commission Forestry Commission Industrial Development Commission State Highway Department

California	Resources Agency
	Department of Parks and Recreation
	Department of Navigation and Ocean
	   Development
	Department of Conservation
	   Division of Forestry
	Department of Fish and Game
	Department of Water Resources
		Department of Public Works
		Bureau of Health Education,
		   Physical Education, and
		   Recreation
		State Lands Commission
		Water Pollution Control
		Department of Health
		California Transportation Agency
		Wildlife Conservation Board
		California Coastal Zone Conservation
		   Commission

Colorado	Department of Natural Resources
	   Division of Parks and Outdoor
	     Recreation
	   Division of Wildlife
		State Historical Society
		Department of Highways
		State Board of Land Commissioners

Connecticut	State Department of Environmental
	   Protection
		State Department of Environmental
		   Protection
		State Department of Health
		State Department of Transportation

Delaware	Department of Natural Resources
	   and Environmental Control
	   Division of Parks and Recreation
	   Division of Fish and Wildlife
	   Division of Soil and Water
	     Conservation
	   Division of Environmental Control
	Department of Community Affairs
	   and Economic Development
	   Division of Economic Development
	Department of State
	   Division of Historical and Cultural
	     Affairs
	Department of Public Safety
	Department of Health and
	   Social Services
		State Archives Commission
		State Highway Department
		State Development Department
		State Board of Health
		Water and Air Resources Commission
		Soil and Water Conservation
		   Commission

Florida	Department of Natural Resources
	   Division of Recreation and Parks
	Game and Fresh Water Fish Commission
	Department of Education
		Department of Agriculture and
		   Consumer Services
		   Division of Forestry
		Department of Transportation
		Department of State
		   Division of Archives, History and
		     Record Management
		Department of Health and
		   Rehabilitative Services
		Department of Environmental Regulation
		Department of Community Affairs
		Department of Administration

Georgia	Georgia Department of Natural Resources	Jekyll Island State Park Authority Stone Mountain Memorial Authority Lake Lanier Development Authority Georgia Department of Transportation

Hawaii	Department of Land and Natural
	   Resources
	   State Parks Division
	   Fish and Game Division
	   Forestry Division
		Department of Transportation
		   Harbors Division

Idaho	State Park Board Fish and Game Commission	State Forestry Department Department of Transportation State Department of Tourism and Industrial Development State Historical Society State Land Department

Illinois	Department of Conservation
	    Division of Parks
	    Division of Historic Sites
	    Division of Land Management
	    Division of Wildlife Resources
	    Division of Fisheries
	    Division of Forestry
		Department of Public Works and
		    Buildings
		Department of Registration and
		    Education
		Department of Public Health
		Illinois State Youth Commission
		Department of Business and Economic
		    Development

Indiana	Department of Natural Resources
	    Division of Fish and Wildlife
	    Division of Forestry
	    Division of State Parks
	    Division of Reservoir Management
	    Division of Nature Preserves
	    Division of Museums and Memorials
	    Division of Outdoor Recreation
		State Highway Department
		State Board of Health
		State Commission on Aging and the
		    Aged and the Governor's
		    Youth Council
		Division of Tourism

Iowa	State Conservation Commission
	    Division of Administration
	    Division of Fish and Game
	    Division of Land and Waters
		State Soil Conservation Committee
		Iowa Development Commission
		State Department of Transportation
		Office of Planning and Programming

Kansas	State Park and Resources Authority Forestry, Fish, and Game Commission Joint Council on Recreation	State Department of Transportation State Recreation Consultant State Historical Society Department of Economic Development Water Resources Board
Kentucky	Department of Fish and Wildlife Department of Parks Heritage Commission Division of Forestry Division of Special Programs	Division of Water Division of Conservation Bureau of Highways Historical Society

Louisiana	State Parks and Recreation
	    Commission
	Wildlife and Fisheries Commission
		Department of Highways
		Department of Public Works
		Department of Commerce and Industry
		State Land Office
		Louisiana Tourist Development
		    Commission

Maine	Department of Inland Fisheries and Game Baxter State Park Authority Department of Conservation	Atlantic Sea Run Salmon Commission Department of Sea and Shore Fisheries Water Improvement Commission Department of Economic Development State Highway Commission Department of Health and Welfare

Maryland	Department of Natural Resources
	    Capital Programs Administration
	    Maryland Forest Service
	    Maryland Park Service
	    Maryland Wildlife Administration
	    Maryland Fisheries Administration
	    Natural Resource Police Force
	Department of State Planning
		Water Pollution Control Commission
		State Highway Administration
		Department of Economic and
		    Community Development

Massachusetts	Department of Environmental Management	Department of Public Health
	Division of Fisheries and Game	Department of Commerce
	Division of Water Resources	Department of Correction
	Division of Forests and Parks	Department of Youth Services
	Division of Marine Fisheries	Department of Fisheries, Wildlife, and Recreational Vehicles
	Metropolitan District Commission	
	Parks Engineering Division	
	Department of Public Works	
	Fisheries	
	Forestry	
	Wildlife	
	Bureau of Water Management	
	Water Development Service	
	Water Quality Control	
	Commission on Pollution	
	Air Pollution Control	
	Solid Waste Management	
Minnesota	Department of Conservation	Department of Highways
	Division of Forestry	Historical Society
	Division of Game and Fish	Iron Range Resources and Rehabilitation Commission
	Division of Parks and Recreation	Pollution Control Agency
	Division of Enforcement and Field Service	State Planning Agency
		Minnesota Resources Commission
		Minnesota-Wisconsin Boundary Area Commission
		Department of Economic Development
Mississippi	Mississippi Game and Fish Commission	Pat Harrison Waterway District
	Mississippi Park Commission	Pearl River Basin Development District
	Mississippi Bureau of Outdoor Recreation	Tombigbee River Valley Water Management District
	(Branch of Park Commission)	Mississippi Department of Archives and History
		Mississippi State Highway Department
		Grand Gulf Military Monument Commission
		Pearl River Valley Water Supply District
		Mississippi State Board of Health
		Mississippi Board of Water Commission.
		Mississippi Agricultural and Industrial Board
		Yellow Creek Watershed District
		Bienville Recreation District
		Mississippi Boat and Water Safety Commission
Missouri	State Conservation Commission	State Highway Commission
	State Department of Natural Resources	Division of Commerce and Industrial Development
	State Tourism Commission	
Montana	State Fish and Game Commission	Board of Land Commissioners
	Park Division	Office of State Forester
	State Highway Commission	State Highway Department
		Board of Health
		State Historical Society
		State Water Conservation Board

Nebraska	Game and Parks Commission	Department of Health Department of Roads State Historical Society Department of Economic Development Natural Resources Commission Extension Division — Univ. of Nebraska
Nevada	Department of Conservation and Natural Resources Fish and Game Commission Division of Parks	Department of Economic Development Department of Highways State Museum Division of Forestry

New Hampshire	Department of Resources and
	   Economic Development
	Division of Parks
	Fish and Game Department
		Natural Resources Council
		Water Resources Board
		Water Pollution Commission
		State Historical Commission
		Department of Public Works and
		   Highways

New Jersey	Department of Environmental
	   Protection
	Division of Parks & Forestry
	Division of Fish, Game, and
	   Shellfisheries
	Division of Water Resources
	Division of Marine Services
		Department of Community Affairs
		   Division of State & Regional
		    Planning
		   Division of Local Government
		    Services
		Department of Transportation
		Department of Health

New Mexico	Department of Game and Fish
	State Park and Recreation
	   Commission
	State Planning Office
	   Division of Recreation and
	    Historic Preservation
		Department of Development
		New Mexico State Highway Department
		Museum of New Mexico
		Department of Education

New York	The Office of Parks and Recreation
	   Park and Recreation Services
	   Recreation Services
	   Operations and Maintenance
	   Marine and Recreational Vehicles
	   Historic Preservation
	   National Register and Survey
	   Historic Archeology
	Department of Environmental
	   Conservation
	   Division of Lands and Forests
	   Forest Recreation
	   Division of Fish and Game
	   Division of Marine Resources
		Department of Health
		Department of Public Works
		Department of Education

North Carolina	Department of Natural and Economic
	   Resources
	   Grants Administration
	   Division of Resource Planning
	    and Evaluation
	   Division of Parks and Recreation
	   Division of Community Assistance
	   Regional Offices
	   Division of Economic Development
	   Travel Development
	   Wildlife Resources Commission
		Department of Cultural Resources
		Department of Transportation

North Dakota	State Outdoor Recreation Agency State Park Service State Game and Fish Department State Forest Service State Water Commission	State Health Department State Historical Society State Soil Conservation Committee State Highway Department State Travel Department Economic Development Commission

Ohio	Department of Natural Resources
	    Division of Parks and Recreation
	    Division of Wildlife
	    Division of Watercraft
	    Division of Forestry
	    Division of Critical Areas and
	      Preserves
		Department of Highways
		Department of Economic and
		    Community Development
		Department of Health
		Department of Commerce (publicity)
		Department of Public Works
		Historical Society
		Muskingum Conservancy District
		Miami Conservancy District
		Department of Agriculture
		Department of Education

Oklahoma	Department of Tourism and
	    Recreation
	    Division of State Lodges
	    Division of State Parks
	Office of Outdoor Recreation
	    and Planning
	Wildlife Conservation Department
	    Fisheries Division
	    Game Division
		Department of Agriculture
		    Division of Forestry
		Department of Highways

Oregon	Department of Transportation, Parks
	    and Recreation Branch
	Fish and Wildlife Commission
	Marine Board
	Fair Board
	Assistant of the Governor, Natural
	    Resources
		Division of State Lands
		Department of Forestry
		Columbia River Gorge Commission
		State Engineer
		Department of Environmental Quality

Pennsylvania	Department of Community Affairs Department of Forests and Water State Fish Commission State Game Commission	Department of Commerce Department of Welfare Department of Health Department of Transportation Historical and Museum Commission Office of State Planning and Development

Rhode Island	Department of Natural Resources
	    Division of Parks and Recreation
	    Division of Forest Environment
	    Division of Fish and Wildlife
	    Division of Coastal Resources
	    Division of Planning and
	      Development
	    Division of Boating Safety
		Department of Health
		Department of Economic Development
		    Division of Tourist Promotion
		Department of Administration
		    Statewide Planning Division

South Carolina	Wildlife Resources Department Forestry Commission Department of Parks, Recreation, and Tourism	Highway Department State Board of Health Water Pollution Control Authority State Development Board State Budget and Control Board Public Service Authority

South Dakota	Department of Game, Fish, and Parks
	    Game and Fish Division
	    Parks and Recreation Division
	    Custer State Park
		Commissioner of School and Public
		    Lands
		Department of Highways
		Department of History
		Water Resources Commission
		State Planning Commission

Tennessee	Department of Conservation
	    Division of State Parks
	    Division of Forestry
	    Division of Planning and
	      Development
	    Wildlife Resources Agency
	    Department of Tourism
		Department of Transportation

Texas	Texas Parks and Wildlife Department	Texas State Department of Highways
		    and Public Transportation
		Texas Tourist Development Agency
		Texas State Department of
		    Community Affairs
		State River Authorities
		General Land Office
		Texas Water Development Board
		Texas Water Quality Board
		Texas Air Control Board
		Texas Historical Commission

Utah	Department of Natural Resources
	    Outdoor Recreation Agency
	    Division of Parks and Recreation
	    Division of Fish and Game
	    Division of Provo-Jordan River
	      Parkway Authority
		Utah State Department of
		    Transportation
		Utah Travel Council
		Division of the Great Salt Lake
		Utah National Guard
		Division of State Lands
		Division of State History
		Division of Water Resources

Vermont	Agency of Environmental
	    Conservation
	Department of Forests, Parks, &
	    Recreation
	Department of Fish and Game
	Interagency Committee on Natural
	    Resources
	Department of Water Resources
	Water Resources Board
		Agency of Transportation
		    Department of Highways
		Agency of Development and
		    Community Affairs
		    Department of Development
		Agency of Human Services
		    Department of Health
		    Office on Aging
		Vermont Council on the Arts
		Department of Education

Virginia	Department of Conservation and
	    Economic Development
	    Division of Forestry
	    Division of Parks
	Commission of Game and Inland
	    Fisheries
	Commission of Outdoor Recreation
	Interagency Committee on Recreation
		Department of Highways
		Breaks Interstate Park Commission
		Water Control Board
		Department of Health
		Commission of Fisheries
		Agencies Administering Historic Sites
		Historic Landmark Commission

Washington	Department of Natural Resources
	State Parks and Recreation
	    Commission
	Department of Game
	Interagency Committee for Outdoor
	    Recreation
	Department of Fisheries
		Highway Department
		Department of Health
		Department of Ecology
		Department of Commerce and
		    Economic Development
		Office of Community Development
		Department of Water Resources

West Virginia	Department of Natural Resources	State Road Commission
	Division of Game and Fish	Department of Health
	Division of Forestry	Department of Agriculture
	Division of Parks and Recreation	Department of Education
	Division of Water Resources	
	Division of Reclamation	
	Public Lands Corporation	
	Department of Commerce	
	Office of Federal-State Relations	
Wisconsin	Department of Natural Resources	Department of Natural Resources
	Division of Forestry, Wildlife, and Recreation	Division of Environmental Standards
	Division of Tourism and Commercial Recreation	Division of Enforcement
		Department of Business Development
		State Historical Society
		Department of Transportation
Wyoming	Wyoming Recreation Commission	Wyoming Highway Department
	Wyoming Game & Fish Commission	State Forestry Division
	Wyoming Board of Charities and Reform	
	Wyoming Travel Commission	

State Liaison Officers

Each state has an outdoor recreation liaison officer, whose responsibility it is to coordinate the state outdoor recreation plan with the agencies of the federal government. This state officer works primarily with the Federal Bureau of Outdoor Recreation, but also performs some coordinating functions with other federal agencies. Following are the addresses of the liaison offices:

ALABAMA
Department of Conservation and Natural
  Resources
Administrative Building
Montgomery, Alabama 36104

ALASKA
Alaska Division of Parks
323 E. Fourth Avenue
Anchorage, Alaska 99811

AMERICAN SAMOA
Environmental Quality Commission
Office of the Governor
Pago Pago, Tutuila
American Samoa 96920

ARIZONA
Outdoor Recreation Coordinating
  Commission
4433 N. 19th Avenue, Suite 203
Phoenix, Arizona 85015

ARKANSAS
Adm. of OR Grants
Arkansas Department of Planning
400 Train Station Square
Victory at Markham
Little Rock, Arkansas 72201

CALIFORNIA
Department of Parks & Recreation
1416 9th Street, Room 1311
Sacramento, California 95814

COLORADO
Division of Parks & Outdoor Recreation
Department of Natural Resources
1845 Sherman Street, Room 101
Denver, Colorado 80203

CONNECTICUT
Department of Environmental Protection
State Office Building
Hartford, Connecticut 06115

DELAWARE
Dept. of Natural Resources and
Environmental Control
Edward Tatnall Building
Dover, Delaware 19901

DISTRICT OF COLUMBIA
D.C. Recreation Department
3149 16th Street, N.W.
Washington, D.C. 20010

FLORIDA
Division of Recreation & Parks
Department of Natural Resources
Crown Bldg. — 202 Blount Street
Tallahassee, Florida 32304

GEORGIA
State Dept. of Natural Resources
270 Washington Street, S.W.
Atlanta, Georgia 30334

GUAM
Bureau of Budget & Mgt. Research
Territory of Guam
Office of the Governor
Agana, Guam 96910

HAWAII
Dept. of Planning & Economic
Development
State Capitol
Honolulu, Hawaii 96813

IDAHO
Idaho Dept. of Parks & Recreation
Statehouse
Boise, Idaho 83707

ILLINOIS
Department of Conservation
602 State Office Building
Springfield, Illinois 62706

INDIANA
Department of Natural Resources
608 State Office Building
Indianapolis, Indiana 46204

IOWA
State Conservation Commission
State Office Building
300 Fourth Street
Des Moines, Iowa 50319

KANSAS
State Park & Resources Authority
801 Harrison
Topeka, Kansas 66612

KENTUCKY
State Department of Parks
Capitol Plaza Tower, 10th Floor
Frankfort, Kentucky 40601

LOUISIANA
State Parks & Recreation Commission
State Land & Natural Resources Bldg.
P.O. Drawer 1111, 625 N. 4th Street
Baton Rouge, Louisiana 70821

MAINE
Supervisor of Federal Aid
Bureau of Parks & Recreation
Department of Conservation
Statehouse
Augusta, Maine 04301

MARYLAND
Dept. of Natural Resources
State Office Building
Annapolis, Maryland 21401

MASSACHUSETTS
Dept. of Natural Resources
State Office Bldg., Gov't. Center
100 Cambridge Street
Boston, Massachusetts 02202

MICHIGAN
Office of Planning Services
Michigan Dept. of Natural Resources
Stevens T. Mason Bldg.
Lansing, Michigan 48926

MINNESOTA
Dept. of Natural Resources
301 Centennial Building
658 Cedar Street
St. Paul, Minnesota 55101

MISSISSIPPI
Outdoor Recreation Director
Mississippi Park System
Robert E. Lee Building
Jackson, Mississippi 39201

MISSOURI
Dept. of Natural Resources
1203 Jefferson Bldg., Box 176
Jefferson City, Missouri 65101

MONTANA
Recreation & Parks Division
Montana Dept. of Fish and Game
Mitchell Building
Helena, Montana 59601

NEBRASKA
Game and Parks Commission
2200 N. 33rd Street
P.O. Box 30370
Lincoln, Nebraska 68503

NEVADA
Dept. of Conservation & Natural
  Resources
Nye Building, Room 214
Carson City, Nevada 89701

NEW HAMPSHIRE
Dept. of Resources and Economic
  Development
State House Annex
Concord, New Hampshire 03301

NEW JERSEY
Dept. of Environmental Protection
John Fitch Plaza, P.O. Box 1390
Trenton, New Jersey 08625

NEW MEXICO
State Planning Office
Executive-Legislative Bldg., Room 403
Santa Fe, New Mexico 87503

NEW YORK
Office of Parks and Recreation
South Swan Street Building
Albany, New York 12223

NORTH CAROLINA
Dept. of Natural and Economic
  Resources
P.O. Box 27687
Raleigh, North Carolina 27611

NORTH DAKOTA
State Outdoor Recreation Agency
State Office Building
900 East Boulevard
Bismarck, North Dakota 58501

OHIO
Dept. of Natural Resources
1952 Belcher Dr., Fountain Sq.
Columbus, Ohio 43224

OKLAHOMA
Division of State Parks
Tourism & Recreation Dept.
500 Will Rogers Memorial Bldg.
Oklahoma City, Oklahoma 73105

OREGON
State Parks Superintendent
300 State Highway Building
Salem, Oregon 97310

PENNSYLVANIA
Secretary of Community Affairs
P.O. Box 155
Harrisburg, Pennsylvania 17120

PUERTO RICO
Public Parks & Recreation
  Administration
P.O. Box 3207
San Juan, Puerto Rico 00904

RHODE ISLAND
Department of Natural Resources
Veteran's Memorial Building
83 Park Street
Providence, Rhode Island 02903

SOUTH CAROLINA
Bureau of Outdoor Recreation
Dept. of Parks, Recreation, & Tourism
P.O. Box 1358
Columbia, South Carolina 29202

SOUTH DAKOTA
S. Dakota Dept. of Game, Fish, & Parks
State Office Building #1
Pierre, South Dakota 57501

TENNESSEE
Department of Conservation
2611 West End Avenue
Nashville, Tennessee 37203

TEXAS
Parks and Wildlife Department
John H. Reagan Building
Austin, Texas 78701

UTAH
Department of Natural Resources
438 State Capitol Building
Salt Lake City, Utah 84114

VERMONT
Director of Planning Division
Agency of Environmental Conservation
Statehouse
Montpelier, Vermont 05602

VIRGIN ISLANDS
Dept. of Conservation and Cultural
  Affairs
P.O. Box 578
Charlotte Amalie
St. Thomas, Virgin Islands 00801

VIRGINIA
Va. Commission of Outdoor Recreation
803 East Broad Street
Richmond, Virginia 23219

WASHINGTON
Interagency Committee for Outdoor
  Recreation
4800 Capitol Boulevard
Tumwater, Washington 98504

WEST VIRGINIA
State Liaison Officer
Office of the Governor
State Capitol
Charleston, West Virginia 25305

WISCONSIN
Department of Natural Resources
P.O. Box 450
Madison, Wisconsin 53701

WYOMING
Wyoming Recreation Commission
604 E. 25th St.
Cheyenne, Wyoming 82002

Chapter 8 Local Government Participation

Providing park and recreation facilities has been an accepted function of local governments for over a century. In 1853, New York City acquired 700 acres for Central Park, and a decade later Philadelphia acquired the site for Fairmont Park. In 1895, Essex County, New Jersey, became the first county to purchase a park site. Today hundreds of local governments administer park and recreation systems, and they are rapidly expanding their functions in this field. Local governments are striving to develop and preserve a recreational environment. The National Association of Counties strongly supports adequate parks and open spaces:

> We cannot afford to abuse our natural environment, scar our scenic wonders, and destroy our historic sites. Densely populated metropolitan areas should not be devoid of open spaces and parks. If all Americans are to enjoy their precarious heritage, every community must initiate a park and recreation program. — National Association of Counties.

The responsibility for providing local park and recreation opportunities must be fixed, and the essential tools — money, leadership, facilities, equipment, and supplies — must be provided systematically and continuously. A citizens' council representing the various interested groups should be active, and a board or commission officially responsible for direction of a public recreation and park system should be established. As part of the complete community plan, the voluntary and private agencies can provide additional opportunities for individual and group recreation.

Legal Aspects

Time is running out for the development of enabling legislation which will allow local governments to preserve urban land for open spaces and recreation. Soon there will be no open spaces to preserve. — National Association of Counties.

The legal basis for local government participation in the field of parks, recreation, and open space preservation is provided by state *enabling laws, local charters,* and *ordinances.* These legal instruments authorize local governments to establish agencies to operate park and recreation systems. They also permit local governments to acquire land and spend public funds for land, buildings, and programs. Other powers are also granted, such as authority to join with other local governments in cooperative efforts.

Enabling Legislation

Before a local government may provide park and recreation service it must be empowered by the state to do so. State enabling laws authorize local governments to establish, maintain, and operate park and recreation systems. These laws specifically empower local governments to acquire and develop necessary land and facilities, to create an agency to administer the park and recreation system, and to finance the system. In some states, such as Utah and California, the state law specifies the exact organization that must be established to administer the program. Other states allow great flexibility on this matter. For example, the North Carolina enabling statute, applicable to cities, counties, and towns, provides that local park and recreation systems may be conducted just as any other function of the local government is conducted. However, local elected officials are authorized to create recreation boards or commissions by ordinance or resolution if such appears to be in the best interest of the people.

In most states, enabling laws allow local governments to acquire land and buildings for park and recreation purposes by negotiated purchase, donation, bequest, or lease. Most cities, and in some states counties, may condemn land for park purposes (by right of eminent domain).

Some state recreation and park enabling laws empower school districts, municipalities, counties, and other units of local government to join with one another to establish, own, operate, and maintain park and recreation systems. For example, the *Michigan* law permits any two or more units of local government to join forces in providing recreation facilities. The expenses of the joint operation are apportioned among the participating agencies. The laws of *Idaho* and *Oregon* and the laws of several other states permit these same arrangements. The *Iowa* law authorizes the creation of county conservation boards, and permits them to cooperate with appropriate state and federal agencies, as well as

Our surroundings can enrich or impoverish our lives. Thus conserving and improving our environment can add immeasurably to private and public happiness.

— Hubert H. Humphrey

There is no substitute for a beautiful home environment.

cities, towns, villages, or other county conservation boards, to establish and maintain park and recreation systems.

It is essential that local government officials be familiar with the state recreation and park enabling laws, so that they may establish and effectively operate a local park and recreation system within the provisions of the state laws.

Local Charters and Ordinances

Cities and counties operating under home-rule *charters* have the authority to establish and operate park and recreation systems under their general power to promote the welfare, safety, health, peace, and morals of citizens (in other words, the police power). Charter provisions related to parks and recreation usually call for creation of a park and recreation department, and provide for appointment of a director of parks and recreation, and often for the formation of an advisory board. The charter usually outlines the duties of both the director and the board. Sometimes charters vest the authority to establish, develop, and maintain the park and recreation system in an administrative board, which in turn selects the head of the park and recreation department.

A local government not acting under home-rule may, by use of an *ordinance*, create a park and recreation department, and an administrative board. The ordi-

> The best beauty is not that beauty found far away and seen only once in a long while, but the beauty in our everyday environment, a pleasant yard, a well-designed neighborhood, open space at the end of the street.

nance usually indicates the manner in which the park and recreation director and the administrative board are selected and outlines their duties. Often the ordinance permits the park and recreation director or the administrative board to pass regulations and rules pertaining to uses of parks and recreation facilities. Typical rules indicate speed limits to be observed in parks, closing hours of facilities, and types of conduct allowed.

Following are specific features that are essential in an *ordinance* or *charter* used to establish a recreation and parks department:

1. Name of the department;
2. Designation of the managing authority (board, commission, council);
3. Outline of the powers, responsibilities, and duties of the managing authority;
4. Authorization and provisions for hiring and supervising personnel;
5. Authorization for cooperative agreements and relationships with other agencies;
6. Authorization for the acquisition and management of areas and facilities;
7. Authorization for methods of financing the department;
8. Description of limitations in programming, if any;
9. Description of the nature of records and reports to be kept by the department.

Finance

Financing a strong park and recreation system requires a steady flow of funds. Funds are needed to acquire areas and facilities, to employ qualified leaders, to purchase supplies and equipment, and to maintain the parks, community centers, and other facilities that are essential for a well-rounded program.

Financial needs are normally of two kinds: *current operating expenses* and *capital outlay*. The current operating funds ordinarily come from appropriations, special recreation taxes, and fees and charges. The funds for capital outlay usually come from bond issues, special assessments, donations, and government grants.

Local governments are usually authorized to appropriate from the general fund such sums as may seem necessary. In most states, special taxes may be levied by local governments. The voters are asked to approve the levy in some states, while in other cases elected officials retain full taxing authority. For example, in *Georgia* the law permits funds to be allocated from the general funds or to be raised by a special tax levied on all taxable property. A minimum of 10 percent of the qualified voters of a municipality or county can petition the governing board to impose such tax. Then the issue must be approved by the voters before the tax can be levied. In the absence of a petition, the governing board may submit the tax question to the voters on its own initiative. In *Colorado* and several other states the local government authorities may levy a special tax for parks and recreation of their own choice without approval from the voters.

Most local governments have authority to issue bonds to finance capital improvements. As with special tax levies, voters are usually asked to approve the bond issues by vote, and a limit to bonded indebtedness is usually placed by the state government. Money is also received on occasions by grant, bequest, or donation. Fees and charges can usually be imposed on the use of special facilities such as golf courses, zoos, etc., and money can also be raised by renting facilities controlled by the recreation and parks department. Most local governments may grant concessions and share the profits with the concessionaires.

Since the mid 1960s money from the Land and Water Conservation Fund, which is administered by the federal Bureau of Outdoor Recreation, has been a boon to many local governments. A large number of tracts of land that have been purchased and developed by local governments by use of this source of funding could never have been purchased and developed otherwise.

Case Study on Finance
Milwaukee County, Wisconsin

The Milwaukee County, Wisconsin, Park Commission has an annual budget of over $25 million, split about 50 percent for capital development and 50 percent for operations and maintenance. Financing for capital improvement comes from county bond issues, federal and state grants-in-aid, fees, and concession receipts. Operating funds are derived from taxes, state grants-in-aid, fees, and concession receipts. Recreation is handled by the city of Milwaukee and the other municipalities in the county (all of Milwaukee County's 242 square miles is incorporated; its population is 1,200,000).

The principal source of financing for the Park Commission is annual appropriations by the county Board of Supervisors. It is an established policy of the Park Commission to avail itself of any and all grants-in-aid, either federal or state. Currently, the county is participating in the Wisconsin Outdoor Recreation Aid Program (ORAP), which provides 50 percent land acquisition funds from cigarette tax monies, and the U.S. Department of Housing and Urban Development.

In addition, the county is partially dependent on the following: (a) the federal Land and Water Conservation Fund, which provides 50 percent land acquisition and development assistance; (b) federal aids for scenic roads and parkway acquisition and development; (c) the federal urban renewal program, which can provide cleared land for park purposes; (d) special grant programs for specific facilities, such as senior-citizen centers or programs for the handicapped; (e) the federal Department of Agriculture's "Operation Greenspan," which provides funds for the conversion of crop-land to noncrop uses, including recreation.

The Park Commission also receives substantial revenue from various fees. This revenue is credited to the Milwaukee County general funds, and available to the Park Commission only upon reappropriation by the Board of Supervisors. Revenue from fees amounted to an estimated well over a million dollars per year from such things as golf course rentals and equipment sales, a county-operated refectory, bathhouse and pool charges, marina rentals, and clubhouse rentals. Revenue from the Milwaukee County Stadium amounts to about a half million dollars.

Generally speaking, the Park Commission is totally dependent upon the annual appropriation of monies by the Milwaukee County Board of Supervisors. The one exception to that rule is that federal and state grant-in-aid funds are paid directly into the Park Commission's Land Acquisition Fund. The total amount of this fund is usually held to $1 million per year. Therefore, if federal and state grants amount to $600,000 in any one year, the county board would appropriate $400,000 in additional funds. If no federal or state funds are received in a year, the board would appropriate the entire $1 million.

Case Study on Finance
Cleveland Metropolitan Park District

The funds available to the Park District consist of receipts from tax levies upon all real estate within the district, and miscellaneous receipts from district operations. These funds are paid into the office of the Cuyahoga County Treasurer, who acts as treasurer for the Board. Funds can be withdrawn only upon an order from the Board of Park Commissioners. Approximately 70 percent of Park District funds are derived from taxes and 30 percent from golf course greens fees, concessions, ranger court fines, property rentals, and state sales tax returned for local government use and the Metroparks Zoo.

The law permits the Board to levy a tax, not in excess of .05 mill within the 10-mill limitation, the exact amount to be determined by the County Budget Commission, without approval by the voters in the district. Any additional tax funds needed and requested by the Board must be approved by a majority of the votes cast in the district at a general election.

For several years the County Budget Commission has allocated .05 mill of general taxes for park district use. The tax yield at this rate has not yet been adequate to acquire, develop, and maintain the park system. Consequently, since 1921, at ten-year intervals the Board has asked and received vote approval for additional tax levies. Two voted levies have been collected each year since 1924. One .15 mill levy, which will expire in 1978, was available for land purchases, development, and maintenance. The second levy, expiring in 1981, was for .084 mill and could be used only for the purchase and development of land.

Two other levies have been added more recently. One .27 mill levy will expire in 1978 and one .35 mill levy will expire in 1984. Both of these levies are for land purchases, development, protection, and promotion of the Park District.

Approximately $7 million per year is produced by the tax levies, and about $3 million per year from fees, concessions, rentals, etc.

Organization

Even though the effectiveness of any organization depends mostly on the people in it, a correct organizational structure can greatly enhance the operation. It can help keep everyone pulling in the same direction. Local organizations for parks and recreation are generally of two types: (a) a combined department of recreation and parks, or (b) separate recreation and park departments. The departments are usually either at the city level or the county level. However, in some cases, special park and recreation districts are established which do not comply with either city or county boundaries. Park and recreation systems are sometimes administered through the school organization, in which case they usually comply with the boundaries of the school district or districts.

Combined Department

Some communities that have combined parks and recreation into one department are Fresno, California; Lincoln, Nebraska; Ashville, North Carolina; Provo, Utah; Syracuse, New York; and Fort Worth, Texas. Currently the overwhelming trend is in this direction. Where new departments are now being established, virtually 100 percent are combined departments of parks and recreation.

Perhaps the greatest arguments for consolidation into a single department are increased efficiency, economy, and improved services. It seems reasonable that the programming agency (recreation) and facilities-managing agency (parks) should be under a single authority.

Separate Departments

During the early development of local governments, the first departments having to do with parks and recreation were separate, and they acquired and maintained land, leaving the programming to the individuals who used the resources. As a need for leadership in activities developed, local governing bodies provided legislation and the organizational structure for recreation departments. The two departments then enjoyed equal status but had different authority and separate administrative responsibilities.

Under separate departments the rendering of efficient and equitable service to the community placed a premium on close coordination between the two departments. In Cincinnati, Ohio, where separate departments are currently operating, officials believe that the duties of each are sufficiently divergent to justify two departments. Another type of separation is illustrated in Monroe County, New York, where the county coordinates major land purchases and leaves programming (which varies considerably in different communities) to the towns.

The major disadvantages of separate departments are: (a) they generally compete for budgetary appropriations; (b) often the leaders involved are unwilling or unable to coordinate the efforts of the two departments; and (c) the departments are often, but not always, more expensive to operate because of duplication of equipment and personnel.

Special Districts

In some states special park districts are legal political subdivisions and consequently not accountable to any city or county government inside their jurisdiction. They are formed under the terms of enabling state legislation to meet certain local needs not satisfied by existing governments. Special districts are accepted by the state as regional complements to both local and state park systems. They are allowed to levy taxes and issue bonds with voter approval. Special districts have the following special characteristics: (a) they are organized entities usually performing only a single function; (b) they can sue and be sued, make contracts, and own and dispose of property; (c) they have considerable fiscal and administrative independence from other governmental units; and (d) where they have taxing and borrowing power they are frequently exempt from tax and debt limits imposed on city and county governments.

The growth of special districts has been significant. Between 1955 and 1962, the number of park and recreation districts in the United States increased from 194 to

> Surely we are wise enough to recognize that man needs more than the steel and concrete environment of urban civilization. He must also have the sanctuary of unspoiled land, a place of solitude where he may turn his thoughts inward...to wonder at the miracle of creation.
>
> — Alan Bible

Too much living in too little space always results in poverty of one kind or another.

488, and expenditures by districts rose from $60,000,000 in 1957 to $92,000,000 in 1962. Between 1962 and 1970 the number of special districts continued to increase, but at a reduced rate, and during the last half decade the popularity of special districts has clearly declined. Depending on their specific purpose, special districts may be responsible for recreation programming or for park land and open space acquisition and development, or both.

One example of a special district is North Jeffco Metropolitan Recreation and Park District, an 84-square-mile rural area in the northeast corner of Jefferson County, Colorado. It has the authority to "plan, promote, develop, maintain, supervise, and administer all park and recreation facilities and programs necessary to serve all present and future residents of the district." The district is governed by an elected five-member policy-making board of directors. By contrast, the Cleveland (Ohio) Metropolitan Park District is concerned primarily with only land acquisition and maintenance, but it works closely with civic groups and individuals in promoting use of district-owned land. It is governed by a three-member board of commissioners appointed by the senior judge of the county probate court.

In some instances the creation of park districts has resulted from default. Lack of adequate services by the local governments because of insufficient funds is one frequent reason. Another reason is often a need for a well-rounded program of facilities and areas which local government is not providing because of limited outlook or because of concentration on a single type of facility. The special district then may step into a void to provide a broader range of opportunities for the people. However, despite the fact that special districts have sometimes proved responsive to people's needs, their use has caused numerous problems to other units of local government. The fact that special districts are superimposed upon existing governmental units often causes conflicts. Special districts tend to become obsessed with their single function or limited purpose to the exclusion of broader complementary considerations. The multiplicity of districts makes effective control and citizen participation difficult. Generally, special districts are not recommended, but in a few instances they seem to be the best solution to the local problems.

The state of Iowa has established a law that results in a kind of special outdoor-recreation district. The law states that the purposes of the legislation are:

> To create a county conservation board and to authorize counties to acquire, develop, maintain, and make available to the inhabitants of the county public parks, preserves, parkways, playgrounds, recreation centers, county forests, wildlife and other conservation areas and to promote and preserve the health and welfare of the people, to encourage the orderly development and conservation of natural resources, and to cultivate good citizenship by providing adequate programs of public recreation.

This legislation delegates to the county board of supervisors the responsibility for appointing a five-member conservation board. Members must be selected on the basis of demonstrated interest in conservation matters and they serve without pay. To finance land purchase and development, the board of supervisors can levy an annual tax of not more than one mill on the assessed valuation of all real and personal property subject to taxation in the county.

Almost all of the 99 counties of Iowa have established conservation boards and have acquired 27,875 acres of park land. Even though special districts are usually best avoided, the Iowa structure, maintaining an elected government body as the responsible administrative focal point, may be a valid adoption.

School District Operation

For the past two decades many professional recreation and park planners have strongly encouraged recreational use of school facilities and school use of recreation facilities. This approach has been advanced under the "park-school" and "community-school" concepts. The "park-school" is a facility and consists of one or more school buildings constructed on or adjacent to a parksite. The "community-school" is a modern concept of community education in which the school is conceived as an agency that makes maximum use of its facilities and other resources to serve both the educational and recreational needs of the community. It is a "lighted-schoolhouse" concept.

The most efficient method of implementing cooperative school and community use of facilities is to do joint recreation, park, and educational planning from the start. That is, each recreational and educational facility or area is originally planned and constructed for joint use by the two departments. Even though this approach is a valuable one, it is apparent that all the recreation and park needs of the people cannot be satisfied through cooperation with the school system. Much of the public recreation demand is for golf courses, swimming areas, boat-launching facilities, hiking trails, and shaded picnic areas, most of which are outside the range of the school district's interest, jurisdiction, and financial capacity. For this reason the school districts are usually not in a position to operate an adequate total park and recreation system. However, the school district can make a significant contribution to the park and recreation program and can reap much benefit from such coopera-

City of Richmond
Department of Recreation and Parks

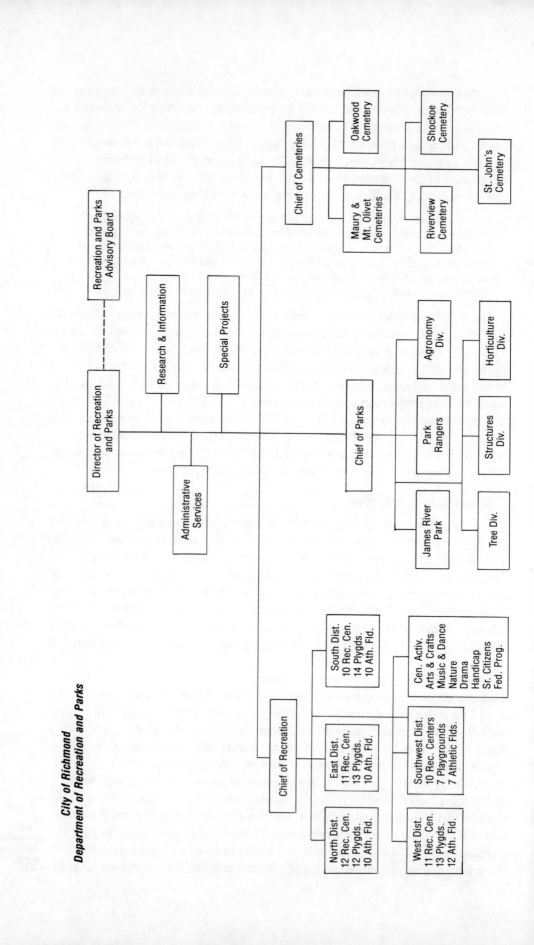

tion. The school district and other local government bodies should cooperate to the utmost in the planning and use of areas and facilities.

Internal Organization

Regardless of whether the department is at the city, county, special district, or school district level, it must be organized to fit the specific situation under which it functions. Localities differ from one another, and no one type of organization is suitable in every instance. The particular organization selected must be complementary to the total governmental organization in the particular case, and it must be designed to fit the specific needs of the people in that locality. It is questionable whether duplicate organizations could be recommended in any two major cities or counties of the nation. Following are case studies that illustrate the internal organization of two park and recreation departments.

Case Study on Organization
Richmond, Virginia

Richmond city covers 62 square miles and has a population of 249,621. The Department of Recreation and Parks has an annual operating budget of $5,943,300 and a capital budget of $955,600. The department employs 225 full-time and 60 seasonal maintenance men, 27 professional administrators, 147 full-time recreation leaders, and 424 seasonal recreation leaders. The park system contains 1169 acres of developed areas divided into 23 parks, 59 playfields with 300 acres, and 528 acres of parks on school sites. In addition, the department administers seven cemeteries, 31 gymnasiums, and 35 community centers.

The director of the Department of Recreation and Parks is appointed by the city manager. The department staff, regulated by civil service, is divided into four units.

Administrative Division. Maintains all records and controls pertaining to the budget, payroll, personnel, purchases and contracts, inventories, public information and services to the operating bureaus.

Bureau of Recreation. Is responsible for planning, organizing, promoting, and conducting recreation programs. Also provides services and coordination to civic groups and organizations.

Bureau of Parks. Maintains, constructs, and polices all recreation areas and facilities and has charge of the street tree program. Schedules the use of areas and facilities for which permits are issued.

Bureau of Cemeteries. Maintains, operates, and polices municipal cemeteries.

To assist the department in its service to the community the city charter specifies the establishment of a Recreation and Parks Advisory Board. It consists of nine members, of whom one must be a member of the school board appointed by the school board and one must be a member of the planning commission appointed by the commission. The remaining seven are appointed by the City Council for terms of three years.

Case Study on Organization
Maricopa County, Arizona

Maricopa County is located in southwestern Arizona with a population of 1,230,000 and a land area of 9226 square miles (5,904,740 acres). The city of Phoenix is the county seat and the largest incorporated area with a 1975 population of 775,500. The County Parks and Recreation Department is responsible for the management and development of 93,546 acres of park land consisting of nine regional and five community park sites.

Maricopa County Parks and Recreation Department
Functional Chart

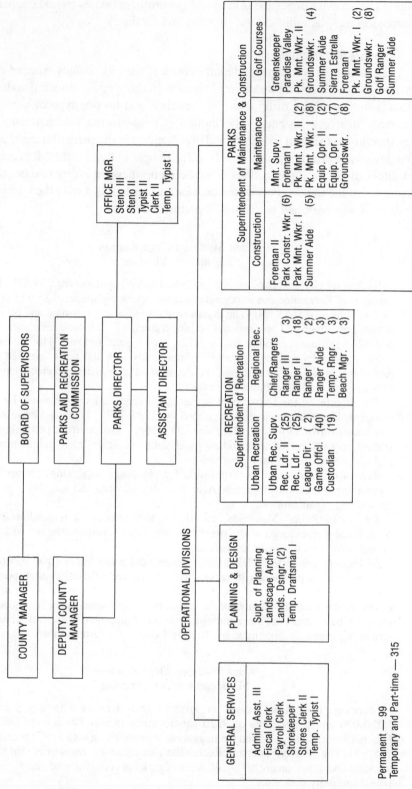

Desirable ocean beach space will be one of the most difficult outdoor recreation resources to provide in adequate amounts in the future. This is because beach activities have become very popular, and the amount of desirable public beach is very restricted.

The Department operates two golf courses, lake programs, shooting ranges (including one of the largest range facilities in the country), archery ranges and field courses, resident nature center, hiking and horse trails, picnic areas, gymkhana and community center, and other park-related facilities. In addition, a wide variety of recreation programs are offered at 22 sites throughout the County, nine of which are year-round.

The annual operating budget for the 1975-76 fiscal year was $1,462,435 and provided for a full-time staff of 99 employees. The Department is presently in an active park development phase and is cooperating with various city, county, state and federal agencies in an effort to expand the open space and recreation opportunities available to the residents of the Maricopa County.

Planning

One of the most important steps toward achieving an adequate park and recreation system is the development of a park and open space plan, which establishes priorities for the acquisition of areas based on existing and projected needs. Such a plan is a systematic approach to (a) determining the needs of people now and in the future, (b) ascertaining existing and future deficiencies by relating anticipated supply and demand, and (c) initiating a program to eliminate any deficiencies. The park and open space plan should be one element of the community's total blueprint for the future, the comprehensive plan.

Local park and recreation planning should be closely coordinated with the state outdoor-recreation comprehensive plan. Every state has developed such a plan that will be updated periodically. Among other things the state plan defines the role that local governments should play in satisfying outdoor recreation needs. Local government units should, in turn, recognize their role and plan accordingly, so that local needs may be identified and included in the state plan. This is especially important inasmuch as the state outdoor-recreation plan is the basis for the approval of Land and Water Conservation Fund Grants, provided to help eliminate outdoor-recreation deficiencies.

Local planners should also be aware of the nationwide outdoor-recreation plan published by the Bureau of Outdoor Recreation. This plan will be updated at five-year intervals. Although not based specifically on state and local plans, the nationwide plan will identify national outdoor-recreation trends and deficiencies, and this will help provide guidance for planners at all levels of government.

Who Makes the Plan?

The responsibility for park and recreation planning is usually entrusted to one of two public agencies — the local planning agency, or the park and recreation agency. In a survey conducted by the National Association of Counties Research Foundation, park and recreation directors replied that most plans were drawn up by local planners in cooperation with the park and recreation agency. This procedure was followed in such localities as San Antonio, Texas; Spokane County, Washington; and Rochester, Minnesota. The local planning agency has access to population data and other basic information. In addition, it is well situated to correlate the park and recreation plan with other elements, as it develops the comprehensive plan for total community growth.

In some cities and counties the park and recreation department draws up the master plan and submits it to the planning department. The planners then coordinate it with other segments of the total community plan. If this approach is used, measures must be taken to avoid duplication of effort and conflicts. If each public agency plans separately from other agencies, the parks department may learn to its dismay that the choice location for a park has been scheduled for a freeway or some other public use. In most cases it is advisable to let the local planning agency prepare the master plan with assistance from the park and recreation department. The park and recreation officials can then help the elected officials execute the plan by proposing acquisition of particular sites and preparing designs for their development. Sometimes planners also give advice on these aspects.

Assistance from numerous private planning firms is available to cities and counties that are developing their first plan or revising an old one. Among the many jurisdictions that have sought professional guidance and objective views of consultants are Hamden, Connecticut; St. Louis County, Missouri; and Richmond, California. Professional consultants may advise local officials on proper techniques and procedures for developing a plan, or they may actually prepare the entire plan. Local officials may avoid disappointment in the work done by professional planners if they inform the consultants of the approximate price citizens can and will pay for a park and recreation system, and if they furnish the consultants with as much background information and as much direction as possible.

Recreation planning is not static. Plans written to bring and channel change are themselves the stimuli for further change. Thus the documents should be updated periodically — every five years, or as the need dictates.

Although no one has developed a single best method for developing a plan, many planners agree that the procedure generally can be separated into three major phases: (a) collection of data on present recreation supply and demand, including population and existing facilities, areas and programs; (b) analysis of future park and recreation needs of the people; and (c) formulation of proposals to meet present needs. Before the first phase of the planning process is undertaken, principles for recreation and park planning should be developed. Among the basic principles are the following:

1. Planning should be based on (a) accurate estimates of present and future needs, taking into account past trends and emerging tendencies; and (b) comprehensive and thorough evaluation of public park and recreation areas.
2. In order to avoid unnecessary duplication, the plan should take into account services provided by private agencies, institutions, and commercial recreation enterprises.
3. The plan should take into account the recreation and park plans of areas lying adjacent to the area being planned, as well as within that area. Furthermore, the plans should be coordinated with regional, state, and national agencies having interests in that area.
4. Realistic park and recreation use and space standards should be established and adopted, and the plan should be based on them.
5. The park and recreation system should be planned on a sound financial basis.
6. After adoption of the plan there should be periodic review, reevaluation and revision, every five years at least.

Implementing the Plan

Little has been accomplished in comprehensive planning until the final phase is entered — that of transforming the blueprint into reality. Acreage must be obtained and developed as called for in the plan. Land can be developed at a later date, possibly with the help of citizen groups, but it must be acquired promptly before the price skyrockets or the land is developed for other uses.

Elaborate priority schedules for the purchase and development of areas and facilities are used by many local governments. When developing a priority schedule, the park and recreation agency must balance short-range and long-range needs. Cities and counties can eliminate some immediate deficiencies by establishing new areas and at the same time can prevent identical problems from developing in the future by initiating a long-range acquisition plan. Discussion of buying and developing parks and open-space facilities is idle talk unless accompanied by an adequate budgeting program.

Zoning

In some localities officials are now taking steps to preserve open spaces in new residential areas by enacting *cluster or density-zoning ordinances*. A cluster-zoning ordinance establishes an overall density for the area, usually in terms of acreage for each dwelling unit, but it allows the developer to reduce the lot sizes and group the homes as long as the overall density is maintained. One section of the tract may be developed at a high density with the remaining portions developed at a lower density, or all development may be centered in one section with the remaining open space preserved for park and recreation purposes. Ordinances often stipulate whether the open space is to be retained in private ownership or dedicated to the local government. Both the community and the developer may reap aesthetic, recreational, and economic benefits from cluster developments. Local government officials find cluster developments a practical way to preserve adequate open space.

A unique example of cluster development is in Reston, Virginia, a 7000-acre planned community located 18 miles from Washington, D.C. Here 42 percent of the land was set aside by the developers for public use. Lakes, golf courses, swimming pools, park, woods, tennis courts, and other recreational facilities were constructed on the land.

Frederick County, Maryland, amended its zoning ordinance to provide for cluster developments. The purpose of the zoning amendment is to permit flexibility in planning new subdivisions which will result in (a) a maximum choice in types of environment in living units available to the public; (b) adequate open space and recreation areas; (c) a pattern of development which preserves trees, outstanding natural environment, geologic features, and social stability; (d) a creative approach to the use of land and related physical environment; (e) a stable residential environment in harmony with natural surroundings, providing desirable living conditions.

Cluster-zoning ordinances should clearly indicate whether open space is to be retained and maintained by private organizations or by the local government. Three methods of ownership and maintenance have been used in the United States with various degrees of success. In New Jersey, open space is dedicated to the local government for operation and maintenance. In some other states a special district whose boundaries correspond to those of the development is created by local ordinance or charter, and the district owns and maintains the property. The third alternative is a nonprofit home-owners' corporation which is created to own and maintain the open spaces within the particular area.

The ordinance of Frederick County, Maryland, provides for the formation of home-owners' associations to improve, operate, and maintain common open space and facilities, including recreation facilities. Each lot owner and/or home owner in the planned unit is automatically a member and must assume a proportionate amount of the financial responsibility, based on a thorough and realistic study of the cost of acquiring and developing parks and facilities, coupled with an analysis of the amount of money available from various sources. The comprehensive plan and the accompanying capital improvement program are adopted by the local governing board after public hearings have been held. The responsibility of the park and recreation officials, along with the community planners, is to keep the elected officials well informed of the needs relative to the plan and to persuade the officials to follow the plan.

In many cities and counties local officials have adopted *land dedication* ordinances that require subdivision developers to dedicate a portion of the subdivision as permanent open space or to make a cash payment to the local government in lieu of dedicating the land. Such ordinances are predicated on the grounds that each

Happy are the children who can find interesting outdoor recreation opportunities close to home.

Providing an adequate outdoor recreation environment near large cities is our greatest problem.

subdivision increases the demand for open space and recreation areas, and that each subdivider should be required to furnish open space for the community in relation to the need he creates by building homes. This is justified on the same basis as the requirement to install streets, sidewalks, and other community improvements in connection with subdivisions. Theoretically the developer recovers the monetary loss of contributing land or money by raising the price of her or his homes. Thus the home owners who will benefit most from the open space pay for it ultimately.

In view of our vast increase in population, and the strong trend toward urbanization, it is essential that zoning ordinances be established and enforced to prevent overcrowded conditions. Adequate zoning for parks and open spaces can greatly improve living conditions in urban areas and can result in increased property values.

Case Study on Planning
Los Angeles County

Big, bustling Los Angeles County critically analyzed an existing California law (AB 1150, Section 11546, Business and Professional Code) that authorizes cities and counties to acquire parkland by a method considered legally controversial in many states. The state law empowers cities and counties to acquire by ordinance the dedication of land, cash payment in lieu thereof, or a combination of both as a condition for subdivision map approval.

In cooperation with the Los Angeles County Division of the California League of Cities, county park and recreation officials attempted to answer some vital questions before deciding to adopt an ordinance under the enabling law. Their questions and answers included the following:

Q. Should local government have an option of accepting the dedication of land or a fee? **A.** In California's case, the answer is "yes," except for subdivisions of less than 50 lots where the builder has a right to pay a fee if he chooses. For subdivisions of over 50 lots, a combination of land and fee can be required.

Q. How is the fee determined? **A.** In Los Angeles County the fee is based upon the value of the land required.

Q. How is the amount of land required to be dedicated determined? **A.** The ordinance implementing the enabling legislation must set up standards to provide for a determination of the percentage of the subdivision to be dedicated. Additionally, the local government must have adopted a general recreation plan containing recreation land requirements.

Q. May fees be used for developing, as well as acquiring, land? **A.** California law permits fees to be used for development of facilities which would serve basically local needs, such as swings, slides, or wading pools. However, it is not the intention of the law to include improvements designed to serve large numbers of people residing outside the immediate area of the park.

Q. Must the land or recreation facility be located within the subdivision? **A.** California law permits the location of the facility outside the subdivision if it is designed for local use and is close enough to the subdivision to permit use by its residents.

Q. Is there a requirement relating to when the park or recreation facilities acquired will be developed? **A.** Yes; however, the requirement only needs to specify when development should commence. Such initial development can be minimal.

Q. Are industrial subdivisions exempt from the local ordinance permitted by the enabling legislation? **A.** Yes.

Q. Should a local government give credit for land a developer proposes to maintain as permanent open space within his subdivision for the use of its residents? (Such private recreation facilities within large developments often have the desirable effects of reducing the demand for local public recreation facilities.) **A.** It is suggested that if credit for such land is given, the developer be required to guarantee that the private recreation areas will be maintained permanently. This means that building and use rights for other than recreation purposes must be relinquished and a "successor in interest" (a condominium or home association) be created by covenant or other legal procedure. This can be accomplished as part of the subdivision's proceedings and approval.

Although the county board of supervisors abides by the policy of acquiring and developing regional parks primarily, it also provides community facilities in unincorporated areas. If a neighborhood park is subsequently annexed by a municipality, the park is turned over to that municipality in fee title without remuneration. However, the transferred park must be retained as a public recreation facility.

Land Acquisition

The amount of land available for all uses is essentially fixed, but demands for it continue to increase. As our population expands, so does the need to use the same tract of land for competing purposes. Acquisition of adequate park, recreation, and open-space acreage to meet the needs of tomorrow's population presents a challenge to all city and county officials. This challenge will steadily increase.

Land is being consumed for subdivisions at an alarming rate. An open-space report published by Fairfax County, Virginia, indicates that if the present rate of consumption of open land continues for two more decades (160-200 acres per 1000 new residents), the entire county will soon be eaten up in urban sprawl, and all of the desirable tracts of open land will have vanished.

In Berks County, Pennsylvania, not only are more acres being consumed to meet increased demand for residential developments, but dwelling unit densities are decreasing. The Berks County Planning Commission reports that, whereas 1 acre of land supported almost 20 dwelling units in previous years, the same amount is generally used by only two to four units today. In addition to increased consumption for residential purposes, more land is needed for wider highways and larger manufacturing establishments. Bigger shopping centers surrounded by more expansive parking spaces are commonplace.

The price of land, especially sites suitable for parks, is rising spectacularly. Some public officials believe a crisis is developing. The Bureau of Outdoor Recreation, in its publication *Recreation Land Price Escalation,* reports that land values generally are rising throughout the nation at the rate of 5 to 10 percent annually, and the value of land suitable for recreation is increasing at an even higher rate. Because there is not enough land suitably located to satisfy all demands, and because prices are rising so rapidly, the amount available must be wisely allocated among competing uses.

Most Americans cherish their outdoor heritage. As more people concentrate into urban and suburban areas, they need a greater opportunity for outdoor recreation near their homes and jobs. They want clean air and water, quiet, a chance to observe birds and animals living free and untamed.

Before public officials embark upon a land-acquisition program, a clearly defined policy should be established. A policy statement sets forth the goal of the acquisition program and indicates methods public officials may use to achieve that goal.

Westchester County, New York, has developed a land-acquisition policy worthy of note. The policy is based on (a) anticipated population size and characteristics by the year 2000; (b) number of acres required to meet the recreation needs (standard of 12 acres per 1000 projected population); (c) general area of greatest need; and (d) type of land and facility needed. The land acquisition policy is composed of the following elements:

1. Recognition that establishment and operation of lands, facilities, and programs to serve active and passive recreation interests and cultural needs is a governmental responsibility.
2. Recognition that all four levels of government — municipal, county, state, and federal — must cooperate to serve recreation interests.
3. Division of responsibility among all four levels of government according to types of resources and programs appropriately provided by each level, and the areas served by various facilities. Municipalities and school districts are responsible for acquiring lands, developing facilities, and operating programs at neighborhood and community level. Totlots, horticultural displays, and local passive parks are provided by this level of government. The county supplements local actions by providing large parks attracting visitors from throughout the country.

By the year 2000, 18,000 acres (6180 acres more than Westchester County possessed in 1976) will be needed to provide recreation for an anticipated population of 1.5 million. Because 80 percent of these people will live in the southern part of the county, emphasis will be placed on acquiring lands conveniently accessible to this population concentration. The policy stresses the need to buy land immediately, before it is developed for another use. In addition to user-oriented facilities to serve the southern half of the county, prime targets of purchase include waterfront lands, natural conservation areas, and scenic areas.

Methods of Acquisition

Land for public use is obtained in a variety of ways, and resourceful public officials will explore the use of all of them. The most successful and widely used method is negotiation with the owner on price and then *cash purchase*. In some cases payments can be spread over a long period by agreeing to buy the tract on installments. Tax delinquent land, usually marginal in character and value, is often acquired for certain purposes at a very low price. Occasionally it is necessary for local government to exercise the *right of eminent domain,* which is a provision in the law allowing agencies of government to condemn privately owned land and acquire it for public use at the appraised market value. This right is usually used as a last resort, but sometimes it serves as a useful protective measure on behalf of public interest. *Donation* is another form by which local governments acquire land that is particularly suitable for park and recreation development. Some departments have been able to acquire a large portion of their park land by this method. Where law permits, local officials have often enacted subdivision regulations demanding *dedication of park sites* in new subdivisions or *cash payment* in lieu thereof.

In addition to acquiring complete title to a tract of land, some local officials have experimented with buying less than full title rights through the use of *scenic easements, right of way accesses,* and *conservation easements.* Also property and buildings are sometimes *leased* by local governments on long-term agreements.

Chapter 9 Outdoor Recreation on Private Lands

Of all the various sectors of outdoor recreation we know less about the private sector than any other one. Government-owned recreation areas are rather clearly identified, and the roles of most government agencies with regard to outdoor recreation are defined. The same is somewhat true about nongovernment organizations. But in the case of privately owned resources the information is not so exact and much desired information is simply not available. Luckily there are a few specific facts and some rather broad generalizations that can be stated.

Often it is assumed that the only method of protecting the public's interest with respect to outdoor recreation opportunities is the public ownership of land. But outright acquisition of recreation land is not the only answer. Indeed in many cases it may not even be the best one. Scenic easements, purchase of right-of-ways, tax abatement programs, hunting and fishing rights, and sale-lease-back arrangements offer an array of tools which should be used. Sometimes bureaucratic inertia has blinded us to these opportunities because they seem like too much trouble or simply because they have not customarily been used. In the future it is going to be necessary to utilize all of these approaches in connection with public use of private land for outdoor recreation. Further, diligent efforts are going to be needed to create and maintain workable arrangements between private landowners and members of the public who want to use the land for recreation.

Of the 2.3 billion acres of land and water in the United States about 60 percent of it is in private ownership. Some of the privately owned land and water is especially designed and managed as outdoor recreation enterprises, but the great majority is managed primarily for the production of commodities of one sort or another. Often the land and water serve secondary uses, of which one is recreation.

Outdoor recreation on private lands can be logically divided into two general categories: (a) that occurring on areas which are unimproved for recreation, where recreation is a secondary use (such as agricultural and grazing areas which are also used for hunting and fishing in season), and (b) that occurring on areas especially improved to accommodate recreationists (outdoor recreation enterprises). Considering these two categories combined, a great amount of outdoor recreation is provided on privately owned land and water.

Private Lands Unimproved for Recreation

Privately owned lands unimproved for recreation are those lands where there has been no special planning or preparation to accommodate recreationists and where the resources are not managed primarily for recreation. Such resources are simply available in their present condition for people to use to a limited extent under certain conditions. Examples of unimproved privately owned resources for recreation are forest lands owned by individuals or companies, privately owned lakes and streams, and farm and grazing lands on which people do such activities as hunting, fishing, horseback riding, and sightseeing. Of the approximately 1.4 billion acres in the United States in private ownership it is estimated that over 50 percent of it has some outdoor recreation value, and most of it is available to the public for recreation under prescribed conditions. Probably bird and small game hunting are the most frequent activities on unimproved private areas, and the majority of this kind of hunting is done on private lands. Also a great amount of fishing is done on private unimproved resources.

The main problem associated with recreational use of private lands is maintaining good relations between landowners and recreationists. As the demand for recreation increases recreationists will need to become more and more cognizant of the landowners' problems which derive from public use of the land. Increased efforts to keep landowners and the public compatible with each other will be needed.

Recreation on Privately Owned Improved Areas

Many areas are specifically designed and managed to accommodate the outdoor recreationists. These are mostly recreation enterprises operated to produce profit. Among these are private camps, commercial camp and picnic grounds, resorts, dude ranches, commercial beaches, yacht clubs, golf courses, boat clubs, ski areas, shooting preserves, vacation farms, riding stables, guiding and outfitting enterprises, private power companies, and special historic philanthropic sites.

Like any other profit producing business, recreation enterprises must be appeal-

Recreation on private land is a privilege, not a legal right. In the future this source of recreation will be ever more essential if the needs of the people are to be met.

Nature study on private unimproved land.

ing to the potential paying customers and managed in a way that leaves the customers satisfied and willing to return again and again.

Resorts

Recreation resorts are perhaps the most widespread of all privately owned outdoor recreation enterprises. They range in type from waterfront hotels, cottages, and motels, usually situated on very small sites and providing only such activities as swimming and sunbathing, to huge sprawling complexes on sites of a thousand or more acres where even the most difficult-to-please guest can find some interesting activity.

More than 50 percent of the resorts in the nation are owned by companies or corporations. About 40 percent are owned by individuals or families and the remaining resorts are owned by private clubs, partnerships, or nonprofit groups. They range in size from less than one acre to more than 30,000 acres, but two-thirds of them are 50 acres or more. According to the Bureau of Outdoor Recreation about three-fourths of the land included in resorts is managed especially for recreational purposes. Water sports are by far the most popular activities at resorts, with swimming being the most popular single activity. Fishing, boating, golf, and water skiing follow in that order.

The great resort movement in the United States started in the 1920s when continental travel began to boom. The movement has gradually gained momentum since then, and is now increasing at a faster rate than ever before. Because of the greater mobility and the increased income of the American people, recreation resorts are gaining in popularity faster than ever.

Ski Areas

Snow skiing, one of the most fascinating of outdoor sports, has grown tremendously in popularity during the last two decades. Formerly considered to be a sport for only the young and the daring, it is now enjoyed increasingly by adults and many older folks. An estimated 7 to 8 million people ski in the United States according to the National Ski Association of America, and this number is increasing by 12 to 15 percent annually. There are more than 650 ski areas in the nation. Twenty-five percent of these are rather limited and are situated on less than 50 acres. Twenty percent of the areas are on large tracts of more than 500 acres. Over two-thirds of the total acreage in all ski areas is devoted principally to recreational use. Of course the most popular activity is skiing, but other activities are tobogganing, sledding, cross-country touring, sightseeing, snowmobiling, ice-skating, and swimming where heated pools are available. Many ski areas have been developed into year-round resorts, providing different types of activities each season of the year.

Shooting Preserves

A shooting preserve is privately owned or leased acreage on which artificially propagated game is released for the purpose of hunting, usually for a fee over an extended season. Good game cover is especially planned and cultivated. Game birds are carefully bred and reared. At maturity they are released to the various areas of the preserve. There are more than 1550 identified shooting preserves in the United States. Not all of these are operated on a commercial public basis. Many are private club operations while others function solely for the personal pleasure of single landowners and their invited guests. No two shooting preserves are alike. Some operate as full-fledged resorts with many attractive features and comforts for all members of a sportsman's family. Other preserves simply provide daily fee hunting with no frills. Charges to the public vary depending upon the facilities and services offered. Some preserves charge by the number of birds bagged, others by the number released, and others by still different methods. In all instances the sportsman and shooting preserve operator agree on costs before the sportsman enters the hunting field.

More than half of the identified shooting preserves are owned by individuals or families. About 20 percent are owned by private clubs and 20 percent by companies or corporations. The remaining preserves are owned by partnerships or through some other arrangement. Numerous preserves offer a wide variety of both land-based and water-based recreation. Of course, hunting is the predominant activity, and this is often combined with fishing. Other activities commonly offered are picnicking, camping, hiking, horseback riding, trap, skeet and target shooting, dog training, and other outdoor related forms of recreation.

Guest (Dude) Ranches

A number of ranches in the United States provide vacation facilities for guests. Many of the ranches are primarily working ranches where the guests (dudes) provide additional revenue and their entertainment is closely related to the work of the ranch. Conversely, at some other ranches the fee paid by the guests is the major source of income. Here the care of ranch livestock and the production of crops frequently are of secondary interest. Nearly half of the identified dude ranches in the United States consist of a thousand acres or more. Some are less than a hundred acres while others approach 100,000 acres in size. The most popular activity on dude ranches is horseback riding, followed by fishing, swimming, and hunting. Other popular activities are cookouts and picnics, camping, boating, pack trips and trail rides, and hiking. The great majority of the dude ranches are in the western states and most of them, of course, are especially designed to have a western atmosphere about them.

Vacation Farms

Many city dwellers are sampling another very different way of life through farm vacations. A number of farm families are making their homes and their meadows, woods, streams, and ponds available to paying guests. These guests often bring with them new interests and new ideas welcomed by the farm families involved. Guests benefit from the clean fresh air, from the country scenery, from being free to walk virtually wherever they choose with no restrictions, from basking in the sun and shade, and from helping with farm chores. There are more than 240 identified vacation farms in the United States. Eight percent of these range from 100 to 500 acres in size. Ten percent are less than 100 acres, and 10 percent are larger than 500 acres. There is a remarkably wide variety of recreation facilities and opportunities on the farms and on public lands nearby. Among the more popular activities are fishing, swimming, boating, hunting, hiking, horseback riding, picnicking, camping, cookouts, and lawn games. Some vacation farms include golf courses, swimming pools and other such specialized facilities. Vacation farms are on the increase and are becoming ever more popular among city dwellers.

Campgrounds

Camp areas come in a variety of types. One of the best known categories is publicly owned campgrounds such as those found in national and state parks and forests or those operated by some local communities. Organized (resident) camps for children are a second category. Ordinarily these camps use the same grounds year after year and have at least a few permanent buildings. A smaller number of permanent camps are for adults. A third type is day camps for children whose parents cannot or do not want to send them to resident camps. Usually these camps are in or near urban areas because travel time must be kept as short as possible. A fourth category of camping, and the one that this discussion is mainly concerned with, is privately owned campgrounds where families can pitch tents or park trailers

> A farm must be more than a corn-and-beef factory: it must support quail and pheasants, rabbits and foxes. A park must be more than a picnic spot or camping area: it must have squirrels and pigeons, or bear and elk. A refuge must be more than a waterfowl area: it must have muskrats and raccoons and a whole community of other living things or it fails to live up to its potential for existence.
>
> — Rogers C. B. Morton

or campers for a fee. There are more than 800 identified commercial campgrounds of this type. Practically all of these occupy a small number of acres (100 acres or less) and many of them occupy only five to 20 acres. However, there are a few commercial campgrounds which occupy several thousand acres. In addition to camping, the more prevalent activities available at commercial camp sites are swimming, picnicking, fishing and boating.

Outfitting and Hunting and Fishing Camps

Specialized camps for hunters and anglers are provided in various localities throughout the nation. Such camps are, of course, concentrated in the areas where game and fish are abundant. Typically, these camps consist of a relatively small acreage where living accommodations and certain recreational facilities are provided, and are adjacent to large tracts of public or private land which is abundant with fish and game. Usually the services provided include outfitting and guided hunts and fishing trips. In the case of guided hunts the game is often guaranteed. In addition to hunting and fishing, in some places outfitters and guides provide river float trips, canoe trips, and wilderness pack trips on horseback for those interested in unusual scenery and high adventure.

Industrial Tree Farms

Privately owned forest and timber lands serve as an important recreational outlet for thousands of Americans each year. These forests are fine examples of private enterprise serving the expanding outdoor recreation need of the public. In many such forests there is rarely a waiting line for picnic tables, fireplaces, and campsites. Most of the facilities are free or cost very little, and some of the forests are located within short driving distances of highly populated areas.

Interesting facts concerning recreation facilities provided on privately owned forest lands were uncovered recently by a survey conducted by the American Forest Institute of Washington, D.C. Among the facts are:

1. A total of 61.4 million acres of privately owned forest land is open to the public for recreation.

2. Within these lands there are more than 86,000 miles of privately owned roads open to visitors.

3. An additional 700,000 acres of natural and artificial lakes are available to the public.

This willingness to welcome the public is not new. Hunters have enjoyed these privileges for many years. However, the company owners of these lands seem to

Hunting on private land.

Fishing in privately owned lakes and ponds is becoming more prevalent. It offers improved opportunities for both sportsmen and landowners.

have sensed the pressing demands being made on municipalities and other public agencies for more parks and consequently recreational opportunities on privately owned forests have been greatly expanded in recent years. In effect, the actions of the owners have reduced the burdens on tax-supported park and recreation agencies.

A survey done by the American Forest Products Industry, Inc., in 1972 gave some specific and revealing findings. It was found that more than 1,500,000 people, including hunters, anglers, campers, picnickers, and skiers, used industrial forest lands annually for various forms of recreation. More than 96 percent of the land included in the survey was open to certain forms of public recreation. In most cases it was available at no cost. It was found that the most frequent activities participated in on commercial timber lands were hunting and fishing. Over 125,000 big game animals were bagged annaully on the lands of the 455 companies included in the survey. Thirty-one of the companies employed game and fish management specialists. Some companies transported hunters and fishermen to remote sections of their land whenever possible and hauled bagged game to accessible public highways without charge. The survey indicated that fishing was permitted on practically all the areas.

Sixty-five of the companies operated 137 free public parks with a total of more than 3400 acres. Most of these parks were equipped with camp, picnic, sanitary,

Children pursuing outdoor play on privately owned forest land.

> A beautiful America will require the effort of government at every level, of business, and of private groups. Above all, it will require the concern and action of individual citizens, alert to danger, determined to improve the quality of their surroundings, resisting blight, demanding and building beauty for themselves and their children.
>
> — Lyndon B. Johnson

water, and play facilities. Some had covered shelters, boat ramps, swimming areas, bathhouses, et cetera. Six areas made provisions for skiing and three provided ice-skating opportunities. It was indicated that 31 companies planned additional parks within one year, and 67 companies had plans for additional parks some time later. Seven companies actually employed professional park planners to guide the development of their recreational areas.

Tree farm parks are most prevalent in the Pacific Northwest and are considerably less common in other portions of the nation. The major problems faced by industrial tree farm owners with regard to public recreation are vandalism, damage to timber, forest fires, and damage to operating equipment.

Commercial Beaches

In many sections of the United States most of the shoreline has been developed with private homes (vacation or year-round) and thus is not available for public recreation. In other sections hotels, motels, and private clubs have acquired relatively long stretches of private waterfront. State, national, and local parks provide the general public with its major chance to enjoy the unique qualities of our many miles of shoreline. Unfortunately, these facilities are limited in number. Competition for the small amount of shoreline not already developed is keen and the price of ownership is beyond the means of most people. In many areas of the nation commercial beaches provide the only opportunity for people of limited means to enjoy, for a small fee, swimming, sunbathing, and, in some places, boating and fishing. Commercial beaches are to be found along the shores of many rivers, lakes, and bays. Still others are located along the shores of the Atlantic and Pacific Oceans and the Gulf of Mexico. According to the Bureau of Outdoor Recreation commercial beaches vary in size from less than one-half acre to more than 1600 acres. The most popular activities by far are swimming and sunbathing, followed by picnicking, boating, fishing, camping, and outdoor games. The great majority of commercial beaches are located in the eastern and midwestern portions of the nation with a few beaches located in the Southwest and Far West.

Yacht Clubs

Pleasure boats are no longer solely the playthings of the well-to-do. The accelerated interest and ability of people to own boats of all kinds are reflected in the increasing number of yacht clubs, and in their growing memberships. There are more than 1200 identified yacht clubs in the United States. These clubs vary from the long established ones to those so new they are still seeking sites on which to build docks and clubhouses. Yacht clubs also vary in the types of memberships and the types of boats owned by members. Typically, yacht clubs do not occupy large acreages. Approximately 65 percent of the yacht clubs occupy 5 acres or less, while only about 15 percent occupy 15 acres or more. Of course, the most popular activities at yacht clubs are boating and boat racing, including sailing. Other popular activities are swimming, fishing, picnicking, tennis, and social activities. Many of the clubs are commercial-type operations where their facilities are available to nonmembers at established fees. Yacht clubs, along with boating in general, are increasing at an ever accelerated rate, and numerous new clubs are being added each year. One of the great restricting factors in the establishment of new yacht clubs is the declining availability of suitable facilities and areas to accommodate them.

Boat Clubs

Boat clubs differ from yacht clubs chiefly in the kinds of boats owned by members. Outboard motor boats of various sizes and the smaller inboard boats are the principal types found in boat clubs, while sailboats and inboard motor cruisers as well as some outboard boats are typically found at yacht clubs. There are over 500 identified boat clubs in the United States. Like yacht clubs, these clubs are located on small acreages ordinarily between 1 and 5 acres. They serve primarily their own members but in many cases services are available to nonmembers at a fee. The most popular recreational activity at boat clubs is, of course, boating. Other activities in their order of popularity are picnicking, swimming, camping, and water skiing.

Industrial Recreation Areas

Many industrial firms provide outdoor recreational areas for their employees. Sometimes these areas are adjacent to the industrial plant and in other cases they are displaced from the plant location. The areas vary considerably in size, ranging from only a few acres to over a thousand acres in some cases. The most popular activity on industrial outdoor recreation areas is picnicking, followed by outdoor games, swimming, fishing, hunting, camping, and golf. Industrial recreation is gradually and steadily increasing in popularity. It is one of the important fringe benefits offered by many of the industrial establishments.

Private Power Companies

Where such need is clearly demonstrated a number of private power companies have provided opportunity for fishing, boating, camping, picnicking, and other water-related interests at their reservoirs. Usually these services to the public are free of charge, but sometimes nominal fees are charged to help offset the expenses of providing the recreational opportunities.

Special Attractions

Certain specialized attractions such as some historic and philanthropic sites have great meaning to the public, and their management and maintenance are largely underwritten by private endowments. Examples of such sites are Mount Vernon and Williamsburg, Virginia. From time to time new sites are added to the long list of sites that already exist.

Technical and Financial Assistance

Various sources exist where a private citizen or enterprise may receive technical or financial assistance. At the state level technical assistance may be obtained from faculty members of many state universities and colleges, and from some private universities. Such faculty members are typically assigned to the University Department of Recreation, but in certain cases assistance might be sought from specialists in business, economics, or site planning. The land grant university in each state includes the State Extension Service. In a number of states the Extension Service has on its staff one or more recreation specialists who work with private enterprises as well as local government units in the promotion and planning of better recreation opportunities. Some state governments have an agency such as a Park and Recreation Department which provides consultation services to private enterprises.

Besides the assistance that is available at the state level, federal agencies provide certain kinds of assistance. The Small Business Administration will provide low interest loans for private projects which qualify. The Area Redevelopment Administration will provide low interest loans and in some cases grants of money for private projects located in designated ARA districts. Through the Rural Area Development program (administered through the State Extension Service) technical assistance is available on any approved project that contributes to Rural Area Development. Programs of the Agricultural Stability and Conservation Service and the Soil Conservation Service provide both technical and financial assistance for certain private conservation projects. These programs and their uses for outdoor recreation are described on pages 87-89.

Possibly the best source of information within each state is the State Outdoor Recreation Liaison Officer (each state has one) who is responsible for coordinating federal and state programs in outdoor recreation. A list of the liaison offices appears at the end of Chapter 7.

Summary Statements

Based on information reported more than a decade ago by the Outdoor Recreation Resources Review Commission, combined with current information from the Bureau of Outdoor Recreation and other government sources, several summary statements can be made.

1. There are over 153,000 outdoor recreation enterprises in the private sector. The total acreage associated with these enterprises is estimated at more than 44,000,000 acres, with 35,000,000 of these acres devoted entirely to outdoor recreation use. Ninety-six percent of the recreational acres are land and four percent are water.

2. About one half of the patrons of outdoor recreation enterprises come from outside the county in which the enterprise is located, while the other half of the

patrons come from within the county. However, this percentage varies considerably with different enterprises.

3. The number of private outdoor recreation enterprises has almost doubled in the last decade, and many of those that existed previously have expanded.

4. About 50 percent of the enterprises are operating partly on borrowed money, and only about 5 percent of these have loans from the federal government.

5. A majority of the guest ranches, campgrounds, shooting preserves, hunting and fishing camps and vacation farm enterprises are owned by individuals or families. Companies or corporations own most of the resorts and resort hotels, commercial beaches, ski areas, and industrial employee recreation areas. Yacht, boat, and golf club facilities are usually owned by the clubs themselves.

6. The land on which recreational facilities are located is usually operator-owned at recreation resorts, campgrounds, beaches, resort hotels, industrial employee recreation areas, hunting and fishing camps, and most vacation farms, while a majority of the ranch, ski area, and shooting preserve operators lease at least part of their land, and more than half of the boat clubs and nearly half of the yacht clubs are on land wholly leased.

7. Generally the campgrounds, beaches, yacht and boat clubs, and industrial recreation areas tend toward small holdings and more intensive land uses. Conversely, hunting and fishing camps, dude ranches, shooting preserves, and ski areas tend toward larger holdings and less intensive land use.

8. Swimming is the activity most frequently offered at outdoor recreation enterprises, and it is the most popular one among the users. Among the other more popular activities are camping, boating, picnicking, fishing, hiking, and golf.

9. The operator's personality pretty well sets the tone for the outdoor recreation enterprise. To be successful the operator must know the mechanics of good business management, be able to handle people effectively, and be willing to provide the guests with satisfying services so they will feel they have received their money's worth. The enterprise must be managed in such a way that it sells itself to the paying public.

10. Apparently there is no single optimal size of recreation enterprise in any of the various types of enterprises. The optimal size varies with the management ability of the operator, the labor force's dependability, the location of the business, the seasonal fluctuations, the degree and quality of competition, and other factors.

11. Vandalism, trash (litter), and fires in that order were the most frequently mentioned problems by the operators. These problems account for about 75 percent of all problems.

12. High, relatively fixed costs that vary little in relation to the number of guests are a burden to many recreation enterprises. Those involving livestock feeding, advertising, and caretaking expenses are examples. Liability insurance is almost prohibitively expensive for beach and ski enterprises and those involving the use of horses or wild animals.

13. Activities requiring extensive areas (riding, hunting, fishing, etc.) account for 54 percent of all new facilities that have been added recently; water sports (boating, water skiing, swimming, etc.) for 34 percent; intensive sports for 4 percent; and miscellaneous sports and activities for the remaining 8 percent.

14. Owners (usually companies and corporations) of a number of facilities open to the public for recreation in effect subsidize public recreation by providing outstanding opportunities for the public's enjoyment at less than actual cost. Such situations should be recognized as contributing to the public welfare and should be further encouraged.

15. There is need for agencies at all levels of government to initiate informational and educational programs to help improve the behavior of persons using private recreational facilities. Private recreation as an industry could effectively cooperate in this effort.

Obviously there is still much information that has not been gathered about the private sector of outdoor recreation. We still know relatively little about all of the services that are provided and we know even less about the potential services of private outdoor recreation. But in spite of what we do not know, some valuable information has been gathered and, from this, some important generalizations can be made. (a) The private sector makes a very significant contribution to the outdoor recreation of the American people. (b) The demand for outdoor recreation on private resources is increasing at a steady rate. (c) Private landowners are becoming more aware of the opportunity to increase their income and at the same time provide a worthy public service by developing the recreational potential of their privately owned resources.

If private landowners and operators of private outdoor recreation enterprises, along with public agencies and the people using private recreational resources, will all work together toward the common goal, the total supply of outdoor recreation available to the public will be steadily increased and the satisfaction the public gains from the use of these resources will be multiplied.

Chapter 10 Outdoor Recreation Resources — Supply and Demand

Fifty years ago Senator Robert La Follette made a solemn plea when he said, "It is urgently essential to save for the human race the things on which a peaceful, progressive, happy life can be founded." His reference was to the great domain of the outdoors — his theme preservation and conservation. With the passing of the years, the significance of this warning and its relevance have become steadily more apparent.

While the out-of-doors has always been important to Americans and, while the availability of outdoor recreation has long been of public concern, in recent years it has taken on new dimensions. The growing population — with more leisure time, and living largely in cities — has brought about problems different from those envisioned by even the most farsighted leaders in the past. In recent decades the whole nature of the American society has changed, and this has brought about a new demand for outdoor recreation.

The seeds of the problem were sown in the early 1920s when, after World War I, the work week was shortened, personal income was increased, automobiles came into general use, and the highway system was expanded. For the first time in our history, people in large numbers had leisure time, could find ways to get from one place to another, and could afford to go. New kinds of recreation — boating, for example — became available to the average person. Public recreation areas — many of them ill-suited to mass use — were not prepared for the great wave of enthusiasts that was about to come.

A second great thrust in the demand for outdoor recreation followed World War II. The trends, which were already apparent before the war, developed with increased rapidity. More urbanization, more leisure time, higher incomes, and more of numerous other factors caused continued escalation of the demand for outdoor recreation. The trend has not let up, and it appears that it will continue during the foreseeable future.

The adequacy of any commodity is expressed in the relationship between its *supply* and *demand*. When the supply equals or exceeds the demand the supply is adequate, at least for the present. One important question facing us now is whether the resources for outdoor recreation are adequately meeting even the current demand for them. A more crucial question is "How long can the supply continue to meet the demand when the demand is increasing at a tremendous rate?"

The Demand

The magnitude of outdoor recreation in the U.S. is great, and so is its variety. On a single body of water some people boat, some water ski, some canoe or sail, some fish, while still others swim on or under the surface. Some walk on the surface of the earth, some dig in it for archeological relics, while others descend into caves or go aloft in gliders or planes. We are coming to use the land, water, and air in every conceivable manner to pursue our interests and enrich our lives.

These activities take place during vacation, on overnight trips, on outings, and whenever we can find a few hours available. Our steadily increasing participation in these activities has long amazed observers, but never so much as now.

Some of our pursuits are very complex and expensive in time and money, but at present it is the simple pleasures Americans seek the most. By far the most popular activities are pleasure driving and walking; together, they account for about 40 percent of the total annual outdoor participation. Other activities that are very popular are those which require the least preparation or specialized equipment — playing

A sunny day at Hempton Beach, New Hampshire.

Midday in Yellowstone National Park.

games and swimming (in summer, swimming goes up almost to the top of the list), sightseeing, bicycling, fishing, attending sports events, and picnicking. Sports that require specialized equipment, skills, or conditions — such as skiing, mountain climbing, skin diving, and sailing — rank low in frequency. They do not rank low, however, in intensity of personal involvement. Those who participate in these specialized skills do so often and with great enthusiasm. Whether it is pride or skill, a sense of fraternity, or perhaps the thrill of danger, a powerful motivating force is at work; and one has only to listen to skin divers and skiers "talking shop" to grasp how compelling these kinds of activities can be.

The Bureau of Outdoor Recreation estimated that in 1960 Americans engaged in the major forms of summertime outdoor-recreation activities on 4.28 billion occasions. By 1965 the number had increased by 51 percent to 6.48 billion. By 1970 that number had increased to 7.42 billion, and in 1975 it was 8.33 billion. It is predicted that by 1980 participation in these summertime activities will have increased by more than 100 percent over the 1960 figure, to 9 billion occasions. And by the year 2000 participation will increase by 300 percent over 1960, to an astounding 12.84 billion occasions. These trends in participation indicate that outdoor recreation is increasing faster than the population. During the 40 years from 1960 to 2000 the population will increase by about 160 percent while outdoor recreation will triple. This is another way of saying that by A.D. 2000 on the average each person will participate in outdoor recreation almost twice as often as in 1960. Figure 12 shows

People minus space equals poverty. This is true whether that space is a slum dwelling, a college classroom, a job opportunity, or a National Park.
— Marya Mannes

16,846,000,000

10,128,000,000

4,282,000,000

1960   1980   2000

Figure 12. Graph showing predicted increases in outdoor recreation participation in 1980 and 2000 as compared to 1960.

the predicted increase in summertime outdoor-recreation participation at 20-year intervals from 1960 to 2000. The predictions are based on past and present trends. Participation in outdoor recreation during other seasons of the year will undoubtedly parallel the trends of summertime activities.

Demand for Particular Activities

According to information from the Bureau of Outdoor Recreation, the most popular *summertime* outdoor activity is walking for pleasure. This is followed closely by swimming, driving for pleasure, outdoor games, sports, and bicycling. Other activities, in order of their popularity, are sightseeing, picnicking, fishing, attending outdoor sports contests, boating, nature walks, camping, horseback riding, water skiing, and hiking. Figure 13 shows in graphic form the estimated annual participation in the 15 most popular outdoor-recreation summertime activities. It should be pointed out that only summertime activities were considered in this figure. A number of other important activities such as hunting, skiing, and ice-skating take place during other seasons.

Demand for Particular Resources

Outdoor-recreation areas are typically categorized into three major divisions — resource-based, intermediate, and user-oriented. (a) *Resource-based* areas are essentially the "great outdoor" areas which are in their natural state, unchanged and unimproved. These areas are found in such places as the forests, national parks, and

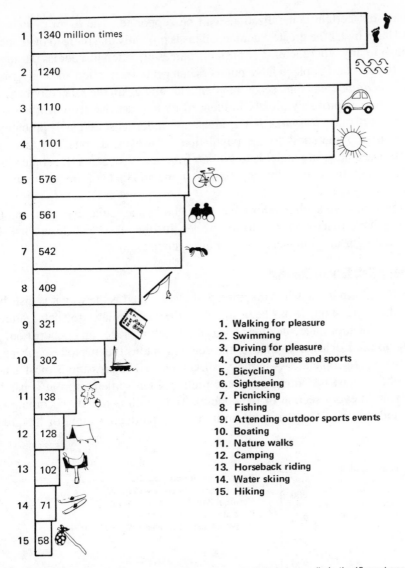

1	1340 million times
2	1240
3	1110
4	1101
5	576
6	561
7	542
8	409
9	321
10	302
11	138
12	128
13	102
14	71
15	58

1. Walking for pleasure
2. Swimming
3. Driving for pleasure
4. Outdoor games and sports
5. Bicycling
6. Sightseeing
7. Picnicking
8. Fishing
9. Attending outdoor sports events
10. Boating
11. Nature walks
12. Camping
13. Horseback riding
14. Water skiing
15. Hiking

Figure 13. Graph showing number of occasions Americans participated annually in the 15 most popular summertime outdoor-recreation activities.

the great public domain. For the most part these areas are relatively remote from most of the nation's population. (b) *Intermediate* areas, which are more accessible, are such areas as state parks and forests, fairly accessible bodies of water, and other such areas which are normally within a few hours' drive from the using population. Typically, these areas have some improvements, possess less of the natural state, and are less wild than the resource-based areas. (c) *User-oriented* areas are those outdoor areas designed and constructed to accommodate specific forms of active participation. They include areas for swimming, picnicking, skiing, skating, and other such activities. Typically, these areas are readily accessible to the using public.

Specific-use figures are not available for comparing the demand for these three divisions, but certain generalizations can be supported. The *user-oriented* areas seem to have by far the greatest demand. This is probably due more to their accessibility than to any other factor. User-oriented areas are often just across the street or around the corner. People in large numbers can get to them often and conveniently. The *intermediate* areas rank second in demand, and again the relatively heavy use of these areas is probably greatly influenced by the fact that they can be reached within a short time. *Resource-based* areas are under least demand, probably because of their remoteness to the population. However, despite this fact, some resource-based areas are under heavy strain from users. In general, people will use most frequently those areas that are close to home and that require minimum effort and expense to reach.

Visitor trends are available for areas managed by particular agencies, and these trends can have much meaning to the reader. In Figures 14 and 15 are listed the visitor trends for areas managed by certain agencies.

Factors Relating to Demand

Equally as important as the magnitude of the demand is the way it is distributed among the population. It has been found that demand relates to such features as geographic location, age, income, level of education, race, and occupation.

Geographic Location. Whatever the demand is for, it seems to be concentrated where the most people are — in metropolitan areas. The pressure is most acute in the Northeast, fast becoming one large metropolitan settlement, but it has been building up in every section of the country. The South is rapidly becoming more urban, and the West Coast is well on its way to producing some of the greatest

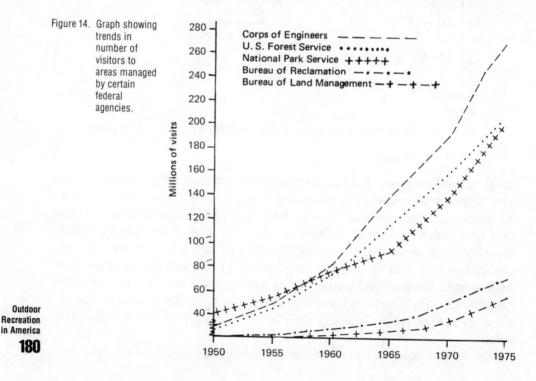

Figure 14. Graph showing trends in number of visitors to areas managed by certain federal agencies.

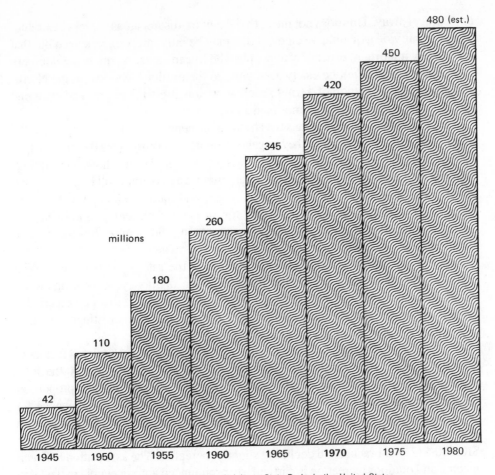

Figure 15. Graph showing trends in number of visits to State Parks in the United States.

conglomerations of population. Even the wide-open states of the farm belt are feeling the pressure, as a once predominantly agricultural population continues to move to the cities. Outdoor pleasures that used to be taken for granted are proving harder to come by.

A metropolitan population must get most of its recreation in the metropolitan region, and for all practical purposes, the existence of extensive areas elsewhere is little compensation for lack of them at home. The great bulk of the outdoor-recreation demand must be satisfied in the after-work and weekend hours; therefore, even though Americans are highly mobile they seek most of their recreation close to home. Even on vacation trips the majority seek recreation only one or two

Thomas Carlyle once said to an American: "Ye may boast o'yer dimocracy, or any ither 'cracy, or any kind of poleetical roobish; but the reason why yer laboring folk are so happy is that ye have a vost deal o'land for a verra few people."

— Josiah Strong

days' travel away. This does not mean that the more distant areas are less desirable. They can provide a qualitative element that may be only rarely experienced but that can be very important, especially to people who live in cities. A park or a wilderness in the Far West may not be easily accessible to the millions who live in the Northeast. But the anticipation of a trip to such an area is itself important, and even one visit can have a long-lasting emotional impact.

Age. Of all the factors, *age* has the sharpest influence. As might be expected, the older people become, the less they engage in outdoor activity. This decline is especially noticeable in the more active pursuits — cycling, hiking, horseback riding, water skiing, and camping. But even in late middle age people still engage in such activities as swimming, motorboating, fishing, and nature walks. And there are types of recreation — walking or driving for pleasure, sightseeing, and fishing — where participation rates are impressive even among old people. But the general picture is one of declining activity with advancing years.

Income. Income has a discernible effect upon the rate of participation. With activities that demand a substantial outlay of time or money — boating, water skiing, horseback riding, and the like — it is hardly surprising that participation is higher among those who have the finances to participate. Interestingly enough, however, the upper income groups also do more walking.

Some of the differences between income groups are due to such related factors as education, occupation, and age. The very low rate of participation by the low-income groups, for example, can be partially accounted for by the high proportion of older people, many of them retired, in this bracket. Even after allowance for these factors, however, it is clear that income itself has a decided influence. In general, participation tends to go up with income, reaching a maximum in the $10,000-$12,000 bracket and declining slightly thereafter. The association between income and outdoor recreation is particularly pronounced among people in the large metropolitan areas where outdoor recreation opportunities are less accessible, and therefore more expensive.

Education. Education affects participation much the same as income does; generally speaking, the more of it people have up to a certain point the more they are likely to participate. This is particularly the case in swimming, golf and numerous other games, sightseeing, walking, and driving for pleasure. In some activities, the correlation is not very consistent.

The Supply

Because of the various trends already mentioned, such as increasing population, greater mobility, higher incomes, better education, and more leisure time, the demand for outdoor recreation has increased at an astounding rate in recent years. All indications are that the increase will continue at the same rate, if not faster, in the future. How long will the supply be able to meet this increasing demand?

We know that recreation is determined primarily by what people do, why they do it, and what effect it has on them. Exactly where they do it is often of minor importance. However, this is not always true because certain types of recreation require terrain and resources of particular qualities.

In the United States there is a total of 3,615,211 square miles of land and water.

> We have become great in a material sense because of the lavish use of our resources, and we have just reason to be proud of our growth. But the time has come to inquire seriously what will happen when our forests are gone, when the coal, the iron, the oil, and the gas are exhausted, when the soils have been still further impoverished and washed into the streams, polluting the rivers, denuding the fields, and obstructing navigation.
> — Theodore Roosevelt, 1908

Just what portion of this is suitable for outdoor recreation of one kind or another is difficult to determine. But a good portion of it has some recreation value in its present state, and much of it could be improved to have more recreational value than at present. Trees and grass can be grown, playfields can be laid out, and pools and lakes created on very ordinary kinds of land. Such improvements can add greatly to the recreation potential of any area. Also, fish and game can be planted and scenic areas developed, within limitations.

A somewhat intelligent appraisal of the supply of our nation's outdoor-recreation resources can be made from the classification of user-oriented, intermediate, and resource-based recreation areas. As explained earlier, the *user-oriented* areas are those improved areas that are immediately accessible to the users, such as city and county parks and playfields. *Resource-based* areas are those areas with particular natural outdoor qualities, commonly described as the "great outdoors." Included in this category are national parks and national forests. The areas in between these two extremes — state parks and state forests — are labeled *intermediate areas*. Of course, there are overlaps: some of the larger and more wild state parks, such as Custer State Park in South Dakota, would fit better into the resource-based category, while some other state parks are very similar to city and county parks and would be categorized as user-oriented. But, for the most part, the three types of areas have quite distinct qualities in terms of size, use, and degree of artificial improvements.

User-oriented Areas

The National Recreation and Park Association estimates that in 1976 there were approximately 1.8 million acres of city and county parks and playfields in the United States. These acres comprise most of our user-oriented outdoor-recreation public areas. According to the standards recommended by that Association and agreed upon by many park and recreation experts, there should currently be about a half million additional acres of such areas. This means that we are already well behind in meeting the needs of the public as interpreted by the recreation and park professionals. Based on present and predicted trends in population and outdoor recreation participation, it is calculated that a minimum of 1.5 million acres of user-oriented recreation areas ought to be added by the year 2000, bringing the total to 3.3 million acres. Clawson[1] goes so far as to predict that by the year 2000, 5 million acres of this type of recreation land will be needed. We now have 1.8 million

[1]Marion Clawson, *Land and Water for Recreation*, Rand McNally & Co., Chicago, 1963, p. 67.

A multiple use user-oriented area.

acres, and during recent years that land has been increased by about 30 thousand acres per year. It is clear that unless a great increase in the rate of acquisition is made in the near future, the needs of the people will not be met. In fact, assuming that trends toward increased leisure and increased urbanization continue, by the year 2000 the situation with regard to user-oriented areas could be critical.

One of the encouraging things about user-oriented areas is that the potential supply is almost unlimited because users do not require land with any hard-to-find features. Practically any piece of real estate can be developed into a desirable user-oriented recreation area. But, whether sufficient areas will be developed where the people need them, before the needed land is committed to other permanent use, is the serious question. For additional information about the supply of user-oriented areas, refer to Chapter 4.

Intermediate Areas

In this category there are currently about 3400 state parks in the United States, comprising over 8 million acres. Also there are several million acres of state forests and an estimated 4.8 million acres of federally owned reservoirs and other resources that fall into the intermediate category. Adding to these a few city and county parks and forests which are intermediate in nature, and privately owned intermediate areas available for public use, it is estimated that this type now extends over 27 million acres.

Even though some parts of the country have an adequate supply of intermediate areas for the present, other parts, particularly the Eastern Seaboard, are already critically deficient in this respect. An additional 5 million acres of these areas could be justified at the present time to fully meet public demands. Experts tend to agree that by the year 2000 an additional 3.5 million acres of intermediate areas will not be in excess of public needs.

Although beauty and other natural characteristics are desirable, popular intermediate areas can be created on land and water that are rather common in type, by making some simple and limited improvements. Often the construction of a boat-launching ramp on a lake, an access road into a scenic area, or picnic and camp facilities in desirable locations can greatly enhance the usefulness of potential intermediate areas. Such areas can often be developed from land that has low value for agriculture, forestry, or industry. Because there is so much flexibility in location of intermediate areas, the cost of acquisition per acre can usually be kept within reason. If the public officials responsible for providing such areas act prudently and with sufficient dispatch, intermediate areas can be provided to adequately meet future needs. But early planning and action are required. Public officials must keep ahead of the rapidly increasing demand for intermediate areas.

For more information about the supply of specific kinds of intermediate areas, such as state parks or state forests, refer to Chapter 6. For information about federal reservoirs, refer to Chapter 7.

Most state parks, such as this one in Wisconsin, are classified as intermediate areas.

> Beyond brick and mortar, away from the sound of cities ... over the hills to God's country ... where health and happiness take root ... and where nature quickens physical, mental and spiritual guidance ...
>
> — John P. Saylor

Resource-based Areas

Resource-based areas provide unique kinds of recreational opportunities not available in other settings. These great-outdoor areas are where people experiment with nature in its unmodified state, where they find and enjoy the country not molded by human influence, still in the condition in which nature developed it. Generally, resource-based areas are relatively remote. Therefore, most people visit these areas less frequently. Yet, in terms of total number of visits, certain resource-based areas (national parks, for example) are receiving very heavy use, and the trend is strongly toward using them more. Lack of time and money still keep many people from traveling to distant natural areas, but the trends toward increased leisure time, more income, and greater mobility point strongly toward a great escalation in the use of these areas. Most outdoor recreation experts agree that these areas will increase proportionately faster than either of the other two types.

In terms of total acres, the supply of resource-based areas seems sufficient. We have about 187 million acres of national forests, slightly less than one acre per citizen, 31 million acres in our national park system, and many millions of additional acres in the form of reservoirs, wildlife refuges, and public domain. There is a total of more than 250 million acres of federally owned land potentially available for resource-based recreation. In addition to the federally owned land, considerable state land falls into this category, and in certain sections of the country a large amount of privately owned land is accessible to the public on a limited basis and under certain conditions.

Of course, all of the resource-based land is not high in recreation potential. For example, a majority of the public domain has very limited potential because most of it is unattractive and unproductive wasteland. Only a portion of our national forests has high recreation potential. Of the 187 million acres in the national forest reserve, the Forest Service has identified about 16 million acres for outdoor recreation, of which about 80 thousand acres are improved camp and picnic sites and the rest unimproved wilderness. The remaining 171 million acres of national forests are used for only certain kinds of recreation on a very limited basis. The total amount of federally owned land now identified as primarily for recreation exceeds 40 million acres. This is a sizable amount of land, about one-fifth acre per U.S. citizen.

Despite the large number of total acres of resource-based land and the rather large amount of this land with high potential for recreation, there are still some serious problems with regard to resource-based recreation areas. Among the more difficult are the following:

1. Prospects for increasing the present total acreage are decidedly limited because most of the resource-based land of high recreation potential is already in public ownership and at present under heavy use. The supply of land in its natural

Even before there was a single resort there was an America worth seeing. Resource-based area.

state is simply not going to increase. In fact, it will steadily diminish as people continue to domesticate more of it. No matter how hard we try it is not conceivable that more than a few million acres can be added to our present supply of publicly owned resource-based recreation land.

2. Most of the highest quality resource-based areas are already under heavy recreation use. Many such areas have been established as part of the national park system or as forest recreation areas or wilderness areas. As additional areas are needed to meet the increased demand, people will of necessity have to use areas that they had previously considered second-rate. The first-rate areas can accommodate only a certain amount of human traffic and still remain first-rate. As these areas become saturated, people will simply have to resort to second-, then third-, then fourth-choice areas.

3. As high quality resource-based areas become more crowded, they will need to be placed under more severe use restrictions. This means that the users will have to adjust to increased regimentation, shorter visits, and less privacy. The adjustment will be difficult for many people.

4. People will need to create some new kinds of activities to substitute for some of the more traditional ones that will not be able to persist. For example, the supply of game and fish will not continue to meet the needs of all those who will want to hunt and fish. In most parts of the nation severe restrictions on these activities are already in effect. The same restrictions will follow in other regions where the supply is not yet under great pressure. Similar trends will follow in such activities as boating, camping, and even sightseeing in the more scenic areas.

The face and character of our country are determined by what we do with America and its resources...

— Thomas Jefferson

In order to meet the resource-based recreation needs of the people in the near and long-range future, public officials will need to continue to acquire desirable resource-based areas at every opportunity, and they will need to develop these areas in such a way as to accommodate as many people as possible without destroying the character of the areas. In this respect a serious problem will be to determine priorities of use and to resolve conflicts of interests where the land is under heavy demand for various uses.

While resource-based recreation areas will receive the greatest proportional increase in future demand, they are the areas that are most likely to suffer from overcrowding, because their unique natural qualities which draw people to them are easily destroyed.

While too much use destroys the physical features of a natural area it destroys at the same time the intellectual and emotional experiences that people seek. The serenity, the sense of being close to nature, and the scenic beauty can all quickly vanish in the face of extensive roads, trodden vegetation, and the bustle of large numbers of people. In the past outdoor-recreation enthusiasts have jealously guarded against commercial exploitation of high-potential recreation areas by interests such as mining, agriculture, etc. But in the future the greatest threat to these areas will come from overuse by recreationists themselves. For more information about the supply of resource-based areas refer to Chapters 5 and 6.

Distribution of the Supply

The extent of present and future outdoor-recreation areas is only one important aspect of supply. Of equal importance is the distribution of the supply in relation to the distribution of people. Actually, the distribution of user-oriented areas corresponds rather well with the population. The amount of such areas per capita varies very little from one general region to another. However, there is great variation among individual cities and counties within regions. Typically, the more sparsely populated areas, such as the Rocky Mountain states and the Great Plains region, have less user-oriented acreage per capita than the most densely populated regions.

Intermediate areas correspond less to population distribution than user-oriented areas, yet in a general sense the intermediate areas are located close to the population. For example, the heavily populated states have the most extensive state park and state forest systems. New York and California are good examples. Heavily populated states tend to have more water areas that are developed for recreational use. For the most part, intermediate areas are concentrated in the general location where the population is concentrated. But there are some obvious exceptions to this.

The distribution of most resource-based land is very poor. That is to say, most of the choice areas are not near the people. Let's review some of the important facts in regard to this matter.

1. More than 80 percent of the federally owned resource-based land is in the western states, where only 16 percent of the people live. People in these states have come to depend on the use of federal land to the extent that they have neglected the development of user-oriented and intermediate areas.

2. The majority of our large cities are in the four great population centers of our

nation: the Eastern Seaboard, the Great Lakes region, the Gulf area, and the Pacific Coast. Of these regions the Pacific Coast is the only one that has anywhere near its share of publicly owned resource-based areas. The other three regions are practically void of any large tracts of such land. This means that, to a large segment of those living in big cities, resource-based areas are out of convenient reach.

3. The trend in population is slightly westward but is still not away from the four great population centers. The population increase will continue to be more rapid on the Pacific Coast and in the midwest regions, but the trend will continue toward further urbanization of all the highly populated areas. This means that those who have much in the way of resource-based areas will continue to have much, although less than previously, while in the future those who have little will have even less.

The distribution of outdoor-recreation land has great significance for present and future planning. It means that the people in the areas of heavy population and little resource-based land must recognize that state, county, and city governments, in cooperation with private landowners, must carry the burden of providing close-to-home recreation areas for a rapidly increasing population, while at the same time the people who live in areas of less population, where there is an abundance of federally owned land, must assume more responsibility for the development of user-oriented and intermediate areas to supplement federal land. This will be very important, because in the future greatly increased numbers of people will be able to travel from cities to the great outdoors. It will therefore be less available to those who live close by and who have tended to claim rights to it.

Spotlight on Certain Resources

Certain kinds of outdoor recreation resources are receiving an unusual amount of attention on a national scale. In connection with some of the resources much is being accomplished toward providing better recreation opportunities.

Recreation Trails

Hiking trails can provide the entire family with the most economical and perhaps the most varied outdoor recreation experience. Thus it is fortunate that a national trails system has already been initiated (see National Trails System Act of 1968 in Chapter 5). In addition to the trails which will be included in the national system, there seems to be a strong move to develop other trails for hiking and bicycling at local levels. The national trails system will include *national scenic trails, national recreation trails,* and *connecting trails.*

Two great trails have already been established: the world-famous Appalachian Trail, extending 2000 miles across the East, and the more rugged Pacific Crest Trail, which extends approximately 2300 miles in a north-south direction near the West Coast. The Appalachian Trail is for foot traffic only, whereas the Pacific Crest Trail is for both foot hikers and horseback riders. No motor vehicles are permitted.

Once man can no longer walk among beauty and wonder at nature, his character, his spirit, and his happiness will wither and die.

It seems probable that the next two scenic trails to receive consideration by Congress will be the Potomac Heritage Trail and the Continental Divide Trail. Studies indicate that both of these routes are of national significance. The Potomac Heritage Trail would follow the banks of that history-rich river for 825 miles beginning at its headwaters in the mountains of Pennsylvania and West Virginia and ending at Chesapeake Bay. No other trail in America offers such a concentrated scenic, cultural, natural, and historic assortment. The Continental Divide Trail would stretch for over 3000 miles through the grandeur of the Rocky Mountains from the Canadian Border to Silver City, New Mexico. It would provide a wide range of both wilderness and western history experiences.

Twelve other potential scenic or history trails which played important roles in shaping the life of this country are as follows: *Chisholm Trail* — over which the herds of longhorns moved from the range of Southern Texas to shipping points in Kansas; *Lewis and Clark Trail* — which extends from St. Louis, Missouri, to the mouth of the Columbia River at the Pacific Coast; *Natchez Trace* — first used by Indians, then trappers and traders, it became the main route between Nashville, Tennessee, and Natchez on the lower Mississippi River; *North Country Trail* — which extends from the Appalachians in Vermont through the Northern states to the Lewis and Clark Trail in South Dakota; *Santa Fe Trail* — the old wagon route between Independence, Missouri, and Santa Fe, New Mexico; *Oregon Trail* — which is the old pioneer route from Independence, Missouri, to Portland, Oregon; *Long Trail* — which extends from Massachusetts through Vermont and into Canada; *Mormon Trail* — which was the route of exodus from Nauvoo, Illinois, to Salt Lake City, Utah.

In addition to the national scenic trails, national recreation trails are beginning to take hold in and around metropolitan areas. The possibilities for such trails are almost endless if we use our imagination and plan ahead. The goal should be hundreds of miles of recreation trails in and around each major city. It is intended that the recreational trails are to be planned by local and state government officials. Such trails which meet the standards set forth for national recreation trails will be eligible for federal cost-sharing from the Land and Water Conservation Fund.

The National Trails System Act of 1968 and other guidelines which have been established at state and local levels for the construction of trails provide only a framework. The framework must be filled by federal, state, and local planners, with much help from recreation- and conservation-minded citizens.

Rivers

Of the 3 million miles of rivers and tributaries in the United States which pour water into the sea, the majority of them have been harnessed in some way for flood control, navigation, hydroelectric power, municipal and industrial water supplies, and irrigation. Cities, factories, and homes have been built on their banks and in many cases they have become dumping grounds for used and unwanted materials. Water use projects have progressed to such a point that there are only a few stretches of the major rivers where the water runs free, unmolested by human development.

Is it possible to have technological progress and also have clean beaches and rivers, great stretches of natural beauty and places where man can go to find the

> All the rivers run into the sea, yet the sea is not full; unto the place from whence the rivers come, thither they return again.
>
> — Ecclesiastes 1:7

silence and privacy he is unable to find in our increasingly urbanized daily life? We must believe that it is possible and work toward continued realization of such condition.

Fortunately there are still some rivers which flow wild and free, largely unspoiled by human handiwork. To help protect some of these stretches of rivers the Wild and Scenic Rivers Act (PL 90-542) was passed in 1968. (For a description of the Act, refer to Chapter 5.)

The Act established the basic principle that certain rivers of the nation should be selected which, with their immediate environments, possess outstanding scenic, recreational, geological, fish and wildlife, historical, cultural, and other similar values, and that these stretches of rivers should be preserved in a free-flowing condition, and protected for the benefit and the enjoyment of present and future generations. In the initial Act (as amended) 10 rivers or sections of rivers have been set aside, and 27 others have been identified for study and possible inclusion in the national system. Those rivers included in the system will be classified and managed under one of the following headings: *wild river, scenic river, recreational river.*

Wild rivers are unpolluted rivers or segments that are free of impoundments, generally inaccessible except by trail, and have essentially primitive shorelines and watersheds. They are vestiges of primitive America. *Scenic rivers* are rivers or segments that are free of impoundments, are accessible in places by roads, but still have shorelines and watersheds that are largely undeveloped and primitive. *Recreational rivers* are rivers or segments that have undergone impoundment or diversion in the past, are readily accessible by road, and have some development along the shorelines.

In addition to including certain rivers into the national system, the federal government encourages state participation by providing that upon request of the state Governor, rivers that have been designated by the state legislature as wild, scenic, or recreational may be protected as part of the national system. In addition, the national Act provides for technical assistance, advice, and encouragement to the states and their political subdivisions and to private organizations in their efforts to identify and establish state and local wild, scenic, and recreational river areas.

State comprehensive outdoor-recreation plans, which are required under the Land and Water Conservation Fund program, consider the need for preserving segments of free-flowing rivers. Several such plans have detailed proposals for the development of state scenic river systems. Financial assistance under the Land and Water Conservation Fund is available on a 50:50 matching basis to plan, acquire, and develop state and local wild, scenic, and recreational river areas. The Federal Bureau of Outdoor Recreation has been specifically designated to provide assistance and coordinate state and local efforts to maintain and enhance free-flowing rivers. State and local rivers which deserve consideration should be brought to the attention of the state outdoor recreation liaison officer.

Beaches

One of the great outdoor-recreation catastrophes of America is described in the fact that the great majority of the beaches are now in private ownership and lost to public use forever. At this point in time this fact seems relatively unimportant except in the heavily populated areas of the east and west coasts. But as the population along the coastlines continues to grow the problem of insufficient public-owned beachland will become greatly magnified. It will be financially prohibitive to reclaim all of the beachland needed for public use in the future. In view of the present circumstance it is imperative that all of the beachland presently in public ownership remain so, and that public agencies be ever watchful for opportunities to acquire additional beach space. Most of the beachland in private ownership serves a very meager purpose in terms of user-hour use.

Artificial Lakes

There are thousands of artificial lakes in the United States and most of them offer some potential for recreation. Few of the larger ones have come into existence without a struggle.

The most notable of the early projects were the lakes constructed under the Tennessee Valley Authority in the 1930s. Many Americans considered that project a curse rather than a blessing. But now it is apparent that with 10 thousand miles of shoreline and over 60 million visitors annually the TVA project is a great recreational asset.

Among the most vocal opponents of artificial lakes have been public officials deploring the loss of land from the tax rolls. But for these people time and experience have brought happy surprises in the profitable recreation industry which has flourished in the areas where lakes have been developed.

The majority of the large lakes have been constructed by the U.S. Army Corps of Engineers, the Bureau of Reclamation, or by some agency under the license of the Federal Power Commission. The federal government now requires the Corps of Engineers and the Bureau of Reclamation to prepare a complete recreation development plan for all of their projects. The Federal Power Commission now requires a plan for public recreation use of lands and waters to be filed as part of all applications for licenses for hydroelectric power projects. The Commission requires that the plan show location of the areas and access roads proposed for camping, picnicking, swimming, boat launching, and sanitary facilities. Thus, virtually every new artificial lake of any size can be expected to give the American people a bonus in the form of well-planned outdoor-recreation opportunities.

It should be recognized that to some extent and in some places artificial lakes are in conflict with the wild and scenic rivers concept and in many situations the choice is very difficult. However, it is important to know that by giving up one form of recreation resource, another form might be gained and the gain might be greater

The health of the eye demands a horizon.

—Ralph Waldo Emerson

than the loss. In this regard each proposed project must be considered on its own merits.

Wilderness Areas

The Wilderness Act, passed in 1964, gave legal protection to 14 million acres of Forest Service land which had already been classified as wilderness and 22 million acres of National Park land. Since that time numerous additional areas have been added to the National Wilderness System. There are many Americans who think that the preservationists have moved too far and too fast toward promoting an extensive wilderness system. But, there are others who think that we still lag far behind in this regard and that 20 to 30 years from now will prove lack of insight and foresight by those who resist the movement.

Actually, the wilderness concept among influential Americans is not new, even though the establishment of a National Wilderness System is of recent origin. Among the early promoters of the modern wilderness idea were Henry Thoreau, Theodore Roosevelt, John Muir, and Aldo Leopold. Based on their observations of a changing civilization due to the Industrial Revolution, these men set the stage for the development of a national wilderness system.

Wilderness as a recreational resource has always been and probably always will be highly controversial, primarily because of its very low density use. The very nature of wilderness dictates that many acres are required for each user. Advocates of wilderness justify it on the basis that it provides a unique kind of recreational experience which is necessary to the sanity of at least a certain segment of the population, and further that it is good for everyone, even those who do not have direct contact with it but have only indirect experiences.

There is no doubt that in the future the wilderness concept will be challenged

To each his own time and his own place.

repeatedly by people who consider it impractical in the face of a rapidly increasing population. There is no question that the concept will need to be modified from time to time and in connection with certain areas as the increased number of people demand more multiple uses of the available land areas. In the meantime the wilderness areas will serve their purpose to the small percentage of the population who are able to spend time there and they will be preserved in their present state for whatever uses the future generations decide are best.

National Parks

The National Park System of the United States (discussed rather thoroughly in Chapter 5) is unique in the history of humankind. Even though certain other countries now have national parks, they are modeled after the National Park System of the United States and they succeeded the origin of our system. The establishment of the first national park in America was a very bold move. It required much groundwork, a certain breed of human being, and unique circumstances.

The National Park System was established with the idea that certain blocks of land should be set aside and maintained in their original conditions, that they should be preserved in their natural states for all time to come. This purist philosophy has already deteriorated to some extent due to the pressures of the masses of people who now utilize national parks. The evolution of change relative to the underlying philosophy and the uses made of these areas is currently underway and it will undoubtedly continue. As a result, certain national parks are operated differently and serve different purposes than were originally intended, and in the future the uses of national park areas will deviate even more from the original intent. Some of the management procedures and policies which were desirable and feasible 50 years ago are no longer practicable, and many of the policies and practices governing the use of national parks at the present time will not be feasible 20 years from now. Certain changes are inevitable in order to accommodate the ever increasing demands of the public.

State Parks

State parks are vital to our times. They can and will play an increasingly important role in cushioning the future inadequacy of the national park system to meet the increasing needs and demands of the public. A well-developed state park system affords people in all geographic areas of the state convenient opportunities to visit attractive natural areas of an intermediary type.

Ordinarily state parks are less remote and less in the natural state than national parks but they are considerably more primitive and natural than municipal parks. Therefore they serve an excellent purpose in affording large numbers of people convenient opportunities to be in touch with nature rather frequently. Most states will find it necessary to place additional emphasis on the development of state park systems, and to be unusually creative and innovative in planning state parks to meet the real needs and interests of the public. These parks will have to be designed to handle large volumes of people and still give them the feeling that they are in touch with nature. The state park movement will be one of the most challenging aspects of outdoor-recreation resource development in the future.

Chapter 11 Economic Impact of Outdoor Recreation

Even though recreation is for the people's enjoyment, its values are not limited to that alone. It also has great economic significance, among other values.

As early as 1968 the Merrill, Lynch brokerage firm, one of America's largest, announced that the annual leisure time market was approaching the $150 billion mark. Further, the firm estimated that by 1980 the leisure market might reach $250 million annually. Merrill, Lynch also stated that in terms of stock values the leisure time market would outperform the improvement of the economy in general.[1]

In 1969 the *U.S. News & World Report* described the leisure market as the fastest growing phase of business in America. It was stated in the article that "affluent Americans with more time on their hands, and money to spend than ever before, have boomed leisure into one of America's biggest businesses. The figure tops the current annual outlay for National Defense."[2]

In 1972 the same magazine said this about the leisure time market: "It is more than the outlay for construction of new homes, it surpasses the total of corporate profits, it is far larger than the aggregate income of the country's exports, and

[1]"Leisure Investment Opportunity in a $150 Billion Market," Securities Research Division, Merrill, Lynch, Pearce, Fenner & Smith, New York, 1968, p. 4.
[2]*U.S. News & World Report*, September 15, 1969, p. 36.

estimates are that the dollar value of leisure time expenditures will more than double during the decade of the 1970s."[3] In 1972 Peter Henle provided information which generally substantiates the claims made by Merrill, Lynch and *U.S. News & World Report.*[4]

The largest items in the retail leisure market are boats, camping vehicles, motor bikes, and ski equipment. The surge to the great outdoors has placed sales of vacation vehicles on a skyrocket course. Travel trailers, motor homes, truck campers, and camping trailers gross over $1.3 billion annually. According to the Recreation Vehicle Institute, the total of such units in service today is over 3 million. Sales in 1976 exceeded 185,000 units. Another emerging giant is the snowmobile. Industrial officials predict that more than 1.2 million snowmobiles are currently in use in the United States and Canada. Snowmobile sales for 1976 approached 400,000 with a total retail value of $480 million.

Snow skiers, now an estimated 4.6 million in number and increasing at the rate of 15 percent annually, rank as lavish spenders. They plunk down approximately $980 million each season getting to the ski slopes and for equipment, lodging, lift passes, and entertainment costs.

Highly popular with an increasing number of Americans is pleasure boating. Americans own more than 10 million boats which tie up at 5650 marinas and docks across the nation. There are over 15 million golfers in the United States who play regularly on about 10,000 golf courses. Tennis is another sport which is enjoying an upsurge, in fact it is currently American's fastest growing sport. Over 10 million Americans play tennis, and they spend about $40 million annually on rackets, balls and accessories. Other millions of fishermen, hunters, archers, mountain climbers, surfers, skin divers, etc., contribute to the burgeoning total.

What it all adds up to is an astonishing picture of America playing in the great outdoors. Behind the scenes serving the ever increasing demands are the muscle and sinew of American industry, and this causes recreation to be strongly interwoven into practically all of the various aspects of the nation's economic system.

Grand Teton National Park in Teton County, Wyoming, was enlarged in 1950. Between 1950 and 1958, the total assessed valuation in the county rose from $4.7 million to $8.2 million; sales and tax receipts rose from $76,457 to $153,706; bank deposits about doubled. Perhaps all of this could not be attributed to the enlarged operation of the park, but certainly the park accounted for much of the increases.

Economists calculated that, in 1975, some 3.6 million visitors to the great Smoky National Park spent over $47 million within a 30-mile radius.

In five counties of Oklahoma, several artificial lakes attract campers and fishermen. The percentage of increase in sales taxes for those five counties was almost double that for the rest of the state during the two years following completion of the lakes.

In 1975, the average per capita expenditure of some 36 million hunters and fishermen in the U.S. was $150 on items directly connected with the sport itself. This resulted in expenditures of well over $5 billion.

[3]*U.S. News & World Report*, April 17, 1972, p. 42.
[4]Peter Henle, "Recent Growth of Paid Leisure for U.S. Workers," *Monthly Labor Review*, March 1972, p. 256.

Many other examples of the economic impact of outdoor recreation could be cited if necessary. But the fact is clear that expenditure in connection with recreation activities is a factor of the first importance in the structure and growth of the American economy.

It is estimated that *recreation activities* account for a $50-60 billion expenditure per year of the total leisure time market. This amount represents a little over 6 percent of the population's income, and that seems to be a conservative estimate. Much of this large expenditure, say about one-half, is for outdoor recreation. This expenditure is represented in the buying of both goods and services in skiing, boating, hunting, fishing, camping, mountain climbing, sightseeing, outdoor photography, and many other activities done in the out-of-doors.

The purchase of recreation goods and services filters all the way through our complicated economic system, causing the total effect to be greater than the amount of the direct expenditure. For example, a recreationist buys a boat from a boat distributor, and that purchase represents a direct expenditure of $3000. To know the impact of that purchase, one must recognize that the boat was made by a manufacturer. The manufacturer purchased certain parts and products from other manufacturers, who in turn purchased certain raw materials which had originally to be taken from the earth. When finally completed, the boat represents $3000 worth of materials and labor, and the economic effects of the materials and labor spread into various aspects of the total economy.

Recreation is also used as a means of upgrading economically disadvantaged rural areas throughout the United States. With assistance from government, many rural landowners have converted their properties into recreational resources — thus attracting increased numbers of visitors to their regions and adding generally to the local economy.

One of the ways in which Indian tribes have improved their economies is through the development of recreation attractions. As an example, when the $110-million Kinzua dam and reservoir was planned for western Pennsylvania, the Bureau of

Recreation is the fourth largest and fastest growing industry in the U.S.

Indian Affairs assisted the Seneca tribe, which was forced to give up much of its property, in developing a huge new tourist program, including shops, lodges, museums, an Indian village, a motel, a 100-boat marina, and an outdoor amphitheater and indoor theater for Indian ceremonials and folklore festivals. It was estimated that this new development would draw several hundred thousand tourists each year. Numerous other such projects have been developed or are presently being developed by other Indian tribes.

Effects of a Particular Outdoor Recreation Development

In order to get further insight into the nature of the economic impact of outdoor recreation, the whole topic can be divided into phases and each phase can be discussed. Let's suppose that a major outdoor recreation attraction is developed, such as a large reservoir, a national recreation area, or a national park.

Land Prices

The fact that an area has natural features which are attractive to people causes the land in that area to be under greater demand than usual. Some people may want to build vacation homes near the recreation attraction. Others will want to build commercial establishments, and some may want to own land for speculative purposes. At any rate, the simple law of supply and demand will cause land prices to escalate and the real estate business will probably boom. The extent to which the escalation

Snowmobiling has enabled large numbers of people to explore the backcountry in winter. Americans and Canadians own over 2 million of these machines.

Power boating and water skiing have become very popular, and these sports involve large expenditures.

occurs will depend mostly upon the ratio of supply and demand of the land as interpreted by the owners and the potential buyers. In some cases land near recreation developments skyrockets while in other cases the escalation is gradual. In any case, those who own land near significant recreation attractions stand to gain as a result of the attraction.

Home Site Development

People tend to want vacation homes and recreation cabins near attractive outdoor-recreation developments. This is one of the factors that stimulates real estate transactions. It also spurs local construction activities and creates a demand for construction materials. In turn, the property values are increased, and this enlarges the tax base in the local county.

Purchase of Goods by Visitors

People coming in large numbers to the area for recreation purchase food, gasoline, clothing, recreation equipment, and supplies, and a host of other goods. Often they stay overnight and require accommodations. It is estimated that on the average tourists in the United States spend about $18 per person per day. At any particular area the average expenditure per day per visitor may be either more or less than that amount, depending on the nature of the area, the economic class of people it attracts, and the goods and services available to the visitors. At any rate, the purchase of goods and services by visitors can be and often is a real boon to the business establishments near outdoor recreation complexes.

More Jobs

The fact that more people visit the area means that more people are employed to provide goods and services to the visitors. Also, additional jobs are created in real estate and construction. In many cases the outdoor-recreation operation itself provides new opportunities for employment. At a national park, for example, a number of people are employed to administer and maintain the park. Often guides and outfitters are under demand to provide tours and excursions.

Effects on Nearby Communities

While boat docks, motels, restaurants, campgrounds, picnic sites, access roads, and the like are being constructed in the recreation area, nearby towns undergo a basic shift in economic, and sometimes in social and political, structure. Broadly speaking, the shift is away from an economy devoted to serving only needs of local residents to one serving the needs of visitors, many of whom have an urban point of view and expect goods and services equal to urban standards. Because local citizens usually want to put their best foot forward for their visitors, they become more conscious of unpaved streets, sidewalks in poor repair, dingy stores, and the absence of good restaurants, and good motels. Often newcomers arrive and start new enterprises or improve old ones. Demands for civic improvements are heard. Long-time community leaders, if they fail to lead the new forces, may find their positions eroded. Of course, the extent to which all of this actually happens is dependent upon, first, the nature and extent of the recreation development, and, second, the ability of the nearby communities to accommodate the needs of the visitors.

Application of Economics to the Total Recreation Experience

As explained in Chapter 1, the total outdoor-recreation experience includes four significant phases: anticipation, preparation, direct experience, and recollection. Each of the phases has its own economic impact, although the impact is nowhere nearly equal for all phases. The second and third phases have the greatest economic significance.

During the *anticipation phase* a person may purchase printed material to gather information about the forthcoming experience and may even do some traveling in an effort to gain desired information on which to formulate future plans. But for the most part the anticipation phase involves little expenditure.

The *preparation phase* typically ranks second in terms of economic impact. During this phase a person may make rather large expenditures for equipment and supplies. For example, a hunting or a fishing trip requires replenishment of equipment. If the trip involves camping, then camping equipment and supplies are needed. Some people purchase boats, canoes, skis, campers, and other items of major expense in preparation for an outdoor-recreation experience.

The *direct experience* extends from the time one leaves the point of departure until one returns. This involves the total expense of the purchase of goods and services during the time of the experience, including travel, food, lodging, equipment, special services, etc. This phase is typically the one involving the greatest expenditure.

The *recollection phase* is relatively insignificant in terms of economic impact but does have some relevance. Film may be developed and one may be prompted to purchase a projector for the showing of the film. Trophies taken in hunting and fishing may be mounted, and various other expenses may be incurred in one's effort to keep alive the memories of the experience.

Economic Impact of Northern
New England Vacation Homes
A Case Study

The Bureau of Outdoor Recreation conducted a study to determine the extent to which occupants of vacation homes in Northern New England (including Maine and parts of Vermont and New Hampshire) participate in outdoor recreation and the amounts they spend in connection with their vacation homes. Following are a few pertinent facts resulting from the study:

1. More than 50 percent of the vacation homes are located on less than one acre of land, but because some of them are in large estates the mean acreage is 16.4 acres.
2. The real value of the homes and the property on which they are located ranges from a few hundred dollars to more than $200,000. The average value is approximately $13,000.
3. On the average, the family income of vacation homeowners is in excess of $12,000 per year.
4. Only 37 percent of the homeowners reside in the Northern New England states. The other 63 percent live in other regions of the Eastern United States.

The Bureau of Outdoor Recreation calculated that there were 28,140 vacation homes in the Northern New England areas included in the study. Further, it was calculated that on the average each homeowner spent $2425 each year locally and $180 elsewhere within the region. If these calculations are correct, then approximately $425 million is spent each year by the occupants of the vacation homes in Northern New England in connection with their use.

It has been estimated by economists that $1000 of direct expenditure by out-of-the-region vacation visitors would add 1.55 times that amount to the region's total economy. This would mean that the total economic impact of the vacation homes in Northern New England is about $658 million annually (1.55 times $425 million of direct expenditures).

Economic Impact of Texoma Reservoir Project
A Case Study

Texoma reservoir, an artificial lake on the Texas-Oklahoma border, was developed in 1945 by the Corps of Engineers primarily for the purposes of flood control and power production. Almost immediately it became a major recreation attraction, which now draws over 10 million visitors per year. Two years after its completion (1947) 2 million people visited the lake. Five years later (1952) the annual visits were 4 million. By 1957 annual attendance had reached 8 million. Now between 10 and 15 million recreationists visit the reservoir each year.

The counties surrounding the lake were historically capital poor. In such cases local leaders usually consider lack of capital to be a prime reason for their past difficulties. But the underlying problem might also be seen as a lack of opportunity for capital to be profitably employed. It might be argued that, if the right combination of natural resources and human talent had been present, capital would have been forthcoming.

The completion of a large reservoir or other significant recreation attraction illustrates the point. A reservoir provides a new opportunity for capital to be profitably used in developing the recreation business, and in closely associated activities. The necessary capital appears, almost all of it from sources outside the communities themselves, and the communities begin the process of growth which local leaders had so long sought from other sources.

There are many ways in which a body of water attracts outside dollars. Three are of particular significance: (a) it attracts visitors who spend large sums at lakeshore resorts; (b) it induces private investors and government agencies to invest money in overnight accommodations for visitors; (c) it attracts newcomers who construct homes and cabins for themselves on or near the shoreline.

In the five counties touching Texoma, direct expenditures by visitors now exceed $34 million annually. Visitor expenditure, it should be kept in mind, is a recurring annual occurrence. It is the chief energizer in the quickening economic pace of the communities involved. Around Texoma, investments in overnight accommodations and other visitor-related construction have further positive impact on the economy.

Economic Impact of the Pearl River Project
A Case Study

One of the best case studies of property escalation is provided in a Bureau of Outdoor Recreation publication entitled Recreation Land Price Escalation. It describes a well-documented situation in the Pearl River Reservoir area near Jackson, Mississippi. A detailed analysis was made of 304 sales involving over 25,000 acres of land adjacent to or within close access to the planned reservoir project. An analysis was also made for the same period of 101 sales transactions covering more than 11,000 acres in a comparable area not influenced by the project, and which served as a control for the study (a standard for comparison). The average price paid per acre of land adjacent to the project showed an average annual increase of slightly less than 9 percent prior to announcement of the project. After the project was announced, prices increased 165 percent the first year, 191 percent the second year, 216 percent the third year, 236 percent the fourth year, and 258 percent the fifth year. The price per acre of the control area for the same period of time continued to increase between 8 to 10 percent per year, the same as it had done during the few years previous.

More Parks in Cities Might Actually Save Money

There is almost always some strong resistance to using property to develop park and recreation areas because public ownership takes the land off the tax roll. But it is possible, according to some sources, that it could be a favor to property taxpayers to buy land and develop parks on a much larger scale than has been planned. This intriguing possibility was outlined in a series of articles in the *San Francisco Chronicle*. The articles called upon the Bay Area to save its open spaces, hillsides, and forests from economic strangulation that is sure to come if they are covered with houses. Following is an excerpt:

> The usual thought that property should not be taken off the rolls is valid only if the property returns more in taxes than it costs in services. Most subdivisions built today do not. The city comes out fairly well as far as subdivision costs go, with the property returning slightly more than it costs. But when you add in the costs of schools and community operations, a house on a 5000 to 10,000 square foot lot comes nowhere near paying for itself in property taxes. It is for this reason that some recreation planning experts say you save money by building parks, because you keep the land

from being developed as subdivisions which require continuing tax subsidies from business and industrial properties.

That's the dollars and cents part of the picture that is most obvious. There are other major, but possibly less obvious, benefits from having extensive open space around cities. For example, property values are higher and the social environment is typically better in neighborhoods where parks and open spaces are abundant than in crowded, row on row, subdivisions.

Certainly people must have homes, and the argument in favor of parks cannot be carried so far as to say that all land now surrounding the city should be made into a huge park. The important thing is to plan wisely and plan now, to set aside the parks where they should be before the land is swallowed up for subdivisions and other purposes.

Estimating the Direct Economic Value of a Park

Placing values on parks in economic terms was for a long time purely an academic exercise. For the most part there has been no practical need for establishing a price because parks are not sold at the market place. Parks have traditionally been a class of public holdings that symbolized the land's character, that imparted dignity and charm, and permitted breathing room within the city and outside cities, and would last forever.

But like practically all else in today's world, parks have lost their "eternal permanence" and by many there are attempts to evaluate them on the basis of economics. Therefore, it is of practical necessity to try to find some economic measures by which to justify the existence of at least some of the parks. This is true of state and federal parks as well as municipal parks.

Clawson and Knetsch described that the immediate value of a park can be roughly measured by surveying the users of the park and finding out how much each one would be willing to pay per use.[5] They used an example of a state park where they indicated that certain users would be willing to pay $5.00, others $4.00, and others lesser amounts. By determining the ratio of users that would pay each amount and by knowing the total number of users it can easily be calculated how much the users would be willing to pay if payment was necessary. In other words this tells how much revenue the park would probably produce if fees were charged. In one sense this could be interpreted as the immediate financial value of the park to the public. However, this procedure does not take into account related values such as the escalation of the value of adjacent property and the influence that the park has on land even farther away, say a half a mile or a mile. Neither does it take into account the general positive feeling that parks cause members of a community to have, even those who never use the parks. The fact that the parks are available and part of the total community plan seems to be a source of social satisfaction.

Another approach that is sometimes used in the case of state parks or national parks is to attempt to calculate the approximate amount of money spent within and close around the park by those who come to visit — in other words, the effect that the park has on the local commerce. This again deals with only one aspect of the value of the park, but it is important information.

[5]Marion Clawson and Jack L. Knetsch, *Economics of Outdoor Recreation*, Baltimore, The John Hopkins Press, 1966.

Certain government resource management agencies, including the Corps of Engineers and the Bureau of Reclamation, have placed estimated values on visits by fisherman, boaters, campers, etc., to calculate the economic value of the recreational characteristics of a project. This procedure provides substantial economic information, but still it is not inclusive of all of the economic values that accrue from the recreational aspects.

Because of the difficulty of arriving at accurate economic estimates, these estimates are seldom used in the settlement of priorities between parks and highways, river developments, power plants, airports, and other such economic-measurable installations.

In the final analysis it seems that the value of a park is what the governing agency thinks it is, and is willing and able to pay for it. This is essentially the same as saying that a rare work of art is worth whatever a buyer is willing to pay. It is not a very precise method of pricing, but in most cases it is the most meaningful one and the one that prevails. However, it is true that some of the procedures of making economic estimates described here might influence the amount that the governing agency is willing to pay, and how persistent the agency might be toward acquiring or holding the park in the face of pressures to do otherwise.

If present social and economic trends continue, expenditure for outdoor recreation will increase at a steady rate. It will gradually become even a greater contributor to the U.S. economy than it is now, and in many localities it will be the number one economic factor.

Chapter 12 The Struggle for a Pleasant Environment

The most important of all outdoor recreation is the kind people find in their every-day living. Whether such recreation exists depends on whether there is a proper environment. Are there convenient places for people to walk and ride bicycles? Are there attractive open spaces where nature can refresh the spirit? Are there streams and lakes for fishing, boating, and dabbling in the water? Are there wooded areas and places for picnics? Or have all of these been buried in culverts or under concrete and asphalt? Can we shape future growth so that recreation is an integral part of daily living? Can we produce a highly livable environment that incorporates the beauties of nature?

Some of our most worthy recreation is simply to experience the sight of natural beauty, or to be in a silent place separated from noise, except perhaps the tinkle of a brook or the chirp of a robin, and to breathe clean and fresh air. To a large number of Americans these seemingly common experiences have become rare. Where most of the people live, attractive natural scenery is scarce. Noise from one source or another constantly rings in the ears, and the air is not clean and fresh. The environment of many Americans has become ugly and polluted.

With respect to nature, archeologists and historians have found that civilizations pass through four stages. In the *first* stage we battle nature for our survival. We attempt to cope with nature and conquer it. In the *second* stage we cooperate with nature in an effort to become domesticated, and nature helps us to produce the goods that we need. After we have first coped with nature, then learned to cooperate **205**

> We shape our physical environment, and afterwards it shapes us.

with it and use it to our advantage, we enter the *third* stage, that of exploiting nature by overharvesting natural resources and overusing natural goods. After recognizing our error and the futility of our approach, we then enter the *fourth* stage, that of rehabilitating nature, attempting to heal the wounds we have caused. The divisions between these four stages are not clear-cut, and at a particular time a society may not be at the same stage with respect to all kinds of natural resources. With respect to many kinds of resources Americans have seemingly passed through the first and second stages, and for the most part have been in the third stage for quite some time. We are now, let us hope, entering into the fourth stage. In many respects we have overharvested and overused our natural resources, and we are still doing so. But at least some of our wiser leaders have recognized this fact and are attempting to lead us into the fourth stage, that of rehabilitating the overused resources. Extensive exploitation of natural resources results in ugliness and certain kinds of pollution which seriously detract from the lives of people.

If the historians were asked to pass final judgment on our nation at this particular juncture of history, they might well conclude that in terms of the energy of the American people, in terms of our technological skill, in terms of the scope of our science, we have reached a pinnacle of material success. Certainly in terms of wealth and what we call progress, we have achieved a level of prosperity no other society or civilization has ever achieved. But simultaneously we have failed to create an overall environment worthy of our wealth and power. We have failed to build handsome cities and to create an environment of order and dignity. Some noteworthy leaders of the world have referred to the large American cities as "catastrophes of continental proportions." As land stewards and builders of cities, we have experienced a large degree of failure, and we will continue to experience such failure unless we lay down new guidelines for growth and shake off the dead dogmas of the past.

It was roughly 350 years ago that a restless adventurous people confronted a virgin land on this continent and began to develop and master it. Out of this confrontation came what is known as our traditional, but now outdated, idea of growth — the American idea of progress. From the very beginning every act that overcame the wilderness was considered good. Subjugation meant growth and growth was next to godliness in the American scheme of things. Since Plymouth Rock, growth and expansion have been synonymous with survival and success. This gospel of growth grew inevitably out of the wilderness settlement. The virgin lands of the New World pitted humans against nature, and as long as the frontiers remained, growth entailed the overpowering of native people, and the triumph over a natural and sometimes hostile environment. For a century or more each individual or group that conquered a native, felled a forest, hacked out a road, laid out a farm, or built a fence was an authentic agent of the American advance.

The pioneers either conquered or they failed to find a foothold and disappeared from the face of the earth like a lost colony. Action was essential and raw courage counted the most. The people leveled forests, plowed up plains, rechanneled

There need to be attractive open spaces where nature can refresh the spirit.

streams, killed off species of animals, segmented the nation with fences. The illusion persisted that even the most ruinous acts were an essential part of building a nation. Growth was progress and progress was growth. That was all the people knew and all they needed to know.

At a later period in American history when this concept of growth was engrafted into our industrial revolution and the machine age, the defilement and spoilage of America really began. Whether it was mining, the cutting of timber, or the building of an industrial plant, we used the quantitative test to measure the worth of any development. It seems that every engineering effort, however ill conceived, was applauded. As a result, in a few places we built with distinction but in most places we did not. In too many cases both our cities and our countryside lack character. Not only have we failed to add but in many cases we have seriously detracted from the dignity of the environment with which we have been entrusted. In this sense we have become immoral and undeserving of the faith placed in us.

> Quality of environment, like freedom, must be protected and achieved anew by each generation.
>
> — Lawrence S. Rockefeller

The true worth of a nation, its inner greatness, lies in the quality of its life rather than its productivity or economic indices. The things that distinguish the "great society" are its orderliness, its sense of history, its intellectual climate, its meaningful tradition, the hospitality it affords the spirit, and the appeal of its overall environment. These qualities determine whether a nation has character. Certainly the United States has many of these attributes of character. But at the same time we are production oriented. We have the most automobiles and the worst junkyards. We are the most mobile people on earth and endure the most congestion. We produce the most energy and have the foulest air. Our factories pour out the most products and our rivers carry the heaviest loads of pollution of any in the world. We have the most goods to sell and the most unsightly signs to advertise them. To a large measure we have exhibited crudeness and lack of sensitivity in the planning and maintenance of our environment. We in this country possess power but lack grace. We have unprecedented prosperity but our country is unclean. We have rich cities but very few handsome ones. This dilemma presents a very practical question of whether during the future we can continue to progress but within more strictly defined guidelines which will protect our environment from further spoliation, and in fact cause it to gradually recover from the damages and injustices which we have already caused. Can we build the character into our land which it deserves but which we have thus far essentially ignored?

The Problem of Ugliness and Pollution

Americans were privileged to start their national life on virtually an unused and unspoiled continent. The country which became the United States was vast and beautiful — a landscape of mountains, valleys, and plains all drained by one of the world's most generous water systems. Here were resources of life, wealth, and enjoyment beyond measure, it seemed to our forefathers, with enough beauty to meet our needs for all time. Yet within a few generations we have fouled the streams, marred the landscape in almost every conceivable manner, built sprawling cities for convenience and not for beauty, and have generally degraded the resources that were so generously willed to us. We have become great contributors to the problem of ugliness and pollution.

Generally, we think of pollution as something we can see, and often this is the case, but there is also pollution that is apparent through senses other than vision: noise pollution and odor pollution. Pollution that contributes to *visual* ugliness is expressed in junkyards, poorly kept buildings and vacant lots, ill-placed and ill-kept sign boards, congested sections of cities, and other displeasing parts of the environment. *Noise* pollution is the presence of too much noise or unpleasant noise. The growling and honking of cars, the clatter of machines, and the constant roar of planes overhead are examples of pollution that detracts from serenity and contri-

No person has the right to neglect the environment. It is the responsibility of every citizen to protect the beauty and purity of the land, the water, and the air.

Where is this beautiful America?

butes to the discomforts of the environment. The United States is the noisiest country in the world, and for many people constant noise causes emotional stress, loss of hearing, and inefficiency. According to the National Council of Noise Abatement, noise pollution costs U.S. industry $2 million daily. *Odor* pollution is of a different type. It results from sulfur fumes and other such chemical wastes caused by industry; from smoke, gasoline, diesel exhaust, and other combustion wastes; and from sewage. Odor pollution, like other kinds of pollution, can detract greatly from the quality of life.

What is happening to America the Beautiful? This recurring question reflects rising frustrations over the nation's increasingly polluted air, dirty streets, and filthy rivers. This pollution, bad enough in itself, reflects something even worse: the dangerous illusion that industrial societies can grow bigger and bigger without regard for the eternal laws of nature.

In the polluting sense, humans are the greatest offenders of all living beings. Each year in the United States we produce 50 billion metal cans plus 30 billion bottles and jars. Many of these containers are made of materials that will last for decades, or even centuries. The average American puts out 1700 pounds of solid waste materials each year, and this rate is rising 4 percent annually. Every day New York City dumps 200 million gallons of raw sewage into the Hudson River or in the ocean adjacent to the New York Bay. Each square mile of Manhattan produces

375,000 pounds of waste per day to be incinerated, and 30 percent of the residue drifts into the air and settles on to the city.

The Mass and Energy Nimbus

Although our urban areas are no more densely populated than cities of other countries or our own cities of the past, they produce more wasteful congestion. Our crowding is basically not a matter of too many people per square mile but rather the enormous amounts of energy and material that accompany each of us. Despite all of the talk about the subject, we still underestimate the magnitude of technological advance and its implications. More than 30 years ago Buckminster Fuller calculated that the total energy generated in the United States was equal to the muscular energy that would be generated if each American had 153 slaves working for him. Today a similar calculation would indicate that each American has the equivalent of 500 slaves. These slaves enable us to increase our own mobility hundreds of times and to toss around incredible masses of materials, altering not only their location and external shapes but also their actual molecular composition. This explains a lot of environmental woes that are otherwise quite mysterious.

Unfortunately, many Americans are still unresponsive to environmental problems in terms of their own behavior. People have a way of brushing off warnings; the threatened penalties seem to lie in the remote future. But it is a dissatisfying fact that inhabitants of drab and chaotic cities or of despoiled countrysides are not free of the consequences even at the present time. They are being punished here and now by being robbed of surroundings that could contribute to a quality life. For them life is presently diminished. It loses point and relish and sense of direction when it is spent amid a haphazard squalor that nature never evolved and humankind never intended.

A good piece of geography is basic — from there on the quality of environment is a matter of human wisdom.

Jet overturns sailboat near National Airport, Washington, D.C.

The Air Pollution Problem

The sheer bulk of big cities slows the cleansing winds. At the same time, rising city heat helps to create thermal inversions (a layer of warmer air above cooler air) that can trap pollutants for days. While United States chimneys belch 70,000 tons of sulfur dioxide every day, 93 million motor vehicles add 250,000 tons of carbon monoxide (nearly 60 percent of smog) and other lethal gases. By the year 2000, about 85 percent of Americans will live in urban areas, driving twice as many automobiles as now and producing twice as much waste products as now (unless countermeasures prove to be effective).

The most alarming characteristic of air pollution is its effect on people's health. It is an established fact that air pollution is a contributing factor to the rising incidence of chronic respiratory diseases — lung cancer, emphysema, bronchitis, and asthma. A less alarming yet highly significant characteristic is its effect on our total environment. In many locations it is ruining our scenery and seriously detracting from the quality of our lives.

Records of the Federal Environmental Protection Agency show that in four days of 1948 polluted air sickened 43 percent of the population of Donora, Pennsylvania, and killed 20; in four days of 1952 it killed 4000 people in London; in 15 days of 1963 it killed 400 people in New York City. Polluted air undoubtedly kills many people in many other places, but they are not counted because the cause of death on

Our fragmented power has outrun our methods of deciding how to use it. Unless we invent means of dealing with technology's side effects, they will bury us.

— Max Ways

death certificates never reads "air pollution," and few cities analyze how many "extra" deaths they record during a siege of severe pollution.

Another way air pollution detracts from our environment is by its effect on vegetation. In practically every urban area it has reduced vegetation from petunias to mighty oaks by from 10 to 20 percent. It kills plants, blights new shoots, damages leaves enough to cut off nourishment, and produces premature old age. Dr. C. Stafford Brandt, chief of the agricultural section of the U.S. Public Health Service's Air Pollution Division, said, "From Washington to Boston and inland for a hundred miles there is not a square mile that is free from air-pollution injury. I don't see how anyone can look at our evidence and not become gravely concerned with the effect on our vegetation." Dr. Brandt went on to point out that one night of heavy industrial output killed $10,000 worth of commercially grown flowers on Staten Island, New York. Most of the pollution is more subtle. Fruit trees grown in normal city air are 10 percent smaller and produce 10 percent less fruit than trees in clean air.

Of the total of 145 million tons of junk that Americans put into their air every year, it is estimated that 52 percent is the colorless and invisible gas called carbon monoxide. The primary source of this waste is from automobile exhaust. The next heaviest portion of poison in the American air, 18 percent, is the sulfur oxides, that come mostly from burning of coal and oil in power plants, factories, and homes. The next most common contaminators of the air are the hydrocarbons, a large group of compounds coming mainly from escaped, unburned fuel, mostly invisible and mostly from automobiles.

Interestingly, air pollution is not confined to large cities of the East, Midwest, and West Coast regions, as evidenced by the following examples: Ed Christopherson, a writer who left Manhattan, New York, for Missoula, Montana, in what used to be known as "the Big Sky Country," stated: "When I lived in New York I used to watch the clinkers come down the air shaft and remember how great the pine-scented evening downdrafts smelled in Missoula . . . Today Missoula is the country's second worst smog area." Mrs. Peter Rose of Denver, Colorado, talking to writer Ben H. Bagdikian, said, "I've got 45 windows in the house, and they need cleaning every week instead of twice a year as they did 20 years ago. It's the same house and the same neighborhood, but the air has become dirty, uncomfortable, and expensive." Dr. La Rele Stephens, a physician in Moscow, Idaho, says he can almost tell by the barometer and the direction of the wind when he will begin getting calls from patients in Lewiston, a town of 13,000 population that is 29 miles away: "When the wind blows the mill fumes over the town or when there is a dead calm, the patients begin to come in with respiratory troubles, nasal congestion, allergies, difficulty in breathing, lots of sneezing."

Today unclean air threatens the health of most Americans, corrodes their property, insults their peace of mind, and obliterates their scenery. Unclean air is no longer the exception in American cities — it is the rule.

The Water Pollution Problem

Industry already devours water on a vast scale — 600,000 gallons to make one ton of synthetic rubber, for example — and the resultant hot water releases the dissolved oxygen in rivers and lakes, killing the bacteria that are needed to decom-

"When you defile the pleasant streams...you massacre a million dreams." John Drinkwater.

Piped-in water pollution.

pose sewage. Meanwhile the ever-mounting sewage is causing other oxygen-robbing processes. By 1985 the burdens of sewage may dangerously deplete the oxygen in portions of all 22 United States river basins. The first massive warning is what happened to Lake Erie, where sewage from Detroit and other cities cut the oxygen content of most of the lake's center to almost zero, turning a once productive inland sea into a sink where life has diminished to practically nothing. It is estimated that over 10 million fish are killed each year by pollution.

It seemed to our predecessors that we had enough good water to meet our needs for all time, but we have demonstrated our destructive ignorance by clogging the capillaries and arteries of our great land with billions of tons of rubbish. Perhaps we were lulled in the early days by the reassuring platitude that "running water purifies itself." Perhaps we simply didn't care. In any case, we have used our creeks, rivers, and lakes — the same ones from which we must draw much of our drinking water — as handy, cheap sewers to carry away every imaginable kind of waste.

We have filled our streams with raw excrement and garbage, laden with disease. We have stained them with oil, coal dust, tar dyes, and chemical liquids discharged by industries. We have burned them with powerful acids that destroy all aquatic life except a stringy, loathsome type of algae. We have turned them gray and murky with silt and sludge, smothering shellfish and other forms of bottom life. We have used them to dispose of residues containing long-lasting poisions, some so powerful that less than one part per million in a stream can kill fish. And, as though to show our contempt for our natural scenery, we have dumped billions of tons of trash in our once lovely waters: cans, worn-out tires, old mattresses, rusty oil drums, refuse from hospitals, broken glass, dead animals, and junked automobiles. It is a dismal fact that we now have seriously contaminated and despoiled most of the rivers and bays in the entire United States.

Honeymooners at Niagara Falls sometimes find the atmosphere less than romantic because the torrent of tainted water often fills the air with a stench like that of rotten eggs. Chesapeake Bay, like most of our major bays, long has been a receptacle for the combined pollution load of a number of dirty rivers, plus sewage and oily wastes from heavy ship traffic. Long ago the Chesapeake's once clear waters became turbid, and its bottom life was choked by silt and sickened by toxic pollutants. Particularly hard hit were the oysters, whose young depend on clean rocks or shell-bars on which to attach themselves. Fifty years ago the Chesapeake was the main harvest ground for the 10 to 12 million bushels of oysters that Maryland then produced. Now, despite advances in oyster culture, the harvest is only one tenth of what it was. Each year hundreds of thousands of acres of shellfish beds along the U.S. shores are "uncertified" by health authorities; that is, they are found to be polluted and cannot be harvested.

Or consider the mighty Hudson, first described in the log book of Henry Hudson's *Half Moon*. As that explorer sailed up the river in 1609, searching for the fabled Northwest Passage, he was disappointed as the water lost its salty taste and

It is a dismal fact that we now have polluted almost every large river, lake, and bay in the entire United States.

> The massive wastes of various sorts that are destroying our surroundings are produced in the course of fulfilling widespread human wants that are in the main reasonable and defensible when viewed individually, but the combined effects are more than the environment can handle.

became fresh. In our times anyone tasting water from the river would be risking his or her life. The Hudson is repeatedly contaminated by raw sewage before it flows past New York City, where it receives another colossal discharge of the stuff, more than 400 million gallons a day. Senator Robert Kennedy, when transferring from one boat to another in New York harbor, looked at the water and said, "If you fall in here you don't drown — you decay."

Mark Twain called the Mississippi Basin "the body of the nation" and wrote lovingly of "the great Mississippi, the magnificent Mississippi, rolling its mile-wide tide, shining in the sun." Today pollution experts call this once proud river the garbage dump of mid-America. Along its winding 4000-mile length the river suffers all the indignities a society can heap on it. Hundreds of towns and cities use it as a sewer. Thousands of factories, packing houses, stockyards, refineries and mills drain into it their assortment of wastes: oils, toxic metals, slaughterhouse offal, pickling liquors, chicken feathers, garbage, chemical sludge, and other horrors. Water birds and fish on the Mississippi have been killed by oil slicks. Spawning beds have been smothered by silt and sludge. Occasionally dead water, robbed of its oxygen by decomposing organic wastes, has slaughtered countless migrating fish.

There are many other examples of the way we have gone to the brink of disaster in our treatment of our water supplies. *Our surface waters are in dangerous condition.* Long ago the immense load of filth and poisons dumped into our streams overwhelmed their natural ability to purify themselves and the volume of wastes discharged by our cities and factories is steadily increasing. Our population, our cities, and our industries all are expanding, while the basic water supply, once thought so plentiful, remains the same. Increasingly, we shall have to reuse the flows of our streams several times before they reach the sea, whether we like it or not. In the great industrial complex of Detroit, where the latest in computerized management is applied to assembly lines, municipal and industrial wastes are handled in Model T style. Among the daily items the Detroit River is supposed to absorb and carry out of sight are 19,000 gallons of oil, more than 200,000 pounds of acid, 2 million pounds of chemical salts, and 100,000 pounds of iron. These are all in addition to the sketchily treated human wastes from a population of several million. The Detroit River is only one of many similarly polluted streams debauching Lake Erie. Some scientists warn that this huge lake is dying. It soon may become a vast greenish sump.[1]

Potentially as tragic as the Detroit, the Hudson, and the Potomac rivers are the once pure mountain lakes such as Lake Tahoe, one of the few remaining unspoiled bodies of water in the world. Seen from an airplane, the bright blue mountain lake, 20 miles long, looks as clear and pure as it was 122 years ago when Captain John C.

[1]John Bird, "Our Dying Waters," *Saturday Evening Post*, April 23, 1966, pp. 29-35, 86-87.

> The lure of water is irresistible — even when that water is clearly unfit as a place to play. Clean water thus is a stark national necessity.

Fremont discovered it. But along some of its coves telltale green splotches are starting to creep out from the shore — algae. Lake Tahoe is in the beginning stages of the process that scientists call "eutrophication," which results in explosive growth of undesirable algae. It can become a chain reaction in which the algae fill the water, then die and decompose, raising a tremendous stink and causing the water to go dead from depletion of its oxygen.[2]

This creeping blight is relatively new at Tahoe. Until recently the high, isolated lake had been largely a summer resort with a few homes scattered around its rocky shores. Then came the boom of people, and, with them, pollution.

Who Are the Polluters?

Unfortunately all of us contribute our share. This was pointed out early by an analysis of who destroyed the purity of the rivers in Illinois. It is well established that there is not a single stretch of a major river in the whole state that is not polluted. Ecologists say that the water is dead, meaning that the rivers no longer have the ability to cleanse and renew themselves. The effluents of big industry did a substantial part of the damage. Sewage from towns and cities has been a major contributor. But, surprisingly, most of the damage to the rivers of Illinois came from farmers who are decent and well-meaning but who, in the pursuit of increasing crop yields, poured onto the land thousands of tons of nitrogen fertilizers. Ingredients of the fertilizers found their way to the rivers by natural drainage, and the result bears the cumbersome name *eutrophication,* which means "dead water." Algae which feed upon the fertilizer drained into the rivers die and as they decay the bacteria which break them down consume the oxygen that once cleansed the rivers of organic wastes.

This is only one example of well-meaning people whose constructive approach toward producing more crops and higher profits has produced serious negative side effects. A similar story could be told relative to the use of DDT and the destructive effects it has had on fish and wildlife. A long list could be made of other similar situations.

The Problem of Land Pollution

Land pollution is primarily a problem of ugliness resulting from a variety of unattractive elements. Within communities ugliness results from many sources: unkept vacant lots, poorly maintained residential areas, unclean streets, and cluttered public areas. Other frequent contributors are industrial complexes, railroad areas, and inner-city-blight areas. The control of ugliness from these various sources is extremely difficult, and it requires the efforts of many responsible citizens and numerous agencies. The basis for such control is the development of a

[2] "Water Pollution: The Blighted Great Lakes" (Life Educational Reprints), Life Education Programs, Box 834 Radio City Post Office, New York, N.Y. 10019.

Shall natural beauty keep giving way to the trash and junk?

beauty-minded public, along with the establishment of policies and the conduct of programs at the local level which will result in the development of well-planned and well-kept communities. Without controls, communities develop into very unsightly places.

Controlling ugliness on the outskirts of communities is somewhat of a different problem than within communities, because municipal agencies have little control over developments beyond the community boundaries. Potential sources of ugliness outside communities are garbage dumps, automobile-salvage areas, too many and poorly designed billboards, improperly designed highways, industrial and mining complexes, land erosion, and careless harvesting of natural resources. Control of these sources of ugliness is the responsibility of certain county, state, and federal government agencies. But such control is directly dependent upon the concept that prevention of ugliness is important — in fact, important enough to prevent misuse of the countryside whether by highways, industries, mining, or whatever. In certain instances some other advantages have to be sacrificed in order to maintain an attractive environment. Practically any kind of development, industrial included, can be reasonably attractive if it is planned and constructed with attractiveness in mind.

A Dream

A child had a dream. He dreamed that outside his window a meadowlark sang, a butterfly darted about the sky, and a squirrel scampered to a treetop. He dreamed that, when he opened the window, clean fresh air rushed in to bid him another happy day in a pleasant surrounding. Looking out he saw a winding and not-much-worn path leading across a landscape to a place of clear water, where he could enter a homemade raft and follow a crooked stream. He dreamed of blue skies and fluffy clouds and all sorts of things and places that children love and want and need. But the dream was truly a dream, for the child awakened into environmental poverty: an unkempt neighborhood, no darting butterfly, no scampering squirrel, no grass-covered hill or clean fresh air, no crooked river or homemade raft, not even solitude. He awoke into no beauty for the eyes to see and no inspiration for the soul to grasp.

How unfortunate that the child had only a dream!

A Challenge

Our increasing population and urbanization add urgency to the need for greater emphasis on recycling of waste products. More people means greater consumption and thus more rapid depletion of natural resources. Also, greater consumption means more waste to dispose of whether in the form of solid wastes or of the pollutants that foul our air and water. Yet much of this waste could be unnecessary. For the most part waste is a human invention. Natural systems are generally closed systems. Energy is transformed into vegetation, vegetation into animal life, and the latter returns to the air and soil to be recycled once again. People, on the other hand, have developed open systems, ending all too often in an open sewer or an open dump. We can no longer afford the indiscriminate waste of our natural resources and neither should we accept as inevitable the mounting costs of waste removal. We must move increasingly toward closed systems that recycle what now are considered wastes back into useful and productive purposes. This poses a major challenge and a major opportunity for private industry.

In dealing with the environment we must learn not how to master nature but how to master ourselves, our institutions, and our technology. We must achieve a new awareness of our dependence on our surroundings and on the natural systems which support all life. But this awareness must be coupled with a full realization of our enormous capacity to alter these surroundings.

In the future we're going to need a large number of "instigators"; people who can handle environmental information from several natural sciences in combination with information from the social sciences. These instigators will have to be able to deal with broad questions involving human values, purposes, and laws that lie beyond and between the specific fields of science. The universities that produced, are producing, and will continue to produce the scientific and technological specialists who have taught us to take the environment apart will now have to prepare the instigators who must take the lead in putting it together again. Finding and preparing such instigators, and keeping them on the track, is going to be extremely difficult, because learning about and dealing with such a broad spectrum of problems is not nearly as easy as being a specialist.

What Is Being Done

There are four important aspects to the control of pollution and ugliness: personal, social, political, and economic. The *personal aspect* involves individual concepts of what a desirable environment is and how important it is to society. Concepts of beauty and ugliness and the desire for an attractive environment are personal qualities partly inherent and partly developed. These concepts are also a part of a person's education. The *social aspect* is expressed in the unity of thought and action by a group, or by society as a whole. Without unified thought and action

Man has lost the capacity to foresee and to forestall. He will end by destroying the earth.

— Albert Schweitzer

little can be accomplished toward controlling the pollution of our environment. Probably of even greater importance is the *political aspect*. Many of the major problems in regard to pollution are of the kind that require the passage and enforcement of laws at various levels, or otherwise governmental influence. Without effective political machinery — that is, without politicians who are committed to fostering a desirable environment — only a limited amount can be accomplished. The fourth aspect, *economics,* is the thorn in our side, because in many cases the control of pollution has been said by industrial management and certain public officials to be unfeasible. Yet what is or is not economically feasible depends to a large extent on priority. When pollution reaches the critical stage, then control becomes feasible even at the expense of industrial or other kinds of development. Seemingly both private enterprise and public organizations will avoid pollution control as long as possible, because it represents a large nonproducing expenditure that increases the cost of operation without increasing the marketability of goods.

Through technology and through carelessness, we have polluted the environment, and there is no question that we have the ability to depollute it. The real question is whether enough of us want action in the correction of pollution. The false assumption that all nature exists only to serve the immediate desires and needs of people is the root of an ecological crisis — one that ranges from the lowly litterbug to the lunacy of nuclear proliferation. This crisis has made it evident that our only choice is to live in harmony with nature, not continually to try to conquer it and exploit it to its limits. Much has been accomplished in recent years, but the struggle to retain a highly livable environment has just begun.

In 1963 the Congress passed the Air Pollution Control Act (now amended and called the Clean Air Act) which represented the first major effort to clean up the air that Americans must breathe. This, along with many good efforts by some states, some local agencies, and some private industries has produced worthy results. Yet the major causes of air pollution still await our solutions. Starting in 1968 the automobile industry has installed antipollution devices on all new cars, but during the near future the increase in the number of cars will more than offset the effectiveness of the antipollution devices now installed. Many industrial plants have reduced their contributions to pollution, but more factories are being built, and the total effect is more pollution instead of less. Some cities are working diligently to reduce pollution caused by incineration of wastes, but the rapid growth of cities offsets most of the results of the improved disposal methods.

Some significant steps have been taken toward solving the problem of pollution of our waters, but this problem remains largely unsolved. In 1965 the Water Quality Act was passed by Congress, giving the states until July 1967 to develop standards of quality to be maintained on interstate streams within their boundaries. The Act also established the Federal Water Pollution Control Administration (FWPCA) to represent the federal government in this field. But, despite its values, the Act is still a compromise, and its effects are quite limited. One of the most serious problems is that one-fourth of our cities and towns still have no sewage treatment plants of any kind, and half of the existing plants are outdated, not of the type that purifies water. Much pressure from the federal government is mounting to cause cities to upgrade their sewage plants, but only moderate progress has been experienced to date. Most public officials seem to want to sweep the problem under the rug, while they concentrate on more glamorous projects.

Some of the more responsible industrial firms have spent goodly amounts of money attempting to improve their methods of disposal of wastes that have previously been dumped into our lakes and rivers. But this represents a non producing expenditure that does not contribute to the marketing of their products, and therefore most industrial management hesitates to make such expenditures.

As a result, despite the fact that some good efforts are being made, our waters are still becoming more polluted day by day. The reason is because our industrial growth and our population growth are progressing more rapidly than our techniques for controlling water pollution. As a result, more garbage will be dumped into our waters this year than last year, and next year will bring another increase.

Land pollution is perhaps less critical than air and water pollution from the standpoint of health. But with regard to an attractive environment, land pollution is perhaps our greatest problem, and it is receiving only moderate attention. A few bold projects designed to beautify blight areas of cities have made a mark on the problem. Billboard control, especially on interstate highways, has progressed. Much has been done to develop a litter-conscious public. And efforts are being made toward soil conservation, reforestation, and rehabilitation of land that has been strip mined. Some of the sore spots still receiving little attention are neglected vacant lots, industrial sites, auto-salvage areas, and crowded residential areas within cities. The President's Council on Recreation and Beautification has been successful in focusing public attention on the problem of ugliness and pollution. The Council has produced guidelines for local action programs, and has stimulated much public interest.

Are We Already Too Late?

The country is beginning to wake up and to tackle its tough problems of pollution and ugliness on some fronts, but in most areas solutions are progressing less rapidly than pollution itself. If we continue to blunder along, setting our sights too low, worrying more about production of goods and immediate costs than the future of our natural resources, much of the countryside may become a disaster area. Will children now being born be able to look upon America and find it fair, inviting, and secure? Or must they accept a despoiled land in which once pleasant streams are open sewers, lakes and bays are cesspools, and beaches are places of peril instead of joy? The key question is: "Can we save our waters, our clean air, our pleasant landscape?" As of now the answer at best is *maybe*.

Stimulus Needed for Local Action

It is significant that most of the pioneering of conservation and outdoor-recreation programs across the country began quite modestly. They were the out-

Many alarms have been sounded, but alarms by themselves do not put out fires.

In the polluting sense, humans are the greatest offenders of all living beings.

Sugar beet waste dumped into this stream in Ohio killed thousands of fish.

growth of an effort by an individual or by a group of people who tried to tackle a particular local problem and who, in tackling the problem, did so with such imagination and skill that they provided a model for others to follow.

The chances are that there are several immediate challenges for your community. It may be that more playgrounds are needed, that a stretch of roadside should be planted, or that a marsh must be saved. The project will be worth doing in its own right, and it may also serve as a wedge for further and broader efforts.

The first step toward action should be to survey the local situation. It is important to become informed about people's needs, interests, and opinions in regard to beautification and pollution control. It is important to know which agencies and citizen groups will help to bring about desired results. Specifically, ask yourself the following questions, for their answer may indicate how action can be stimulated and you might be the one to stimulate it.

How do elected officials stand on the matter of beautification and pollution control? Have they shown any significant interest in improving the environment? Has anyone approached them on the matter? Perhaps they need some public pressure to motivate them to act. You may be the one to convince them of a strong public desire for a beautiful environment.

Is there a planning commission? Every community needs a planning commission in order to have a design by which to grow into a desirable place. The commission members must be creative and foresighted enough to see not only present needs but also the future needs of the community as it grows.

Has a master plan for the community been developed? Without a plan and an agency to implement the plan, a community will grow like Topsy and eventually develop into an undesirable environment.

Is there a park and recreation department? This is the one agency whose primary concern is the provision of adequate public parks and recreation opportunities. If the department has good leadership and sufficient financial and public support it can make a great contribution to the environment and help to assure a highly livable community.

Is there an agency for waste disposal? Waste disposal and trash cleanup are important to the environment. The more densely populated a community becomes, the more attention must be given to this matter.

Is pollution of air and water receiving adequate attention? Does any agency have the power to control sources of air and water pollution and, if so, does it have adequate support, and is it doing the job effectively?

Which civic groups and private organizations are available to join in the effort?

Action for Open Space

It is well agreed that a certain amount of open space in and around populated areas can add to the quality of living. Experience has proven that unless certain spaces are purposely kept open, soon all the land within a populated area is covered with buildings and asphalt. There are three important considerations with regard to open space: (a) amount, (b) convenience of its location, and (c) its quality in terms of recreational value. In analyzing the advisability of retaining land as open space, some specific questions about the land should be answered: (a) Does any part of it

> A successful environmental reform will require much more than piecemeal dosages of technical antidotes for individual environmental problems. It will require a substantial renovation of the American life style.

reflect historic development of the region? (b) Has it any particular natural features of significance, such as unusual or beautiful scenery? (c) Is the soil satisfactory for whatever use it will be put to? Often land along streams and rivers or on mountainsides is valuable and attractive but unsatisfactory for certain uses.

When considering action for open space the following questions should be considered:

1. Would a planning grant be justifiable in the case of your community? If so, such grant might be obtained under the 701 section of the Federal Housing Act under which the Federal Department of Housing and Urban Development can pay two-thirds of the cost for a community planning study.

2. Are there areas in and around your community that would qualify for purchase and development under the Land and Water Conservation Fund Program, which is administered by the Bureau of Outdoor Recreation? This fund is established for the specific purpose of enhancing the purchase and development of outdoor recreation areas.

3. Can the present open space, including parks and playgrounds, be upgraded to serve the public better?

4. Are there any private groups or private individuals who may want to donate land for open space in the community?

5. Would it be desirable and is it possible to zone nearby agricultural land in such a way as to encourage its being retained for agricultural use rather than being developed for residential or other such uses?

6. Are there spots of such historic significance that they should be established as historic sites? Financial assistance in support of such sites is available from the Department of Housing and Urban Development.

7. Would cluster zoning help answer the problems in regard to open space in your community?

Action for a Better Landscape

What does a person perceive while driving home from work? Or on the way to the supermarket? The child on the way to school? And what of the people on the wrong side of town? What do their eyes view? The critical, unifying parts of the community's landscape are the parts that the greatest number experience in common — the focal points.

Ask yourself these questions about the landscape of your community:

1. Is there need for an antilitter drive?

2. Should your community have a clean-up and paint-up day?

3. Do additional trees and flowers need to be planted? If so, which organizations are willing to help?

4. Should you press for underground utility lines?

5. Is the lack of billboard control detracting for the landscape?

> While we indulge in worthy, earnest, but nevertheless limited enterprises such as saving the whooping crane, we fail to notice our own growing eligibility for the title, "endangered species."

6. Is there need for better street benches and park picnic furniture?
7. Would a federal beautification grant be of significant help? Such grants are available through the Department of Housing and Urban Development.

Action for Clean Air and Clean Water

The sources of air and water pollution — smokestacks, untreated sewage releases, and industrial wastes — are mostly in communities, and this is where much of the action must start. Since the passage of the Federal Water Quality Act of 1965, there has been authority for the establishment of water-quality standards for interstate and coastal waters. The Act gives the states the first chance to develop standards for the interstate waters within their jurisdiction. All of the states have now submitted water-quality standards for their interstate waters. The establishment and effective enforcement of these standards will go a long way toward cleaning up our dirty waters.

Federal grants-in-aid are available to help local governments develop sewage control and treatment facilities. Several federal agencies with differing objectives and somewhat different clientele are now actively dispensing grants and other types of assistance for pollution control. For information on the various sources of grants, contact the Federal Water Pollution Control Administration, Department of the Interior.

Most states have agencies that provide some form of technical assistance to communities for water pollution control. The field people of these agencies can help the community evaluate its needs and direct it toward the right assistance.

The 1967 passage of amendments to the Clean Air Act gives the government a new and powerful mandate to move forward with the job of setting air-quality standards and seeing that they are enforced. Through the Division of Air Pollution of the Public Health Service, technical and financial assistance is available to states and local governments. Any community with the legal authority to take air-pollution-control actions within its jurisdiction is eligible for project grants that pay up to two-thirds of the cost of developing, establishing, or improving air-pollution-prevention and control programs. Once the program is under way there will be grants available to air-pollution-control agencies to carry a portion of the cost of running the program.

Most citizens who have fought to control pollution and ugliness have found the battle to be tough. But they have carried on under the inspiration that they were creating a better place for themselves and their children and for all those who follow. It is, without question, a battle worth fighting.

Chapter 13 Education for Outdoor Recreation

In order to determine the role of education in meeting people's outdoor recreation needs, two main groups must be considered: the *consumers* of outdoor recreation and the *producers* of recreation opportunities. The former group is composed of the general public, while the latter group includes those who plan, manage, and administer recreation resources and programs. In the case of both of these aspects of education, sound philosophical concepts must prevail.

Educating the Public for Outdoor Recreation

Education, like life itself, is an ongoing process. It is both basic and essential to human purpose and achievement, yet it is a complex process, about which we have too little information.

We differ from the rest of the biological world in that our character and personality are not determined primarily by heredity. At birth we are open; we are largely unmade and hence what we become is greatly influenced by our experiences, that is, by our education — both formal and informal. Ignorance or neglect of this fact about humankind is fatal to individual and to group welfare. The human individual, uncultivated, is not simply an animal, but something much more undesirable and dangerous than any other biological species, for the animal is made largely by nature and is guided by its special instincts, including certain crucial restraints. Not so with the human, who is subject to powerful emotions and needs and is desperately dependent upon what he or she learns or fails to learn.

The process of "making a person" is education. The growth toward full maturity is a result of the amount and quality of experiences which produce the human characteristics desirable in our society. Thus, it can be said with confidence that knowledge of human nature and about how to provide the optimum in education are the major requirements for an effective, self-repairing society. If education is neglected, then all other human endeavors tend to be secondary and might even eventually be self-defeating and self-destructive.

A most encouraging positive factor is the human being's wonderful potential — our physical, mental, and spiritual possibilities. Yet, as we have clearly seen in modern times, our potential for evil is as great as our potential for good. In fact, our negative characteristics arise and multiply simply from neglect while the positive characteristics require wise and prolonged work to bring about their development.

Few things are more unproductive and destructive than working against the nature of things. Our nature includes some deep-seated hungers. Among the greatest hungers and the more crucial ones from the standpoint of education are (a) the hunger for wholeness, and (b) the hunger for some contact with natural things. In light of this knowledge of human nature, what aspects of modern life threaten us most seriously? What aspects detract from our development and satisfaction? Here are some suggestions: (1) For a large portion of the population, noise, clutter, and crowdedness are common parts of daily life, and these circumstances present a constant threat to effective functioning and to growth and development. These undesirable circumstances have even crept into our educational system. The almost compulsive pushing, rushing, and crowding in education from kindergarten through graduate school have, in many instances, reached epidemic proportions. (2) The increasingly dominant part played by mechanical things threatens to dehumanize humankind and all of its institutions. Too much of this tends to stifle and often destroy the genuinely human characteristics that enrich and ennoble our lives. (3) Closely related to the process of dehumanization is the tendency for all of life to become increasingly artificial or what might be called secondhand. A large proportion of activity in the schools is a pretense. It lacks the quality of direct, meaningful, genuine experience. (4) Our precious sensitivity, one of our most valuable assets, is threatened. Many people who live in crowded conditions cannot hear over the noise, cannot see beyond the clutter, and cannot feel through the confusion and hypocrisy. (5) Modern life for many people is fragmented, broken into small, and often meaningless, parts. This detracts measurably from the fullness concept of life and leaves people with an unfinished feeling.

Human nature has not changed very much, but the conditions under which people live have changed drastically in recent decades. Modern living, much of which is urban, has robbed them of insight into their reason-to-be. It has removed them from the good earth, substituted concrete and asphalt for open spaces, woods, lakes, and streams. Cities have often not been designed and constructed in ways that best meet

Next in importance to freedom and justice is education, without which neither freedom nor justice can be permanently maintained.

— James A. Garfield

Learning the skill of canoeing can add a new dimension to outdoor recreation.

people's needs. As we became urbanized, we did not intend to deprive people of the basics of life; we simply forgot to provide for some of these things. The constrictions, restrictions, and requirements for conformity in crowded living conditions have resulted in much dissatisfaction with life and this in turn has contributed, and is contributing, to complex social problems.

In principle, what special experiences do we need to bring out the best in us? What kinds of conditions need to be present? What kinds of situations need to be developed? Among other things, we need a close and continuing relationship with natural things, with nature unspoiled. We need to understand our oneness with and our intimate relationship to the natural world. We should come to understand, respect, and love nature. Perhaps we would think less of conquering, which is such a pitiful and dangerous myth, and more in terms of understanding and cooperating with the natural order. We need some healing and refreshing experiences, some space and time in which deeper, inner growth can get a start and be nourished. Perhaps most of all, we need to be motivated to reach outside our immediate physical environment and project our thoughts into the deeper meaning of life. We need to live in an environment that nurtures our spirit to grow as it naturally would under stimulating conditions.

As a part of our experience we need to learn skills and gain knowledge, appreciations, interests, and desirable attitudes necessary to receive the utmost benefits from recreational pursuits. And we must learn how to use resources in ways that leave the resources unimpaired for future use. This phase of our education is typically referred to as outdoor education.

The interdependence of outdoor recreation and outdoor education is clear. Each can make the other more meaningful. Education must precede as well as accompany outdoor recreation experiences in order that those experiences may be highly valuable. What we get from recreational experience depends in large part on what we bring in terms of educational background.

Earl Pullias, one of our outstanding modern-day philosophers, claims that some of the important values of education about the outdoors are: (a) It can establish a healing and growth-producing relation with the natural world — the world to which we are so intimately related. (b) It can promote growth in sensitivity, that is, open the self up to wide variety of experiences that nourish and bring to fruition the full richness of human nature. (c) It can assist in the development of habits of withdrawal and renewal which are fundamental to physical, mental, and spiritual health in modern life. Perhaps it can help to slow down and simplify the rushed confusion that characterizes so much of life. (d) It can offset the deadening effect upon the human mind of forever dealing with abstractions — with second-, or third-, or fourth-hand experience — with which modern life is encrusted. The human mind urgently needs direct *experience,* even if it is very simple direct experience.

Categories of Outdoor Education

Outdoor education includes two major categories: *education in the outdoors,* and *education for the outdoors.* The two categories are closely related and they complement each other. The former category occurs in an outdoor environment, while much of that included in the latter category may take place in an indoor setting.

Surfing is one of the more difficult outdoor sports to learn, but it is very popular in certain areas.

L. V. Sharp helped us understand what should be taught in the outdoors, and what can be taught indoors, when he asked,

> ...that those subjects, topics and courses that can best be taught and can best be learned indoors, be taught and learned indoors, while those subjects, topics, and courses that can best be taught and learned out-of-doors, be taught and learned out-of-doors.[1]

His lifetime of writing and teaching was his attempt to show how that latter program could be accomplished.

The following chart will give additional insight into the two categories: education in the outdoors, and education for the outdoors.

Outdoor Education

Education in the Outdoors	Education for the Outdoors
Direct outdoor experiences involving observation, study, and research in outdoor settings such as the following: School Sites Park and Recreation Areas Camps School or Community-owned Forests, Farms, Gardens, Zoos, Sanctuaries, and Preserves State and Federal Land and Water Private Outdoor Resources	The learning of skills and the development of appreciation for activities such as the following: Camp and Survival Skills Casting and Angling Shooting and Hunting Techniques Boating and Small Craft Techniques Aquatics — Swimming, Water Skiing, Skin and Scuba Diving Archery Winter Sports Mountain Climbing Hiking and Bicycling Use of Compass — Mapping and Orienting Outdoor Photography Outdoor Cooking

Other titles that are often used to denote outdoor education or some phase of it are (a) environmental education, (b) conservation education, and (c) resources education. It is important to distinguish between these titles. *Environmental education* is aimed toward understanding the condition of our natural environment, the interaction between us and our environment, environmental changes, and present and potential environmental problems. *Conservation education* is the study of preservation, protection, and conservative and appropriate use of natural resources. *Resources education* is the study of the development, status, and appropriate use of natural resources. Obviously these areas of education are closely related and overlapping, and they are woven into the program known as *outdoor education*. Whatever name is used to represent outdoor education, the program is aimed at equipping people with an awareness of their natural environment and the ability to enjoy, know about, appreciate, and care for their natural surroundings.

The Role of the Schools

The schools are charged with the primary responsibility for most phases of education. However, a host of other agencies supplement and complement the efforts of

[1]Sharp, L. B., "Basic Considerations in Outdoor and Camping Education," *The Bulletin of the National Association of Secondary School Principals* 31:43-47, May 1947.

the schools. It is important to recognize that planned education comes from many different sources, the schools being the primary source.

It is interesting to note that about 60 years ago the Commission on Reorganization of Secondary Schools included as one of its seven cardinal principles of education "the development of knowledge, understanding, and skills, which will enable [a person] to use his leisure in ways which are constructive and satisfying." Later, in 1938, the Educational Policies Commission named "self-realization" as one of the four generalized objectives of education. This stated objective engrosses the concept of constructive use of leisure time. These objectives of education, stated many years ago, already indicated recognition that leisure had to be directed by adequate knowledge and sound attitudes into productive channels. The same objectives have even greater meaning today when we are faced with the urgent and difficult problem of making certain that the steadily increasing leisure time at the disposal of nearly everyone will be used wisely from the standpoint both of the individual and of the community.

The school curriculum for outdoor education may include a host of topics of which some of the more popular ones are nature-conservation principles, the study of bird and wildlife habitats, camping and survival skills, outdoor-living techniques, use of compass and maps, photography, outdoor cooking, hunting and shooting techniques, angling, boating and small watercraft, swimming, hiking, ice-skating, snowshoeing and skiing.

Outdoor education should not be separated from the other subjects, but should integrate the other subjects as much as possible. Figure 16 shows the relationship between outdoor education and other school topics.

The details of the outdoor education curriculum at the different grade levels can be found in textbooks on the subject, but a generalized presentation is given in the chart (Figure 17) prepared from information assembled by Julian W. Smith and others.

Figure 16. Topics which are often integrated with outdoor education.*

*Julian W. Smith, Reynolds E. Carlson, Hugh B. Masters, and George W. Donaldson, *Outdoor Education*, 2nd edition, p. 21, © 1963, 1972. Reprinted by permission of Prentice-Hall, Inc., Englewood Cliffs, N.J.

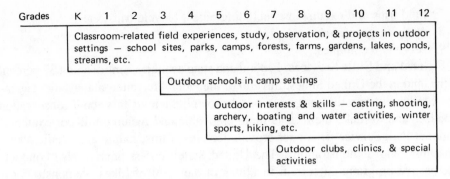

Grades	K	1	2	3	4	5	6	7	8	9	10	11	12

Classroom-related field experiences, study, observation, & projects in outdoor settings — school sites, parks, camps, forests, farms, gardens, lakes, ponds, streams, etc.

Outdoor schools in camp settings

Outdoor interests & skills — casting, shooting, archery, boating and water activities, winter sports, hiking, etc.

Outdoor clubs, clinics, & special activities

Figure 17. Outdoor education curricular contents at different grade levels in schools.*

Contributions by Nonschool Agencies

Education is often equated with formal schooling. But it should be remembered that education takes place in many situations. In our social structure, a wide variety of agencies and organizations more or less share the objectives of schools. In many cases their programs are complementary to that of the schools, providing experiences different from those of the classroom yet related to the same broad purposes. Even though the schools are charged with the major responsibility for outdoor education, these other agencies contribute their share.

Local Recreation and Park Departments. Aside from the schools the agency most directly involved in outdoor education is usually the local recreation and park department. From the time of the establishment of the first parks, one of their main purposes has been to provide aesthetic satisfactions through the maintenance of areas of natural beauty. However, to attain the highest values of these areas, a certain knowledge and understanding of nature are necessary. The interpretive programs of the parks are designed to help visitors gain this knowledge and understanding and to develop appreciation for nature.

Local public park and recreation agencies have particular contributions to make to the outdoor education in the following ways: (a) they provide areas and facilities; (b) they often cooperate with the schools and give direct service to the schools; (c) they offer special programs for those who visit the areas; (d) they sometimes provide interpretive materials in the form of pamphlets and booklets.

More specifically, here are the activities offered through recreation and park departments which contribute to outdoor education:

1. interpretive services, including publications and audio-visual materials;
2. zoos;
3. special interest clubs relating to the out-of-doors;
4. outdoor-related classes;
5. outdoor-related crafts;
6. instruction in outdoor skills such as riflery, fly casting, canoeing, skiing, photography, etc.;

*Julian W. Smith, Reynolds E. Carlson, Hugh B. Masters, and George W. Donaldson, *Outdoor Education*, 2nd edition, p. 21, © 1963, 1972. Reprinted by permission of Prentice-Hall, Inc., Englewood Cliffs, N.J.

7. field trips and excursions, including hikes, bicycle trips, etc.;
8. camping programs;
9. survival techniques.

Federal and State Services. Federal and state agencies control about 37 percent of the land in the United States. Several of the federal resource-management agencies conduct interpretive programs in order to enlighten visitors about conservation practices and to make their visits more enjoyable and meaningful. For example, National Park Service personnel provide lectures, films, nature and scenic hikes, museums, and demonstrations. The United States Forest Service also conducts interpretive programs in certain localities in the form of hikes, demonstrations, interpretive signs, and evening lectures and films. Following is a list of the federal agencies directly involved in outdoor education programs:

Department of Interior
1. National Park Service
2. Fish and Wildlife Service
3. Bureau of Outdoor Recreation
4. Bureau of Reclamation
5. Bureau of Land Management
6. Bureau of Indian Affairs

Department of Agriculture
1. Federal Extension Service
2. United States Forest Service
3. Soil Conservation Service

Agencies in Other Departments
1. Army Corps of Engineers
2. Public Health Service
3. U.S. Office of Education
4. Tennessee Valley Authority

The patterns of state government services vary greatly from state to state. Certain services, however, may be found in all states, even though the administrative structure and the names may differ. States consistently do the following:

1. provide leadership education through colleges and universities or through workshops and institutes;
2. provide services to communities, to local organizations, and to individuals;
3. protect and conserve wildlife and other natural resources;
4. maintain state-owned lands and waters for public use.

The following specific divisions of state government are typically involved in outdoor education:

1. State Department of Education
2. State Parks Department
3. State Department of Fish and Wildlife
4. State Forestry Department

Education is our first ally in the fight to protect our human and natural resources.

Conservation officers teaching children about nature's processes.

5. State Recreation Agency
6. State colleges and universities
7. State Health Agency

Professional and Service Organizations. Several professional and service agencies are particularly well equipped to conduct outdoor education projects. Not bound by the rigid time-and-place requirements of the schools, they escort groups to outdoor environments for both short and extended stays. The schools owe them a debt for their pioneering that has proved the worth of programs subsequently included in the school curriculum. The list of such organizations is a long one, and some of them, along with a brief interpretation of their programs, are mentioned in Chapter 14.

Professional Education

Another responsibility of education in the field of recreation is to prepare persons who will serve as leaders and as planners, interpreters, managers, and administrators of the resources used for recreational purposes. Individuals competent to handle these tasks are commonly known as "professionals." A large number of professional positions now require a bachelor's degree, some of them require a master's degree, and a few require a doctorate. Recreation is now recognized as a profession and it is, in fact, emerging as a very important profession. The demand for competent leadership will increase as people and programs increase. Our colleges have a significant challenge to meet in coming years because sound preparation of leaders is a must.

A profession is regarded as covering a rather broad field, within which there are areas of specialization. Medicine, for example, includes surgery, neurology, pediatrics, and other branches. Engineering includes civil engineering, chemical engineering, and electrical engineering. Recreation similarly has numerous branches, among which are school, municipal, industrial, therapeutic, and outdoor recreation.

Each profession must have an identified body of knowledge — a core content — to which is added material pertaining to the specialized branches. The professional preparation curriculum should provide the combination of core content and specialization required by each branch of the profession. The curricular content in the field of recreation, including outdoor recreation, has recently been the subject of intensive study.

As pointed out by Dana,[2] professional education in outdoor recreation has developed along two distinct but gradually converging lines. It was first associated with physical education, which dealt primarily with body development and sports. These activities obviously promoted health and provided the participants with recreation of a sort, often out-of-doors. Gradually, departments of physical education in the colleges evolved into departments of physical education and health, then into departments of physical education, health, and recreation, always with outdoor recreation receiving relatively little attention except for outdoor sports and camping skills. These were centered on people and on activity, and relatively little attention was given to natural resources.

The second stage of the development of professional preparation in outdoor recreation was through natural resources management. Those who prepared for management of natural resources found the resources being used more and more by recreationists. The problem of management, conservation, and preservation became ever more closely entwined with the recreational use of the land and water resources. The need for special preparation in outdoor recreation became so apparent that courses on outdoor recreation were added to the natural-resources-management curriculum. In some colleges outdoor recreation is now offered as a field of minor specialization.

The first substantial recognition of the values resulting from recreational use of

[2]Samuel T. Dana, *Education and Outdoor Recreation,* Department of the Interior, Bureau of Outdoor Recreation, U.S. Government Printing Office, Washington, D.C., 1968.

These four youngsters had never seen a frog before. They are attending a farm camp operated by a dairy farmer 11 miles from Charlotte. This is their first nature experience and, as the picture indicates, they are fascinated by the frog.

the natural environment came from the National Recreation Association and other private organizations, rather than from educational institutions. The values received strong, but not very lasting, emphasis at the National Conference on Outdoor Recreation called by President Coolidge in 1924. Colleges were slow to stress the preparation of leaders for recreation, and until recently it was apparently not regarded as needing professional direction.

Within the last two decades, this attitude has changed, prompted by the increased numbers of people with more leisure time and more money at their disposal, increased urbanization, and increased ugliness of both rural and urban landscapes. Mounting pressures on limited resources of land and water for a wide variety of uses that are often in competition have combined to create new and difficult problems. The pressures have revealed the need not only for sound public policies but also for professional skill in planning the allocation of resources to their best uses, in integrating outdoor recreation with other uses, in managing recreational resources efficiently, and in directing constructively the activities of those who use them.

As a result, many departments of physical education, health, and recreation have broadened their scope, and some new departments have been developed to deal with recreation. The change in emphasis has led some colleges to establish a department named the Department of Recreation and Park Administration.

Spring — A New Beginning

In rivers and pools...swamplands and woodland greens...across the dunes and in the sunlit meadows...life...with all its beauty...its promise of eternity...is taking place...

A little green shoot that has risen from the earth...now free to ascend ...within the realm of its kind...to whatever beauty it may attain... It breathes...as all living things must do...it drinks...it must rest...and above all it must grow...for if it ceases to grow...it shall cease to live.
— Gwen Frostic

> Great economic and social forces flow with a tidal sweep over communities that are only half conscious of what is befalling them. Wise are those who foresee what time is thus bringing and endeavor to shape institutions and mold men's thought and purpose in accordance with the change that is silently surrounding them.
>
> — John Morley

At the same time, a similar change has taken place in schools of forestry and natural resources. They had long recognized the value of wild lands for recreational use, but they had regarded such use as of relatively minor importance which needed little direction other than the prevention of its interference with uses such as timber production and grazing. Today numerous schools whose primary concern is the management of natural resources offer professional instruction in outdoor recreation, and the number is growing.[3]

The Development of Curriculum Content

The new recognition of recreation in general and outdoor recreation in particular has led to several studies of the curricular content needed to meet modern requirements in these fields. Following are brief discussions of the more significant studies.

AAHPER Studies. One of the first productive efforts was a National Conference on Professional Preparation in Health Education, Physical Education, and Recreation Education, held in 1962 under the auspices of the American Association for Health, Physical Education, and Recreation (AAHPER). The conference emphasized the importance of a strong background of general education, which it felt should comprise 50 percent of a four-year undergraduate program. It considered five years essential for adequate professional preparation, with the understanding that the fifth year might be completed prior to service or after a period of experience. It concluded that the profession itself should determine the nature of professional education and should establish the standards to ensure the competency of practitioners.

With respect to outdoor recreation the conference recognized two specialized program areas — recreation and park administration, and camping and outdoor activities. The scope of the proposed coverage for each of these fields was indicated in some detail, but no attempt was made to prescribe specific courses.

Five years later, in 1967, the same association (AAHPER) held a conference on Graduate Education in Health Education, Physical Education, and Recreation Education. This conference concluded that "three principal areas of emphasis are observable in graduate level recreation education: recreation programming, administration of recreation services, and natural resource management for recreation." The competencies regarded as essential for the latter area included an understanding of the relationships between natural resources and of the principles involved in their management, but not the technical ability to direct their actual management for purposes other than recreation.

[3]*Ibid.*

National Recreation Education Accreditation Project. In 1963 the organization now known as the Federation of National Organizations for Recreation (a council of ten national organizations) initiated a National Recreation Education Accreditation Project. Among the several tasks assigned to it, the committee in charge of the project devoted much attention to curriculum "to prepare persons to live and to help others to live a more enriched life, to serve the community more effectively, and to assure recreation leadership in a variety of settings." The committee divided the proposed professional curriculum into three parts: (a) general education, (b) professional education, and (c) professional emphasis. It recommended that half of the total number of credit hours in the curriculum be devoted to general education for all students, regardless of their specialty in professional recreation. Some of the subjects to be covered are indicated in considerable detail in the committee report. The committee recommended that the majority of the remaining 50 percent of the courses be devoted to professional education, and that those courses be designed to give a broad coverage of subjects that reflect and closely relate to the general field of professional recreation leadership. The remaining courses were to be devoted to professional emphasis, elective courses selected to fill the student's particular specialized interest. This phase the committee divided into three categories: recreation-program supervision, recreation and park administration, and recreation-resources planning.

Panel on Natural Resource Science. In 1965 the National Research Council established through one of its commissions a Panel on Natural Resource Science. One of the tasks assigned to it was the preparation of recommendations for the development of undergraduate programs in the field of renewable natural resources. The panel came to the conclusion that the basic principles, and to a considerable extent the practices, involved in the management of natural resources have much in common, whether the major emphasis is on trees, wildlife, forage, water, or recreation. Therefore, it decided to recommend a unified but flexible approach to education for all aspects of natural-resources management.

The panel's specific proposal was that there be a single curriculum for the education of students preparing for service in the field of renewable natural resources. This curriculum would be followed by all students, but its structure would be such as to meet the needs of those intending to work in different areas, such as forestry, wildlife management, watershed management, recreation management, etc. It would be divided into four parts: (a) a basic core, (b) an area emphasis, (c) professional courses, and (d) electives. The first part would be uniform for all students, while the other three parts would permit specialization.

The panel report did not mention professional preparation in outdoor recreation as an area of specialization, and it did not mention specific courses in outdoor recreation. The report simply treated outdoor recreation as one of the uses of natural resources and, therefore, one of the concerns in resource management. The panel implied that an adequate curriculum leading to specialty in management of a particular kind of natural resource would prepare a person to manage that resource for recreational as well as for other uses.

It is interesting that the recommendations of the three groups agree in emphasizing the importance of a broad foundation in the arts and sciences, to be followed by opportunity for specialization in any of a rather wide variety of fields. These include the many ramifications of recreation in the case of the first two groups (AAHPER and NREAPC), and of conservation and management of renewable natural resources in the case of the third group (PNRS). The scope of the subjects that all three groups proposed to cover in four years is impressive and challenging — to both teachers and students.

College Curricula in Outdoor Recreation

In the United States more than 160 colleges and universities offer curricula leading to a bachelor's degree with a major in recreation. (About an equal number of two-year colleges offer curricula in recreation.) Approximately half of these institutions identify *outdoor recreation* as one of their areas of specialization. It should be recognized that even though a large number of institutions claim a specialization track in outdoor recreation, only a few of them are prepared to offer a truly thorough education to a student in this field. Therefore, any serious-minded student who wants to become a true specialist in outdoor recreation should be highly selective about the institution he or she attends. Only those programs should be considered that are well established and that have in them competent, well-informed teachers. A complete list of the colleges and universities that offer degrees in recreation along with a designation of specialized areas in each program appears in the book listed below.[4] This book is excellent for any student planning to enter any phase of the recreation profession.

The more specialized curricula having to do with *natural resource management for outdoor recreation* are found in colleges of forestry or colleges of natural resources. Following are the universities that offer recreation curricula of this kind.[5]

University of Arizona — Tucson, Arizona 85721
University of California — Berkeley, California 94720
Colorado State University — Fort Collins, Colorado 80521
University of Georgia — Athens, Georgia 30601
Southern Illinois University — Carbondale, Illinois 26901
University of Michigan — Ann Arbor, Michigan 48104
Michigan State University — East Lansing, Michigan 48823
University of Minnesota — Saint Paul, Minnesota 55101
University of Missouri — Columbia, Missouri 65201
University of Montana — Missoula, Montana 59801
University of Nevada — Reno, Nevada 89507
Oklahoma State University — Stillwater, Oklahoma 74074
Oregon State University — Corvallis, Oregon 97331
University of Tennessee — Knoxville, Tennessee 37916
Utah State University — Logan, Utah 84322
Virginia Polytech Institute — Blacksburg, Virginia 24061
University of Washington — Seattle, Washington 98105
West Virginia University — Morgantown, West Virginia 26506

[4]Clayne R. Jensen, *Job Opportunities in Leisure Time Occupations,* Vocational Guidance Manuals, Inc., 620 South Fifth Street, Louisville, Kentucky, 1976, 126 pp.
[5]E. L. Demmon, *Opportunities in Forestry Careers,* Vocational Guidance Manuals, Louisville, Kentucky, 1975.

Chapter 14 Professional, Service, and Educational Organizations

In addition to government agencies and private enterprises involved in outdoor recreation, there are a number of professional and service organizations which carry on various functions in the outdoor-recreation field. In order to get a complete scope of those involved in outdoor recreation and to what extent, it is necessary to become familiar with these citizen organizations, hereafter arranged alphabetically.

American Alliance for Health, Physical Education, and Recreation

The AAHPER, an affiliate of the National Education Association, was created for the purpose of promoting and developing better programs in health, physical education, and recreation. Its major efforts are in connection with school and college programs. It has a staff consultant in several related areas. Its division of recreation gives various kinds of professional leadership, including workshops and conferences on the national and district levels devoted to professional improvement of recreation personnel and school and college programs.

Through the Association, numerous books and pamphlets relating to recreation have been prepared and distributed. It also publishes the monthly *Journal of Physical Education and Recreation* and the *Research Quarterly*. It is financed mostly by membership fees, but does receive some assistance through grants and gifts. It has affiliate organizations in six geographic districts of the United States and in all of the 50 states. The home office is at 1201 16th Street, N.W., Washington, D.C. 20006. **239**

American Camping Association

The American Camping Association was established in 1910 to further the welfare of children and adults of America through camping and to extend the recreational and educational benefits of out-of-doors living. The Association serves as the voice of camp leaders throughout the nation, and it is the organization that stimulates high professional standards among camp leaders and camping agencies. It sponsors national and regional conferences for the purpose of improving camp leadership and camp programs.

The Association publishes *Camping Magazine* eight times a year. It also publishes and distributes several books and pamphlets on camping and related activities. It is financed through membership dues. The home office address is Bradford Woods, Martinsville, Indiana 46151.

American Forestry Association

This Association was founded in 1875. Its purpose is to create an enlightened public with regard to natural resources and the part they play in the social and economic life of the nation. It is the key organization concerned with improving the qualifications of forest management personnel.

The Association has published several booklets, and it publishes a monthly magazine entitled *American Forests*. Also, the Association sponsors national and regional conferences devoted to the improvement of America's forests. Its home address is 1319 18th Street, N.W., Washington, D.C. 20036.

American Power Boat Association

The APBA was established in 1903 for the purpose of developing, improving, and promoting power boat racing as a safe and desirable competitive sport on the individual and family basis. It currently has about 7000 members throughout the nation. Most of the members are people who are primarily interested in supporting boat racing and are not actively involved in competition. The Association is financed primarily through membership fees but also receives money from manufacturers of boats and boating equipment. The address of its headquarters is: The Whittier, 415 Burns Drive, Detroit, Michigan 48214.

American Youth Hostels, Inc.

Youth hostels were first established in Germany by Richard Schirrmann, a young German schoolteacher, in 1909. He envisioned hostels as being places where young city dwellers could stay inexpensively overnight while on walking or cycling trips in the country. Soon the movement spread to other nations, and in 1934 the first American Youth Hostel was established in Northfield, Massachusetts, by Isabel and Monroe Smith, two American schoolteachers.

The present purpose of youth hostels in America is to provide overnight housing to young people particularly who could not afford to stay at more expensive accommodations while traveling throughout the country "under their own steam," hiking, biking, canoeing, on horseback, or skiing.

Each hostel is supervised by carefully chosen houseparents and provides

A father and his son may be closest together when they are fishing far apart.

Happiness is not a station at which to arrive, but a manner of traveling.

adequate sleeping accommodations, cooking, and washing facilities. The hosteler can cook his own food and also enjoy the hostel common room, where young travelers can meet others from all over the world and thus help spread better understanding among people.

The organization is made up of 31 area councils throughout the U.S., with membership and support from individuals and organizations of the various communities. It publishes various pamphlets and booklets designed especially for hostelers. It is financed through membership fees and program fees paid by participants in its hosteling programs. For detailed information about AYH, write for a free folder: American Youth Hostels, Inc., National Campus, Delayslane, Virginia 22025.

Appalachian Mountain Club

The Appalachian Mountain Club was organized in 1876. Its purpose has been and still is the exploration of the mountains of New England and adjacent regions, both for scientific and artistic reasons and to cultivate an interest in geographical studies. More recently the Club has emphasized recreational development of the mountain country in Massachusetts, Maine, and New Hampshire, and in areas of its eight chapters from Delaware to Maine.

It provides trails, shelters, huts, guidebooks, and maps for recreational use. The Club maintains over 500 miles of foot trails, 20 shelters, and a system of huts for use by the public in the White Mountains. It also sponsors instruction in such outdoor activities as snowshoeing, skiing, canoeing, mountain climbing, and trip leadership and safety.

The Club is financed by membership dues. It publishes a monthly magazine called *Appalachia Bulletin* and a semiannual journal, *Appalachia,* and maintains one of the most complete mountaineering libraries in the country. Its home office is at 5 Joy Street, Boston, Massachusetts 02108.

Appalachian Trail Conference, Inc.

The Appalachian Trail Conference was established for the purpose of promoting, constructing, and maintaining continuous trails through the mountain country of the Atlantic Seaboard states, extending from Maine to Georgia. The trails are supplemented by primitive-type camps placed at intervals along the trails. The organization is devoted to conserving the primitive environment of the Appalachian mountain regions.

Four times a year, the Conference publishes the *Appalachian Trailway News*. It also publishes news items and other information of interest to the Appalachian Trail users. It has published ten guide books and numerous pamphlets on the recreational use of the Appalachian Trail country. The organization is financed through membership fees. Its mailing address is P.O. Box 236, Harpers Ferry, West Virginia 25425.

Athletic Institute

This organization was established in 1934 to increase the interest and enthusiasm of the American people for sports activities, and to promote and assist in the development of more and better sports facilities and equipment. The Institute has an extensive sports education and promotion program, and it has published several booklets and pamphlets relative to sports participation, sports facilities, and sports equipment. Further, the Institute has developed numerous audiovisual aids that are used extensively in educational programs. It offers free assistance on problems related to sports programs. The office address is Merchandise Mart, Room 705, Chicago, Illinois 60654.

Council for National Cooperation in Aquatics

The idea of expanding cooperative aquatic efforts at the national level was originated in the fall of 1951 after two years of study and discussions. The original purpose of the Conference for National Cooperation in Aquatics, now called the Council for National Cooperation in Aquatics (CNCA), is to provide a setting in which representatives from the 32 national organizations constituting the council could come together to: (a) report on individual agency programs, plans, and projects, (b) share and discuss common problems, and (c) plan ways of working together on agreed-upon projects. It is intended that this cooperative effort will add to the independent work carried on by the various national groups, and thus advance the entire field of aquatics. The council has published and distributed several books and pamphlets on topics relating to aquatics. The address of the Council headquarters is 3 Hillandale Drive, New Rochelle, New York 10804.

Federation of Professional Organizations for Recreation

The Federation was organized in 1961 for the purpose of providing an exchange of ideas among the executive directors and presidents of the leading professional recreation organizations. There are 20 member associations. Chief projects of the Federation have been concerned with accreditation of recreation curricula and exchange of ideas on association programs. The address of the Federation is 20 North Wacker Drive, Chicago, Illinois 60606.

The Izaak Walton League of America

The Izaak Walton League of America is a 50,000-member citizen action group founded in 1922 to promote the conservation and wise use of our nation's natural resources and the enjoyment and wholesome utilization of America's outdoors. Public education, policy research, citizen involvement, and legal action are fostered through the national, state division, and local chapter levels.

Current priorities include support for strict air and water pollution control standards, regulation of strip mining, rational land use planning, energy conservation, a livable urban environment, and expanded outdoor recreation opportunities. The

---

To go fishing is the chance to wash one's soul with pure air, with the rush of the brook or with the shimmer of the sun on blue water. It brings meekness and inspiration from the decency of nature, charity toward tackle makers, patience toward fish, a mockery of profits and egos, a quieting of hate, a rejoicing that you do not have to decide a darn thing until next week. And it is discipline in the equality of man — for all men are equal before fish.

— Herbert Hoover

League's newest citizen action program is "Save Our Streams — Adopt One," in which citizens improve water quality by "adopting" a stream segment and caring for it year-round.

The League publishes a monthly tabloid entitled *Outdoor America*. The address of the national headquarters is 1800 North Kent Street, Suite 806, Arlington, Virginia 22209.

National Audubon Society

The Audubon Society was established in America in 1905. It strives to advance public understanding of the values and wise use of natural resources.

The Society sponsors four summer study work shops in the United States which are dedicated to developing in adults, particularly teachers, an appreciation for nature and a sense of responsibility for the protection of natural resources. It offers lectures on nature subjects and assistance in the development of community nature centers. The Society owns and operates a number of wildlife sanctuaries. It also does wildlife research, supplies educational materials, and operates model nature centers.

The Society publishes the *Audubon* bimonthly magazine. Also it publishes a magazine entitled *American Birds* six times a year, and distributes several pamphlets. The Society is financed primarily by membership dues but has supplementary incomes from gifts, grants, foundations, film rentals, lecture services, etc. Its home office is 950 Third Avenue, New York, New York 10022.

National Campers and Hikers Association

This Association was established in 1954 for the purpose of educating the public about the conservation of natural resources and especially about the use and values of the outdoors. It sponsors educational services relative to the development of outdoor programs and facilities, and publishes and distributes pamphlets on camping and outdoor living. Also it offers services in trip planning and campsite locations. Its monthly magazine is entitled *Camping Guide*. The Association is financed by membership dues, and its home address is 7172 Transit Road, Buffalo, New York 14221.

National Golf Foundation

The National Golf Foundation was founded in 1936 by the major manufacturers of golf equipment. Its purpose is to increase the opportunities for all Americans to enjoy golf by assisting in the development of more and better golf facilities and golf instructional programs. It places special emphasis on (a) increasing participation in golf, (b) assisting in the design and development of golf facilities, (c) offering consultation workshops and seminars for teachers and coaches, (d) conducting research.

The Foundation is financed by manufacturers of golf equipment and facilities. It publishes and distributes numerous pamphlets and booklets on topics relative to golf facilities, equipment, and programs. The address of its home office is NGF headquarters, 804 Merchandise Mart, Chicago, Illinois 60654.

National Industrial Recreation Association

The National Industrial Recreation Association was incorporated in 1941 in the State of Illinois with national offices at 20 North Wacker Drive, Chicago, Illinois 60606. It currently serves as a national clearing house for the dissemination of information and ideas on employee recreation for 800 member companies in the U.S. and Canada. Its official publication is *Recreation Management,* which reaches 8000 industries ten times a year. NIRA holds annual national and regional conferences and exhibits, plus eight national tournaments. Officers are elected annually.

National Recreation and Park Association

The National Recreation and Park Association is an independent nonprofit service organization dedicated to the conservation of natural resources, the beautification of the environment, and the development, expansion, and improvement of park and recreation leadership, programs, facilities, and services for human growth and community betterment. NRPA is the only independent national organization servicing all aspects of the nation's park and recreation movement. Much of its income is raised through community United Fund campaigns.

NRPA was formed in 1966 by the merger of five pioneer organizations in the park and recreation field: The American Association of Zoological Parks and Aquariums, the American Institute of Park Executives, the American Recreation Society, the National Conference on State Parks, and the National Recreation Association. It has a professional staff located at the headquarters office. Additional professional personnel in five regional offices across the United States provide in-person consultant services to park and recreation agencies and related organizations at the municipal, county, district, and state levels.

To serve each member's special interests, NRPA has seven branches: The Armed Forces Recreation Society, the American Park and Recreation Society, the Commissioners — Board Members Branch, the National Conference on State Parks, the Student Recreation and Park Society, the National Therapeutic Recreation Society, and the Society of Park and Recreation Educators.

NRPA services are generally classified into five primary categories, although some overlap the others: (1) information; (2) education; (3) interagency liaison; (4) public relations; and (5) research.

The Association sponsors numerous annual educational and planning conferences and workshops on the national and district levels. It prepares and distributes numerous books and pamphlets on park and recreation topics. It produces the following periodic publications:

1. *Parks and Recreation Magazine* (monthly) — designed to acquaint the general public with various park and recreation problems, trends, ideas, and policies;

2. *Recreation and Park Yearbook* — a statistical picture of the public park and recreation movement in the United States issued at five-year intervals;

3. *Management Aids* — an annual series of 12 "how to" manuals dealing with specific policy and management functions;

4. *AGBOR (A Guide to Books on Recreation)* — an annotated list of recreation books available for purchase through NRPA's Book Center;

5. Newsletters — a regular series of 12 monthly, bimonthly, and quarterly news digests on topics of specific interest to professionals and lay board members in the park and recreation field;

6. *Playground Summer Notebook* — an annual program, activity, and idea manual for nonprofessional playground leaders;

7. *Park Practice Program* — a series of four park-related idea publications for national, regional, state, and local park administrators;

8. *Journal of Leisure Research* — a quarterly publication highlighting the most recent and pertinent research efforts in parks and recreation;

9. *TR (Therapeutic Recreation)* — a quarterly containing articles of interest to members of the National Therapeutic Recreation Society.

National Rifle Association

The National Rifle Association of America, founded in 1871, is an independent nonprofit organization supported by membership fees. Its purposes are to educate public-spirited citizens in the safe and efficient use of small arms for pleasure and protection; to foster firearms accuracy and safety in law-enforcement agencies, in the Armed Services, and among citizens subject to military duty; to promote good sportsmanship and to foster the conservation and wise use of our renewable wildlife resources; and to further the public welfare, law and order, and U.S. defense.

Following are the more important activities of the NRA:

1. Originator of nationwide Hunter Safety training and Home Firearms Safety courses.

2. Governing body of U.S. competitive rifle and pistol shooting and international skeet and clay pigeon shooting; member of U.S. Olympic Committee and International Shooting Union.

3. Certifying agency for marksmanship, firearms safety and training instructors, and NRA tournament referees.

4. Parent organization of shooting and hunting clubs, and police and military marksmanship units.

5. Sponsor of civilian marksmanship training (since 1871), national rifle and pistol matches and the National Board for Promotion of Rifle Practice (since 1903), and Young Shooters' Training (since 1907).

6. Creator of Hunter's Code of Ethics; Arms Collectors' Uniform Bill of Sale; Nationwide Sighting-In Day, donor of hunting trophy awards and awards for rifle, pistol and shotgun proficiency.

7. Publisher of *The American Rifleman* (NRA's official journal), *The American Hunter, NRA Tournament News* (for competitive shooters), *The NRA Hunting Annual Conservation Yearbook,* and authoritative publications on firearms activity and gun legislation.

The NRA office address is: 1600 Rhode Island Avenue, N.W., Washington D.C. 20036.

National Wildlife Federation

The National Wildlife Federation was organized in 1936 and currently has affiliate organizations in all 50 states, Puerto Rico, the Virgin Islands, and Guam. Its

Along a western river freshly watered horses carry adventurers to their remote destination.

purpose is to encourage the intelligent management of the life-sustaining resources of the earth — its soils, water, forests, plant life, and wildlife — and to promote and encourage the pursuit of knowledge, appreciation, and wise use of these resources. It sponsors an extensive educational program and provides, free of charge, much educational supplementary material in the form of booklets and leaflets. It publishes *National Wildlife* magazine and *International Wildlife,* bimonthly publications; *Ranger Rick's Natural Magazine,* ten issues a year; *Conservation News,* a semimonthly newsletter; *Conservation Report,* published weekly while Congress is in session; and *Conservation Directory,* a listing of conservation organizations and their personnel. The Federation also grants a number of fellowships to graduate students in fields related to natural-resource conservation. The Federation is financed by membership dues, voluntary contributions, and sale of educational materials. Its home office is at 1412 16th Street, N.W., Washington, D.C. 20036.

Nature Conservancy

The Nature Conservancy is a member-governed organization, incorporated in the District of Columbia for nonprofit educational and scientific purposes. It began its work in 1917 as a national committee of the Ecological Society of America. In 1946 this committee organized as an independent group and in 1950 adopted its present name. It promotes the preservation of natural areas of outstanding scientific or aesthetic significance through their actual acquisition by purchase or gift. The Conservancy (a) maintains and manages a system of preservations throughout the United States, (b) raises money to apply toward the acquisition of natural areas, (c) accepts gifts and bequests of land for conservation purposes, (d) assists universities in acquisition of lands for biological research and field study, and (e) assists governmental agencies and local communities in establishing natural parks and open areas.

The Conservancy is financed through gifts from individuals, grants from foundations, and membership dues. It publishes a quarterly bulletin entitled *The Nature Conservancy News,* and it also publishes pamphlets relative to the conservation of natural resources. The Conservancy home office is 1522 K Street, N.W., Washington, D.C. 20005.

Outboard Boating Club of America

This Club was organized in 1928 to promote better boating opportunities for all Americans. Specifically, the Club promotes boating safety, better-boating laws, and improved boating facilities and equipment. It provides information to the public through pamphlets, booklets, and safety posters. It also provides the public with films related to boating, as well as booklets and other materials on how to organize and operate a successful boat club. Some 300 local boat clubs are affiliated with OBC, representing nearly 10,000 boating families.

The Club is financed by membership dues. It publishes a semi-monthly magazine entitled *Outboard Boating*. It also publishes and distributes numerous booklets on boating and boating facilities. Its home office is 401 North Michigan Avenue, Chicago, Illinois 60611.

Sierra Club

The Sierra Club was founded in 1892 by John Muir for the purpose of helping people to explore, enjoy, and learn to protect parks, wilderness, waters, forests, and wildlife resources. It is based on the idea that wild lands can and should continue to exist and that they will if man is intelligent in his use and care of such lands.

The Sierra Club organizes trips of various kinds into wilderness areas in the U.S. and abroad, as well as day and weekend trips operated by local Chapters and Groups. These are generally open to members only. In addition, the Club maintains several Lodges in California and one in British Columbia, organizes clean-up trips on trails, mainly in the Western U.S., and publishes trail guidebooks — the "Totebook" series. It is financed by membership dues, special grants, and the sale of publications. The Club has sponsored numerous high-quality publications, mostly in the form of books. The address of the home office is 530 Bush Street, San Francisco, California 94108.

Sport Fishing Institute

This Institute was organized in 1949 by a group of fishing-tackle manufacturers.

Its primary purpose is to promote better fishing opportunities for the American people, both at the present and in the future. The Institute is organized around three major functions: (a) research in fishery biology, (b) fish conservation education, and (c) professional service to official agencies and key citizen groups. It is financed by contributions from more than 150 manufacturers of fishing tackle and accessories, outboard boats, and boat motors, and other sporting goods used directly or indirectly in connection with fishing, as well as token contributions from many interested individuals.

The Institute has prepared and distributes several booklets on fish conservation. It also publishes monthly the *SFI Bulletin*. Its home address is Suite 503, 719 13th Street, N.W., Washington, D.C. 20005.

Sports Foundation, Inc.

The Sports Foundation, Inc., was established in 1965 as a public, nonprofit organization, to receive and maintain funds exclusively for the promotion of all types of sports. Working under grants from the National Sporting Goods Association, the Foundation sponsors annually the National Gold Medal Awards program. Through this program it selects and honors the nation's outstanding recreation and park departments at the local and state levels. On occasion the Foundation gives special recognition to other agencies that make significant contributions relating to sports and recreation.

The Foundation funds national studies of various kinds which relate to recreation and promotes recreation participation through the sponsorship of educational programs. It provides financial support to several organizations, such as the U.S. Lawn Tennis Federation, the U.S. Ski Team, and the U.S. Olympic Committee.

It encourages participation and facility development in a wide range of recreation activities. The headquarter office is at 717 North Michigan Avenue, Chicago, Illinois 60611.

Wheelman Incorporated

The League of Wheelman, Inc. (L.A.W.), was established prior to 1880, and in 1893 its rolls showed 40,000 members. Due to the development of the automobile and a network of roads built only to accommodate auto traffic, the L.A.W. declined drastically and struggled for several decades for survival. During recent years the L.A.W. has been growing steadily.

Its main objective is to develop and preserve a bicycling environment for the members of the public who enjoy this particular sport. Its members resist city and highway developments which make bicycling inconvenient or impossible, and promote among the public the idea that bicycling is a wholesome and worthy activity for large numbers of people. Inquiries about the organization may be sent to Mrs. Dorothy Hart, 5118 Foster Avenue, Chicago, Illinois 60630.

Chapter 15 A Look into the Future

What we have done in the past and where we stand at the present are both less important than the direction in which we shall head in the future. The past serves as our guide, the present represents our circumstance, and the future holds all of our hopes. In the recent past we have experienced rapid and continuous change, and at present we are experiencing change more rapidly than ever before. In regard to the future, it appears that change will continue to be the mark of the times.

Future Trends in Socioeconomic Forces

Fundamental to the future of outdoor recreation are the social and economic forces that set the stage for trends in outdoor activities. What will be the future of these forces?

The *population* of the United States is increasing at about 1.5 percent annually. This means that where there were 219 million people at the end of 1976 there will be about 245 million by 1985, and over 300 million by 2000.

Of the 219 million people in America, over 75 percent live in urban areas. By 1985, over 77 percent of the 245 million people will be urbanites. By 2000 probably 80 percent of the 300 million people will live in urban America. By then the Eastern Seaboard, the Great Lakes region, the West Coast, and the Southeastern Gulf area will each represent one continuous sprawling urban area. The Great Plains states and the Rocky Mountain region will be much more crowded than they are now, and practically every area of the nation will be approximately twice as densely popu-

> The past is but the beginning of the beginning, and all that is and has been is only the twilight of the dawn.
>
> — H. G. Wells

lated as it was in 1965. Obviously this increase in population will tax our outdoor-recreation areas and facilities to their limits.

As the population increases, our *transportation system* will require a major overhauling. The large urban areas will need extensive underground or elevated transit systems. The surface of the land in those areas will simply not accommodate all of the moving about that people will do. High-speed railway systems will take people rapidly from one point to another within urban and suburban areas. Helicopter shuffle systems within cities will emerge. Rapid air travel up to 2000 miles per hour will become available. The larger waterways will be covered with boats and ships with some skimming across the water up to 80 or 90 miles per hour. Very large numbers of people will be able to travel conveniently to every outdoor recreation attraction.

Personal income has increased steadily since 1940. In 1976 the per capita income of all Americans was $5400. It is hazardous to predict whether the upward trend in income will continue but, assuming that the trend over the last three decades does continue, we can expect that by 1985 the average per capita annual income will be $6000 and by 2000 it may be well over $7000. What the purchasing power of the dollar will be by 1985 or 2000 is anyone's guess, but all indications are that in the future Americans will have more purchasing power than they have at present, and this means they will have more money to buy goods and services of their choice. Many will choose to expand their participation in outdoor recreation.

The average *level of education* as measured by the grade level achieved in school has increased steadily for several decades. All indications point toward a continuation of this trend. Increased education not only results in greater capacity to earn money, but it also expands one's horizon of interests and appreciations in a greater variety of activities, many of which are of the outdoor-recreation type. The demand for outdoor recreation will no doubt increase.

Because more Americans in the future will be even more removed from nature during their daily living, it will be imperative that greater emphasis be placed on education for outdoor recreation. It will be necessary to keep Americans informed on how to enjoy and appreciate the out-of-doors, and how to use it effectively and still conserve it for future use.

Trends strongly indicate that most of the readers of this book will see the day when the *average work week* in America will be 32 hours. It is currently slightly less than 40 hours. Fifty years ago it was nearly 70 hours. They will also see a continued increase in number and length of vacations, and they will see the day when the typical American retires at age 60 as opposed to age 65, the typical retirement age now. At the same time life expectancy will continue to move upward, expanding the period of retirement in both directions. The probable effects of all of this increased leisure time on outdoor-recreation participation are apparent.

During recent decades we have made great advances in *technology and automation*, and these advances have influenced practically every aspect of our lives, including what we do for recreation, where we do it, and how much time we spend doing it. Future trends will continue to be toward increased technology and automation, and these trends will continue to have effects on our outdoor recreation. New methods of participation and new devices used for participation will continue to be developed, and because of this our patterns of outdoor recreation will continually change.

Regardless of how much time, money, education, etc., we have, the factor that determines our living patterns more than anything else is our *philosophy* toward the different aspects of life. The philosophy of Americans toward recreation has changed vastly during recent years. They have come to recognize that recreation is an important part of life to enrich personality and give fulfillment. One of our great challenges at present is to improve the quality of people's recreation in order that it will make a better contribution to them. The elements of worthiness and wholesomeness must be driven harder into people's philosophy of recreation.

This overview of future trends affecting outdoor recreation presents a rather bleak picture, giving the impression that our outdoor areas will be overrun by hordes of people moving about in a rapid and disorganized fashion and exploiting nature in every respect. This could be the case, but it does not need to be and it will not be if we keep ourselves informed about the problems arising and if we have the ingenuity and courage to control the trends by planning ahead for the solution of oncoming problems. The future of outdoor recreation in America can be extremely bright if we now give the topic the attention it deserves. But we must face the fact

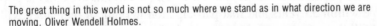

The great thing in this world is not so much where we stand as in what direction we are moving. Oliver Wendell Holmes.

that the future problems will be much larger than those of the past and the present, and the solutions will become increasingly more difficult. Planning for outdoor recreation to meet the needs of the future American population requires the attention of our best thinkers, planners, and organizers. It requires extensive foresight on the part of political and professional leaders, and extensive cooperation by the different levels of government and between government and nongovernment agencies. Finally, education of the masses on the processes of nature, environmental problems, and principles of conservation and preservation needs greatly increased attention.

Man's Future Need for Outdoor Recreation

Americans have undergone great changes in their living patterns, and in many respects great progress has been made. But our basic needs, our desires and hopes, have not changed significantly. We are still a biological species living in an environment with which we have been compatible for thousands of years. We still have the same basic drives, a need to belong, a need for security, and a need to thoroughly enjoy our existence. The great outdoors is deeply imbedded in the American heritage. To us the out-of-doors is a tradition. It is the basis for much of our history. The future will not change this, and neither will it reduce our innate need to be in touch with nature's beauties and wonders. In fact, it appears that as we become ever more urbanized our need for outdoor recreation will steadily increase. The great question is whether in the future the opportunities will be available to satisfy this need.

Future Participation Trends

During the past two decades participation in outdoor recreation has increased faster than the population. Predictions based on past trends are that the population will double within 35 years and that participation in outdoor recreation will triple. Not only will the rate of participation greatly increase, but the emphasis will also change. Until now the great emphasis has been on the simple forms of recreation, such as hiking, cycling, camping, fishing, hunting, sightseeing, and swimming. These common activities will continue to be the popular ones, but some of the more specialized and expensive pursuits will gain rapidly in popularity. Among them will be snow skiing, boating, water skiing, scuba diving, underwater exploration, and specialized photography.

Future Supply and Demand

The supply of basic resources (namely, land and water) for outdoor recreation will not increase. Certain revisions and additions can greatly enhance the usefulness of the resources for recreation purposes, but such revisions do have limited potential. On the other hand, there seems to be no limit to the potential demands on these resources, and it is well established that the demands will escalate at an ever increas-

We should wage a constant war — not a war against people, but a war for people, a war for all those things which are good for all of us.

— Sterling W. Sill

ing rate. This simple relationship between supply and demand means that in the future we will need to (a) identify soon the areas of high recreation potential and prevent them from being committed on a permanent basis to less essential uses, and (b) continue at an increased rate to alter and develop the basic resources so that they will better serve the increased demand for outdoor recreation. This whole matter is a very large and complex problem which involves government at every level, private enterprise, and a large number of professional and service organizations.

Future Economic Impact

The economic impact of outdoor recreation is just gaining momentum. Practically all trends point toward greatly expanded participation in outdoor recreation and more purchasing power per individual American citizen. This combination means only one thing — comparatively more money will be spent by people in pursuit of enjoyment through participation in the out-of-doors. If participation triples during the next 35 years, as predicted by the Bureau of Outdoor Recreation, and if the per capita income increases as predicted, then the economic impact of outdoor recreation will probably increase by four times during this same period. Expenditure for recreation is bound to become an item of the first importance to the American economy. Its potential is exciting, to say the least.

Future Government Involvement

Because of the great increase in outdoor recreation anticipated, it will be necessary for government agencies at all levels to become involved on an enlarged scale, and more interagency cooperation and coordination will be necessary.

In the future the federal government will need to do at least the following:
1. increase its efforts toward identifying, developing, and managing the more desirable recreation attractions on federally owned land;
2. establish in law that certain federal agencies have defined responsibilities in outdoor recreation, where this has not already been done;
3. continue to exert influence to stimulate state and local governments to meet their responsibilities in outdoor recreation;
4. continue to provide grants-in-aid to states and local governments to enhance outdoor recreation developments at the state and local levels.

In the future state governments will need to recognize that
1. long range park and recreation planning will continue to become more essential, and many localities will require state assistance in the form of consultation and planning;
2. state enabling legislation will need constant evaluation and some revision in order to keep pace with changing needs;
3. state parks have more than doubled in number in the last 20 years, and this trend will continue;
4. all public land with high recreation potential will receive heavier use, thus requiring more strict regulations, improved conservation practices, and better systems of maintenance; that in many areas public land is already insufficient and the trend will be toward acquiring more state-owned recreation land and encouraging recreation use of private land;

> Not how long but how well we live should be our major consideration.

5. fish and wildlife resources are already near exhaustion in some states; if hunting, fishing, and other wildlife activities are to continue as a form of recreation, state-conservation programs will have to be improved and expanded;

6. boating, fishing, water skiing, and swimming are rapidly increasing; as a result, more exact regulations governing water sports will be needed in many states; decisions as to which agency is responsible for establishing and enforcing such regulations will demand serious attention;

7. due to increasing population and decreasing open space, more efficient use of land and facilities will become essential; more and better recreation leadership will be in demand; state (and private) universities will be called upon to prepare more recreation leaders specialized in the management of outdoor recreation resources:

8. the demand will greatly increase for improved state highways and access roads into areas with recreation potential;

9. state governments will have to encourage and even offer advice on commercial outdoor-recreation developments;

10. there will be need to better identify the recreational responsibilities of different state agencies in order to reduce duplication and overlap of efforts, and to prevent any void in necessary state services;

11. master planning on both state and local levels will have to be done.

Because American communities are becoming larger and ever more complex it will be necessary for each local government to carry an increased load in supplying needed outdoor-recreation opportunities within the immediate locality. Specifically, local governments will need to

1. do more advance planning with regard to open space and outdoor recreation;

2. acquire key outdoor-recreation sites more in advance of the demand for their use for other purposes;

3. show greater concern for the everyday living environment of people and employ whatever methods are feasible in the particular locality to maintain a respectable and pleasant environment.

Private Land and Private Enterprise

The nongovernment segment will, of necessity, become increasingly involved in outdoor recreation. Government agencies and government resources will simply not be able to meet the rapidly increasing demand for outdoor recreation. The majority of land in the United States (60 percent) is in private ownership. This is especially true in and near the heavily populated areas of the nation. Much of the land has potential for outdoor recreation not yet developed. There is unusual potential on private lands for small game and bird hunting, fishing, picnicking, camping, horseback riding, and numerous other such activities. This potential has not been developed primarily because the demand has not been great enough to motivate private landowners to prepare outdoor-recreation opportunities for the public. Marked progress in this direction has been made in recent years, but the trend has only begun. To develop this vast potential it will be necessary for government agencies to expand their work with private landowners in helping them to establish sound outdoor-recreation operations. As the demand for outdoor recreation increases, many landowners will see opportunities and find ways to capitalize on the demands. At the same time they will serve a worthy public need.

Establishing and Maintaining a Livable Environment

Let it be repeated that the best recreation is that found in one's everyday living, the beauty of one's home surroundings, and the pleasing experiences in daily living. From the outdoor recreation point of view this calls for a "recreation environment" — an environment that contributes to the pleasantness of each day. In order for most future Americans to be able to live in such an environment we will need to reverse our direction in some respects. We will have to find ways to depollute our lakes, bays, and streams which have been so vigorously polluted until now. We will need to take some drastic measures in order to check the polluting of our air — a problem that is still being mostly ignored and yet is recognized as one of our most severe environmental problems. We shall have to face the fact that we cannot destroy matter, we can only change its form. Once we make millions of cars, billions of cans and bottles, and hundreds, thousands, and millions of other objects which eventually become useless, then we must find some respectable method of disposing of them. We must learn that we cannot continue to mar the landscape and clutter it with all sorts of unattractive litter and still have a pleasing environment. Our methods of antipollution have a long way to go before they catch up with our very efficient methods of pollution. In the future great strides must be taken toward all aspects of pollution control if we are to survive, to say nothing of enjoying our environment.

A Bright Future

Of all the things we pursue in the future the greatest one will be, as it has always been, true happiness on a lasting basis. Even though the rapid increase in demand for outdoor recreation has caused great need for concern, this does not necessarily mean than the future is dim. In fact, the future can be very bright if we demonstrate enough interest, ingenuity, and courage to keep ahead of newly developing problems, problems of the kind and magnitude that we have not faced before. If we anticipate future problems, meet them head on, and work out intelligent and timely solutions, then outdoor-recreation opportunities in the future can be even better than they are now, and better than they have been at any time in the past. The outdoors can and should continue to have significant impact on the lives of people and on the development of the nation.

> ...count me among those who look upon the future as a great opportunity.
> — Henry J. Kaiser

Selected References

Action for Clean Water, Izaak Walton League, Glenview, Illinois.

Bagdikian, Ben H., "Death in Our Air," *Saturday Evening Post*, October 8, 1966, pp. 31-35, 106-110.

Barach, Arnold B., *U.S.A. and Its Economic Future*, 2nd edition, Macmillan Co., New York, 1970.

Bathurst, Effie G., and Wilhelmina Hill, *Conservation Experiences for Children*, U.S. Office of Education, U.S. Government Printing Office, Washington, D.C.

Brown, William E., *Island of Hope*, National Recreation and Park Association, Arlington, Virginia, 1971, 1974.

Clawson, Marion, *Land and Water for Recreation*, Rand McNally & Co., Chicago, 1963.

Clawson, Marion, and Jack L. Knetsch, *Economics of Outdoor Recreation*, The John Hopkins Press, Baltimore, 1966.

Community Action for Natural Beauty, Citizens' Advisory Committee on Recreation and Natural Beauty, Washington, D.C.

Community Action Guide for Air Pollution Control, National Association of Counties, Washington, D.C.

Community Action Program for Water Pollution Control, President's Council on Recreation and Beautification, Washington, D.C.

Concepts of Conservation, The Conservation Foundation, Washington, D.C. 1972.

Dana, Samuel T., *Education and Outdoor Recreation,* Department of the Interior, Bureau of Outdoor Recreation, U.S. Government Printing Office, Washington, D.C., 1968.

Demmon, E.L., *Opportunities in Forestry Careers,* Vocational Guidance Manuals, Louisville, Kentucky, 1975.

Diebold, John, *Automation: Its Impact on Business and Labor*, National Planning Association, Planning Pamphlet No. 106, Washington, D.C., May, 1969.

Doell, Charles E., and Louis F. Twardzik, *Elements of Park and Recreation Administration*, 3d edition, Burgess Publishing Company, Minneapolis, 1973.

Fabun, Don, *The Dynamics of Change*, Prentice-Hall, Englewood Cliffs, N.J., 1967.

Fanning, Odom, *Opportunities in Environmental Careers*, Vocational Guidance Manuals, Louisville, Kentucky, 1971, 1975.

Forest Recreation for Profit, United States Department of Agriculture, United States Forest Service, Bulletin #265.

How to Preserve Your Area for Its Natural Value, The Nature Conservancy, Washington, D.C.

Jensen, Clayne R., *Recreation and Leisure Time Careers*, Vocational Guidance Manuals, Louisville, Kentucky, 1976.

Jensen, Clayne R., *Survey of the Outdoor Recreation Responsibilities of State Agencies in the Fifty States*, unpublished study, 1976.

Jensen, Clayne R., and Clark T. Thorstenson, *Issues in Outdoor Recreation*, Burgess Publishing Company, Minneapolis, Minnesota, 1972.

Leopold, Aldo, *A Sand County Almanac and Sketches Here and There*, Oxford University Press, New York, 1949.

LIFE, Educational Reprint 76, "Water Pollution, The Blighted Great Lakes," New York.

LIFE, Educational Reprint 91, "Environment, What Can Be Done?" New York.

Little, Charles E., *Challenge of the Land*, Open Space Action Institute, New York, 1968.

More Attractive Communities for California, California Roadside Council, San Francisco, California, 1970.

National Association of Counties Research Foundation, "Outdoor Recreation," Washington, D.C.

National Association of Counties Research Foundation, "Outdoor Recreation — Land Acquisition," Washington, D.C.

National Association of Counties Research Foundation, "Outdoor Recreation — Legal Aspects," Washington, D.C.

National Association of Counties Research Foundation, "Outdoor Recreation — Organization," Washington, D.C.

National Association of Counties Research Foundation, "Outdoor Recreation — Planning," Washington, D.C.

National Conference on State Parks, "State Park Statistics," National Recreation and Park Association, 1972, 1976.

Nebraskaland Ranch-Farm Vacations, Nebraska Game Commission.

Outdoor Recreation: A New Potential for Cooperation, U.S. Department of Agriculture, Farmer's Cooperation Service, October 1972.

Private Sector Study of Outdoor Recreation Enterprises, Bureau of Outdoor Recreation, Department of the Interior, March 1966.

Recreation on Forest Industry Lands in the United States, American Forest Products Industries, Washington, 1972.

Signs Out of Control, California Roadside Council, San Francisco, California.

Smith, Julian W., Reynold E. Carlson, George W. Donalds, and Hugh G. Masters, *Outdoor Education*, 2nd edition, Prentice-Hall, Englewood Cliffs, N.J., 1972.

Theobald, Robert L., "The Man With the Pencil of Light," *Saturday Review*, August 29, 1964.

Toynbee, Arnold, "Conditions of Survival," *Saturday Review*, August 29, 1964.

United States Department of the Interior, *Federal Assistance in Outdoor Recreation*, U.S. Government Printing Office, Washington, D.C., 1975.

United States Department of the Interior, *Focal Point for Outdoor America*, Bureau of Outdoor Recreation.

United States Department of the Interior, *Our Natural Resources: The Choices Ahead*, Conservation Yearbook Series, No. 10, 1974.

United States Department of the Interior, *Outdoor Recreation, A Legacy for America, A*

Summary of Outdoor Recreation in America 1972-1978, Bureau of Outdoor Recreation, Washington, D.C.

United States Department of the Interior, *Outdoor Recreation Action*, "Bicycling and Hostels," Bureau of Outdoor Recreation, Washington, D.C., Quarterly.

United States Department of the Interior, *Outdoor Recreation Action*, Bureau of Outdoor Recreation, Washington, D.C., Winter 1975.

United States Department of the Interior, *Outdoor Recreation Trends*, U.S. Government Printing Office, Washington, D.C.

United States Department of the Interior, *The Population Challenge*, U.S. Government Printing Office, Washington, D.C., 1972.

United States Department of the Interior, *Private Assistance in Outdoor Recreation*, U.S. Government Printing Office, Washington, D.C.

United States Department of the Interior, *Quest for Quality*, U.S. Government Printing Office, Washington, D.C., 1965.

United States Department of the Interior, *Recreation Land Price Escalation*, Bureau of Outdoor Recreation, Washington, D.C.

United States Department of the Interior, *Saving the Scene*, Conservation Yearbook Series, Number 8.

United States Department of the Interior, *The Third Wave*, U.S. Government Printing Office, Washington, D.C., 1968.

United States Department of the Interior, *With Us on Earth*, Conservation Yearbook Series, Number 8.

Photo Credits

The author would like to express his thanks to the following agencies and individuals for permission to reproduce photographic material supplied by them.

Chapter 2. Page 18, Sun Valley News Bureau; pages 22 (top), 23, and 24, U.S. Forest Service: page 22 (bottom), USDA — Soil Conservation Service.

Chapter 3. Page 26, Bureau of Census, U.S. Department of Commerce; pages 30 and 33, U.S. Bureau of Outdoor Recreation; page 34, U.S. Department of Transportation.

Chapter 5. Page 60 (top), National Park Service; page 60 (bottom) and page 79 (bottom), Utah Travel Council; pages 65, 71, 82, and 85 (bottom), USDA — Soil Conservation Service; pages 85 (top) and 94, U.S. Bureau of Outdoor Recreation.

Chapter 6. Page 101, U.S. Forest Service; page 108, Mel White.

Chapter 7. Page 117, California State Parks Department; page 120, Florida State News Bureau; pages 122 and 125, USDA — Soil Conservation Service.

Chapter 8. Page 141, National Recreation and Park Association; pages 146 and 155 (bottom), U.S. Bureau of Outdoor Recreation.

Chapter 9. Pages 163, 167 (top and bottom), USDA — Soil Conservation Service; page 168, Utah Travel Council.

Chapter 10. Page 176, U.S. Bureau of Outdoor Recreation; page 185, Wisconsin Conservation Department; page 187, Walter Dyke; page 193, National Park Service.

Chapter 11. Page 197, Foto Schaefer; page 198, USDA — Soil Conservation Service; page 199, U.S. Bureau of Reclamation.

Chapter 12. Page 207, National Recreation and Park Association; pages 209 and 217, U.S. Bureau of Outdoor Recreation; page 210, U.S. Department of Housing and Urban Development; page 211, National Park Service; page 213 (bottom), C. P. Schmidt; page 221 (top), Utah Travel Council; page 221 (bottom), courtesy of W. E. Siebel, Ohio County Fish & Game Association.

Chapter 13. Pages 227 and 228, U.S. Bureau of Outdoor Recreation; page 233, Meb Anderson; page 235, Leon Sisk.

Chapter 14. Page 241, U.S. Bureau of Outdoor Recreation; page 247, USDA — Soil Conservation Service.

Chapter 15. Page 253, National Park Service.

Index

A Dream (story), 217
AAHPER (See American Alliance for Health, Physical Education and Recreation)
Acts (See Legislation)
Agriculture, Department of, 89
Agricultural Stabilization and Conservation Service, 87-88
Air pollution, 211-12
Air Quality Act of 1967, 104-5
American Alliance for Health, Physical Education, and Recreation 236, 239
American Camping Association, 240
American Forestry Association, 40
American Powerboat Association, 240
American Youth Hostels, Inc., 240
Appalachian Mountain Club, 242
Appalachian Regional Commission, 92
Appalachian Trail Conference, Inc., 242
Areas, intermediate, 179
Areas, resource based, 178
Areas, user-oriented, 179-80
Aristotle, 4, 35
Athletic Institute, 242
Atomic Energy Commission, 93
Audubon Society, National, 244
Automation and technology, 40
Automobiles, 34-35

Beaches, 192
Beaches, commercial, 169
Bible, Allen, 145
Bird, John, 215
Boat clubs, 170
Braucher, Howard, 6
Brightbill, Charles, 3, 6
Brockman, C. Frank, 6
Brooks, Paul, 64
Bureau of Indian Affairs, 82-83
Bureau of Land Management, 75-76
  areas of, 76
  origin and development of, 75
  recreation involvement of, 75-76
Bureau of Outdoor Recreation, 84-87
  origin and development of, 84
  purposes of, 84-86
  regional offices, 87
Bureau of Reclamation, 72-75
  areas of, 74
  origin and development of, 72-73
  recreation involvement of, 73-74
Butler, George D., 6

California, organization for outdoor recreation, 123-24
Campgrounds, 165

265

Carlson, Reynold E., 6
Charlesworth, James, 4
Cherne, Leo, 37
Cities (See Local government)
Clawson, Marion, 183, 203
Cleveland Metropolitan Park District, 144
Colleges and Universities, 121
Commerce, Department of, 90
Corps of Engineers, 68-72
   areas of, 71-72
   legislation affecting, 69-70
   policies about recreation, 70
   recreation involvement, 70-72
Council for National Cooperation in
   Aquatics, 243
Curricula in outdoor recreation, 238

Dana, Samuel T., 234, 236
Danford, Howard G., 3, 6
Defense, Department of, 90
de Grazia, Sebastian, 3, 6
Demand for outdoor recreation, 176-82
   factors relating to, 180-82
   particular activities, 178
   particular resources, 179-80
Demmon, E. L., 238
Deppe, Theodore R., 6
Desmond, Thomas G., 4
Diebold, John, 41
Disraeli, 4

Economics of outdoor recreation, 195-204
   effects on nearby communities, 200
   effects of specific factors, 198-200
   effects on homesite development, 199
   influence on jobs, 200
   land price trends, 198
   purchase of goods by visitors, 199
Economic Opportunity Act of 1964, 122
Economic Opportunity, Office of, 93
Economic status of Americans (See Income)
Education, effects of, 42-43
Education for outdoor recreation, 225-38
   categories of, 228-29
   nonschool agencies involved, 231-33
   professional preparation, 234-36
   school involvement, 229-30
Elementary and Secondary Education Act of
   1965, 113
Emerson, Ralph Waldo, 192
Endangered Species Act of 1973, 109
Environment, 205-24
   air pollution, 211-12
   future problems of, 257
   land pollution, 216
   pollution and ugliness of, 208-10
   water pollution, 212-16
Environmental Education Act of 1970, 106-7

Environmental Quality Improvement Act of
   1970, 107
Extension Service, U.S.D.A., 89

Federal Boat Safety Act of 1971, 108
Federal government (Also see names of
   specific agencies), 57-96
   basis for involvement in outdoor
   recreation, 57
   legislation, 97-114
   resource management agencies, 58-96
   technical and financial assistance, 84-96,
   97-114
Federal Highway Administration, 83-84
Federal Power Commission, 93
Federal Water Projects Recreation Acts of
   1965, 100-2
Fish and Wildlife (Also see U.S. Fish and
   Wildlife Service), 120
Forests (See State Forests, and U.S. Forest
   Service)
Frostik, Gwen, 235

Garfield, James A., 226
General Services Administration, 93
Gothein, Marie Luise, 48
Greek influence, 48
Greenspan Program, 104
Griswold, Whitney A., 4
Gross national product, 38
Gudea (a Samarian king), 48
Guest ranches, 165

Health, Education and Welfare, Department
   of, 90-91
Henle, Peter, 196
Hutchins, Robert, 4
Higher Education Act of 1965, 113
Highways and roads, 121
Highway Beautification Act of 1965, 104
Hoover, Herbert, 243
Housing Act of 1954, 110-11
Housing and Community Development Act of
   1974, 112
Housing and Urban Development Act of
   1965, 111
Housing and Urban Development,
   Department of, 91
Humphrey, Hubert H., 140
Hunting and Fishing Camps, 166

Income, changes in, 38-40
Industrial recreation areas, 170
Industrial tree farms, 166-69
Interior, Department of, 92
Intermediate outdoor recreation areas, 184-86
Izaak Walton League of America, 243
It Became Part of Him (story), 13-14

Jackson, Henry M., 77, 98
Jefferson, Thomas, 187
Jensen, Clayne R., 238
Johnson, Lyndon B., 59, 169

Kaiser, Henry J., 157
Kennedy, John F., 75
Knetsch, Jack L., 203

Lakes, artificial, 192
Land acquisition, 157-59
Land pollution, 216-17
Land and Water Conservation Fund Program, 99
Legal aspects relating to recreation, 117-18, 140-41
LaGasse, Alfred B., 55
Legislation, federal (Also see specific acts), 97-113
Leisure, meaning of, 2
Leisure time
    daily, weekly, vacation, retirement, 36-37
    meaning of, 2
    significance of, 3
Leisure and work trends, 35-38
Leopold, Aldo, 52
Local government, 139-60
    charters and ordinances, 141-42
    enabling legislation, 140
    financing methods, 142-44
    land acquisition procedures, 157-59
    legal aspects, 140
    planning, 151, 153
    organization for recreation, 144-51
    zoning, 153-57
Los Angeles County, 156

Mannes, Marya, 177
Mannheim, Karl, 44
Mather, Stephen, 52
Meyer, Harold D., 3, 6
Michigan, organization for outdoor recreation, 127-28
Miller, John Eli, 28-29
Miller, Norman P., 3
Milwaukee County, Wisconsin, 143
Miracle County, Arizona, 149-50
Mobility, improvement of, 33-34
Mumford, Lewis, 43
Morley, John, 236
Morton, Roger C. B., 156
Muir, John, 67
Municipal government (See Local government)
MacLean, Janet R., 6

Nash, Jay B., 3, 5, 7

National Campers and Hikers Association, 244
National Environmental Policy Act of 1970, 107
National Forests (See U.S. Forest Service)
National Golf Foundation, 244
National Industrial Education Association, 245
National Outdoor Recreation Plan, 94-96
National Park and Recreation Association, 245
National Park Service, 58-64
    area classification, 59-63
    area by state, 62
    origin and development of, 58-59
National Parks, 194
National Recreation Education Accreditation Project, 237
National Rifle Association, 246
National Trails System Act of 1968, 106
National Wildlife Federation, 246
Natural Historic Preservation Act of 1966, 103-4
Natural resource science, panel on, 237-38
Nature Conservancy, 247
Neumeyer, Esther S., 3
Neumeyer, Martin H., 3
New England, northern sector, 201

Objectives of outdoor recreation, 8-10
Older Americans Act of 1965, 111
Oppenheimer, Robert, 40
Outboard Boating Club of America, 248
Outdoor education, 229
Outdoor recreation
    cultural values of, 17
    definition of, 8
    early development in the U.S., 15-16, 49-50
    early part of the present century, 50-52
    economic impact of, 195-204, 255
    education for, 225-38
    educational values of, 20
    future of, 251-57
    government involvement, future, 255-56
    leadership preparation programs for, 55-56
    need for, future, 254
    participation trends, future, 254
    physiological values of, 19
    post World War II years, 52-53
    psychological values of, 17-18
    resources for, 175
    sociological values of, 19
    spiritual values of, 20
    supply and demand, 175, 254
    technical and financial assistance for, 171
Outdoor Recreation — a Legacy for America (National Plan), 94-96

Outdoor Recreation Resources Review
  Commission (ORRRC), 97-98

Parks (See National Park Service, State Parks
  and local government, parks)
  estimating their value, 203-4
Peattie, Donald Culross, 106
Pearl River Project, 202
Philosophy, changing, 43-45
Pinchot, Gifford, 49-50
Plato, 40
Pollution (Also see Environment), 208-16
  a challenge, 218
  need for local action, 220-24
  what is being done?218-20
  who are the polluters?216
Population trends, 26-30
  United States, 28-30
  world, 26-27
Power companies, 170
Private resources for outdoor recreation,
  161-63, 256
  improved areas, 162
  unimproved areas, 162
Professional preparation of outdoor recreation
  leaders, 55-56, 234-38
Public domain (See Bureau of Land
  Management)
Public Land Law Review Commission, 93
Public Works and Economic Development
  Act of 1965, 111

Recreation, meaning of, 5-7
  activity oriented, 8
  anticipation phase, 10
  classification of, 7-8
  effects on economics, 200-4
  expenditures on, 40
  meaning of, 5-7
  objectives of, 8-10
  participation phase, 10
  planning phase, 10
  quality of, 6-7
  recollection phase, 11
  resource oriented, 8
  total experience, 10-11
Recreation and Public Purposes Act of 1954,
  100
Resorts, 163
Resource-based recreation areas, 186-88
Resources for outdoor recreation, 175-94
  spotlight on certain kinds, 189-94
  distribution of, 188-89
Reuther, Walter, 41
Richmond, Virginia, 148-49
Rivers, 21-24
Rivers for outdoor recreation, 190-92
Robinson, Duane M., 3
Rockefeller, Lawrence S., 207

Roman influence, 48
Roosevelt, Theodore, 49-183
Russell, Bertrand, 4

Santayana, George, 44
Sarnoff, David, 4
Schweitzer, Albert, 218
Shooting Preserves, 164
Sierra Club, 248
Sill, Sterling W., 154
Ski areas, 164
Small Business Administration, 93
Small Reclamation Projects Act, 102
Smith, Julian W., 229-30
Socio-economic forces, 25-46, 251-54
Socrates, 4
Soil Conservation Service, 88-89
Special outdoor recreation attractions, 170
Sports Fishing Institute, 248
Sports Foundation, Inc., 249
State Forests, 120-21
State government
  authority to provide recreation, 115-16
  California, 123-24
  enabling legislation, 117-18
  liaison officers for outdoor recreation,
  135-38
  Michigan, 127-28
  outdoor recreation plan, 122
  public education, 121
  recreation services, 116
  Utah, 125-26
State Government Agencies, involvement in
  outdoor recreation (Also see specific
  agencies), 115-38
State Park Systems, 118-20, 194
Supply and demand of outdoor recreation
  resources, 175-94
Supply of outdoor recreation resources,
  182-89
Sutherland, Willard C., 44

Teale, Edwin Way, 109
Technology and automation, 40
Tennessee Valley Authority, 80-82
  involvement in recreation, 81
  land between the lakes national park, 82
  origin and development of, 80
Texoma Reservoir Project, 201-2
Thoreau, Henry David, 66
Toynbee, Arnold, 4
Trails for outdoor recreation, 189
Transportation, Department of, 92
Travel (See Mobility)

Udall, Stewart, 16, 44
U.S. Army Corps of Engineers (See Corps of
  Engineers)

U.S. Fish and Wildlife Service, 76-80
    origin and development of, 76-77
    recreation involvement of, 77-78
U.S. Forest Service, 64-68
    multiple use concept, 67
    origin and development, 64-65
    recreational use of land, 66-68
    visitors annually, 66
    wilderness and primitive areas, 67
Urbanization, trends towards, 30-33
User-oriented recreation areas, 183-84
Utah, organization for outdoor recreation,
    125-26
Vacation farms, 165
Van Dyke, Henry, 105
Walton, Izaak, 109
Water pollution, 212-16

Water Quality Act of 1965, 103
Water Quality Improvement Act of 1970, 107
Water Resources Development Act of 1974,
    110
Water Resources Research Act of 1964, 102-3
Watershed Protection and Flood Prevention
    Act of 1954, 102
Ways, Max, 211
Wells, H. G., 152
Wheelman, Inc., 249
Wild and Scenic Rivers Act of 1968, 105
Wilderness areas, 193-94
Wilderness System, 99-100
Wildlife (Also see U.S. Wildlife Service), 120
Work and leisure trends, 35-38
Yacht clubs, 169-70